The Hindu Monastery in South India

The Hindu Monastery in South India

Social, Religious, and Artistic Traditions

Nalini Rao

LEXINGTON BOOKS
Lanham • Boulder • New York • London

This book is dedicated to my father, Dr. S.R. Rao, archaeologist and emeritus scientist.

Published by Lexington Books
An Imprint of The Rowman & Littlefield Publishing Group, Inc.
4501 Forbes Boulevard, Suite 200, Lanham, Maryland 20706
www.rowman.com

6 Tinworth Street, London SE11 5AL, United Kingdom

British Library Cataloguing in Publication Information Available

Library of Congress Cataloging-in-Publication Data

Library of Congress Control Number: 2020943001

ISBN: 978-1-7936-2237-2 (cloth)
ISBN: 978-1-7936-2239-6 (pbk)
ISBN: 978-1-7936-2238-9 (electronic)

Contents

List of Figures vii

Preface ix

Acknowledgments xi

Note on Sanskrit Diacritics xiii

1 Introduction: Hindu Monasteries in a Socioreligious Context 1

2 Beginnings and Growth of Śaiva Monasteries in South India 19

3 Vedānta Monasteries: Development, Identity, and Patronage 53

4 The Icon and Relic of the Guru 91

5 Multivalent Symbolism of the *Vṛndāvana* 133

6 Conclusion 155

Appendix 163

Glossary 167

Bibliography 171

Index 203

About the Author 217

List of Figures

Figure 2.1	Students in a *maṭha*	29
Figure 3.1	View of a Ashta *maṭha*, Udipi	73
Figure 3.2	Vidyāpīṭha, Pejawar *maṭha*, Bengaluru	74
Figure 3.3	Rāghvendra Swāmi *maṭha*, Mantralaya	75
Figure 4.1	*Vṛndāvana* of Raghuvarya *Tīrtha, Nava Vṛndāvana*, Anegondi	92
Figure 4.2	*Vṛndāvana* of Vidyānidhi *Tīrtha*, Yaragola	94
Figure 4.3	Votive *vṛndāvana* of Rāghvendra Swāmi, Bengaluru	95
Figure 4.4	*Mūla vṛndāvanas* in *Kṛṣṇa maṭha/temple*, Udipi	96
Figure 4.5	*Vṛndāvanas* in Puthige *maṭha*	96
Figure 4.6	*Mūla vṛndāvana* of Raghottama *Tīrtha*, Tirukoilur	97
Figure 4.7	*Mūla vṛndāvana* of Śripādarāja *Tīrtha*, Mulbagal	97
Figure 4.8	*Mūla vṛndāvana* of Yogindra *Tīrtha*, Srirangam	98
Figure 4.9	*Vṛndāvanas* in Uttaradi *maṭha*, Hospet	99
Figure 4.10	Lord Vāyu	100
Figure 4.11	*Sālagrāmas*	104
Figure 4.12	Memorials stones, Sasvad, Poona District, Maharashtra	117
Figure 4.13	*Nava Vṛndāvana*, Anegondi	118
Figure 5.1	Tulsi Vṛndāvana	137
Figure 6.1	Guru in a *Maṭha*	159

Preface

My interest in the study of Hindu monasteries was sparked by a painting in the Virupaksha temple at Vijayanagara (modern Hampi). It portrayed a spectacular scene of a guru being carried in a palanquin followed by musicians and a large number of people. It reminded me of a royal celebration and spurred my interest in the power and status of the guru particularly within an institution.

Soon afterward, I visited the holy site of Mantralaya and stood before a dramatically displayed icon. It was a massive rectangular stone cube, a boxlike structure. It was carved out of black stone, above which was a small metal icon of a God. Decorated with flowers, silver plates, sandalwood paste, the icon was being worshipped with lights, and incense. I could hear the loud chanting of *mantras*, and hundreds of devotees prostrating to the icon of which they could get merely a glimpse. I was struck by its non-anthropomorphic form. I could connect it to the two popular religious images in India, namely the Śiva *liṅga* and the Buddhist *stūpa*. The icon was a "memorial tomb" of an eminent medieval saint Rāghvendra Swāmi and was indeed memorable.

I was eager to understand the nature of the relation between the 'black' icon, which was that of a guru and a living guru in the monastery. I had numerous queries about the two images of the guru and the God, that touched upon both the sacredness and power of the guru. Why was he worshipped like a God? Was it his charisma, yogic, or even his mystical powers? Why was his memorial not placed within the precincts or sanctum of a temple? What might have been the historical and sociological reasons for the phenomenon of the rise of the guru in medieval India?

I noticed that in a living Hindu monastery, the power and status of the guru was a central element. He is surrounded by a host of disciples and looked upon with utmost reverence. He is worshipped, crowned and accorded royal titles. The guru in a monastery is essentially an ascetic who has renounced the worldly pleasures of life. I was eager to understand more about the power, status, and nature of the guru in the context of the institution of the monastery.

This book is the result of a protracted period of ten years of research, discussion with living gurus and fieldwork on Hindu monasteries in the state of Karnataka, in South India. I found that there are not many books on this topic. My fieldwork involved documenting architectural, literary, and artistic evidences about Hindu monasteries. Since then, I have visited almost every monastic site in South India in order to understand the organizational structure and nature of the institution and more importantly the origin and meaning of the icon of the guru.

Acknowledgments

It has taken a long time to bring out this book. I am particularly indebted to Vishweshwa Tirtha (former head of Pejawar Matha), Satyatma Tirtha (head of Uttaradi Matha), Sugunendra Tirtha (head of Puthige Matha), principals in Vidyapitha, Bengaluru, Prabandhanacharya, Acharya Pandurangi, Pujya Jagadguru Karmayogi Charukeerty Bhattarak Swamiji (head of Jain Math in Sravana Belagola), Suvidyendrateertharu, (former head of Raghavendra Swami Matha, Mantralaya). I owe an enormous debt to Dr. R. L. Brown who inspired me to to begin as well as complete my project. I express my gratitude to Stanley Wolpert, Damodar Sardesai, Ashok Aklujkar, Ingrid Aall, Arnold Kaminsky, Debashish Banerji, Sita Raman, BVK Shastri, Shiva Bajpai and S.R. Rao. I have received great support from Swamy Swahananda, Swamy Sarvadevananda, Ramdas Lamb, Sthaneshwar Timalsina, Christopher Key Chapple, Aneil Rallin, Sundara Adiga, and K.P. Poonacha. My special thanks to, Meena Rao, Nalini Venkatesh, Matteo Barbiero, Vibhu Walia, Indrani Murthy and Choodamani Nandagopal.

Many librarians, and museum curators have been helpful during my field study. I wish to thank those individuals at the Kannada Sahitya Parishad (Bengaluru), Kannada Research Institute (Dharwar), Bengaluru University Library, Mythic Society, Hampi Museum, Epigraphical Society of India (Mysore), Mysore University Library as well as the staff in the Archaeological Survey of India. This project has benefited from the generous assistance of PBRC Grants (SUA). I express my gratitude to all those friends, acquaintances, temple priests, personnel in the monasteries, who have provided valuable assistance in various ways. This book could not have been written without the help of Madhav Rao, who untiringly escorted me to remote villages for my research. I am particularly grateful to Monica Sukumar and Lexington Books for their patience and help in publishing this complex research book. I also thank my husband, Nagaraj, and my daughters, Madhu and Alaka, and Leela, Milan, and Nikhil, for their constant support and encouragement. Finally, the study was made possible through the previous researches of scholars working in the field, all of whom I wish to acknowledge.

Note on Sanskrit Diacritics

I have generally used diacritical marks for Sanskrit and Kannada words, including names of gods, gurus, religious organizations, and texts, but have omitted them on names of kings, monasteries, dynasties, religious affiliations, and the titles of books in endnotes and in the bibliography. Diacritics have been omitted on 'anglicized' words such as Saivism, Saivite, Vaisnavite, Vaisnavism, Vedism, Vedantic, while retaining them on Śaiva, Vaiṣṇava and Pāśupata. There are differences in the usage of diacritics between the term *vṛndāvana* which denotes Guru's *vṛndāvana*; but for the geographical and metaphysical site of Kṛṣṇa, the word is in capital letters, Vṛndāvana, in order to distinguish the multiple usage of the term. Furthermore, words as *maṭha* and *maṭh/mutt* are used following popular pronounciation in the regional language.

Chapter 1

Introduction

Hindu Monasteries in a Socioreligious Context

For millennia, India has been the home of countless ascetics and monks, who have maintained a tradition of philosophical speculation, religious practice, and teaching. Whatever be his religious denomination, sect, or school, the ascetic was revered. He was known by various names, such as *sanyāsī*, *sādhu*, *ṛṣi*, *sant*, *ācārya*, *paṇḍita*, *swāmi*, *yati*, and guru.[1] Ascetics have been the preservers of ancient Vedic beliefs and commentators of religious texts. People greatly desire to listen to his interpretations of scriptures, doctrines, mythological narratives as well as practical advice on how to live as a true Hindu. Few examples of such great ascetics in modern times are Swāmi Prabhupāda, Śri Chandrasekharānanda Sarasvati, Ramana Maharshi, Rāmakṛṣṇa Paramahamsa, Swāmi Vivekānanda, Satya Sai Bāba, Dayānanda Sarasvati, and Śri Bāla Śivayogi. The ascetic is revered by all the three *dharma* traditions of India, Jainism, Buddhism, and Hinduism and his status does not depend on his "belongingness" to any particular denomination or fold.

Hindu ascetics have greatly influenced the trajectory of Indian philosophy and culture, as well as the religious, social, and political institutions. Their value to society is derived from renunciation of worldly pleasures, and more importantly, from their role as a teacher or guru. Despite their power to shape the growth of Hinduism, there are not many institutions or great architecture that were built for the simple saffron robed monk. The Hindu *devālayas* (temples) contain numerous images of gods and goddesses, but rarely do we find images of saints (although they must have played a key role in the construction of temples). Instead, the institution that was organized around the guru was the Hindu monastery known as a *maṭha*. The charismatic leadership of the guru, his ascetic qualities, and philosophical theories sustained the monastery for more than a thousand years and still continues to play a dynamic role in Indian society.

The term "guru" means a teacher, in the narrow sense of the term, but a guru within the institution of a *maṭha* is normally an ascetic, a celibate, and a philosopher-monk. He follows specific rules and norms, beliefs and practices affiliated to the original founder of the organization of the particular *maṭha*. He maintains the *guruparamparā* (lineage of gurus) and is responsible for the interpretation of religious doctrines. Today, an additional function of the guru is the proper guidance in matters of religious and spiritual, at various levels. His learning and charismatic leadership elicits admiration and respect from the community. Although known by various terms, such as *jagadguru* (world teacher),[2] *swāmi*, *ānanda*, and *Tīrtha*, the most common epithet is *ācārya* or simply Guru. In this book, I have distinguished the ascetic head of a monastery as Guru (with a capital G) from gurus who are not affiliated with an organization or head of an institution.

The chief aim of the Hindu monastery is to preserve the body of religious doctrine formulated by its founder (or later Gurus), and to transmit these traditions for an ordered society. The ultimate religious purpose of the *maṭha* is to help the individual to attain *moksha* (liberation) from *samsāra* (bondage hrough attachment). The Guru facilitates his disciples to discover the "true self" which is hidden beneath layers of ignorance, through a discipline of the mind and body, in order to lead a good life. At a collective level, within the monastery and community at large, there is a pervading emphasis on the Guru who has attained liberation through renunciation and thus realized God. This determines the teachings, beliefs, and practices of the disciples, students, devotees, and lay followers. Furthermore, the contributions of the ascetic pontiff to philosophical literature have been extraordinary, particularly those of Vedānta *maṭhas* whose heads have compiled numerous commentaries on the sacred scriptures, *Vedas* and *Upaniṣads*.[3] Often, the Guru solves disputes, and even functions as a fundraiser. Thus, *maṭhas* with the leadership of the Guru have preserved and helped in the transmission of religious and philosophical traditions, thereby, playing an important socioreligious role.

Maṭhas are religious institutions that are distinct particularly to South India. They serve as schools which perform the function of feeding, boarding, lodging, and rest houses for pilgrims. A *maṭha* may be defined as an organized integral system of education, worship, feeding, and lodging, consisting of a community of disciples and headed by a Guru, who is normally an ascetic. *Maṭhas* witnessed a long trajectory of growth till they developed to be of seminal importance to the community. Between the ninth and fourteenth centuries CE there was a proliferation of variety of *maṭhas*: Śaiva, Vaiṣṇava, Vedānta, and Liṅgāyat *maṭhas*, each consisting of regional and local branches. The major monastic orders institutionalized the system through Guru lineage, patronage, individual identity, philosophical theories, religious practices, and icons. During the late medieval period, the status and sacredness of the living Guru was substantiated into an icon, that was worshipped, much like that of the Buddha.

There was no commemorative architecture built for the Hindu Guru till the fourteenth century CE. However, in Karnataka, we find a paradoxical phenomenon of icons with relics of the Guru within one of the denominations of the monastic orders, namely the Dualist order or the Dvaita *maṭha*. The icon of the Guru is in the form of an immovable rectangular stone cube. Below the memorial is enshrined the "whole-body relic" of the deceased Guru. The embalmed body, along with the non-figural monumental "memorial" icon, is known as a *vṛndāvana*. The *vṛndāvana* can also be considered a sepulchral and mortuary icon. Venerated from past seven hundred years in the innumerable Dvaita monasteries (founded by Madhvācārya), *vṛndāvanas* are still in worship and are popular icons. Such an exceptionally interesting image along with the living Guru has played a major role in the life of the community.

This book builds upon the centrality of the Guru and the icon, by investigating into the anomaly of relic worship within Hinduism that considers death as polluting. It examines the historical and religious factors for the institutionalization of the "deceased" Guru. Such a novel phenomenon of mummification and invention of a new iconography of the Guru raises complex questions. What are the origins of the *vṛndāvana*? What were the reasons for the rise of the Guru in medieval India and the mummification of his deceased body? These questions can be best understood in the historical context of *maṭhas*, religious movements, and royal patronage. This book provides an insight into the historical phenomena in the context of the ascetic pontiff, the Guru. His dynamic role as a charismatic religious leader and philosopher was the outgrowth of a complex network system between the king, Guru, and the devotee.

The conundrum of the origins of the non-figural stone icon of whole-body relic of the mummified Guru recalls Buddhist and pre-Buddhist traditions. The "institution of the Buddha" was the *saṅgha* or community of monks, and his commemorative monument was the monumental *stūpa* that contained the relics of the Buddha. A comparison between Hindu and Buddhist monasteries reveals the nature and function of the monastic educational system that kept alive religious teachings and practice during a crucial period of Indian history.

In short, this book is an investigation into the institutionalization of the living and deceased ascetic pontiff (Guru) in Hindu monasteries during the medieval period in South India. The study opens a whole new chapter in the religious history of South Asia. Such a complex investigation into the institutionalization of the living and deceased ascetic Guru in Hindu monasteries between the ninth and seventeenth centuries CE in South India reveals the dynamic traditions of asceticism and bliss, dead and living, sacred and unholy, Guru and God that often cross boundaries.

The Hindu Monastery

The Hindu monastery eludes definition. Scholars have defined it as a monastery or a monastic institution[4] due to its similarity to the Christian monastery where the residential monks pray, have a deep veneration to God, dedicate their lives to the practice and spread of religion, and live in a well-organized community. The Hindu *maṭha* has a more expansive function and a flexible organizational structure than a Christian monastery.[5] Apart from being a place of residence for the ascetic,[6] it is a hut, monastery, place of learning, and a college.[7] In the late medieval period, it grew to be a center of philosophy,[8] as well as a place of worship headed by an ascetic (*sanyāsī*),[9] who has renounced worldly life. Thus, a Hindu *maṭha* may be defined as an organized integral system of education, worship, feeding, and lodging, consisting of a community of disciples who adhere to a set of beliefs affiliated to the original founder and headed by an ascetic guru. In short, a *maṭha* is an educational and ascetic institution, headed by a Guru. Since *maṭhas* went through a gradual growth in structure and organization, nature and function, the above characteristics are more noticeable during late medieval period, from the eleventh century CE. They developed into institutions of seminal importance, thereby forming an integral part of the community.

All *maṭhas* are not similar as they differ in their religious beliefs, rituals, philosophy, organizational structure, imagery, and disciplinary codes. For instance, the followers of Rāmānujācārya, referred to as Śri Vaiṣṇava, worship Viṣṇu and Lakshmi; those of Madhvācārya emphasize ritual and worship the personally conceived deity, which could be any of the ten *avatāras* of Viṣṇu. Its rules of celibacy[10] compared to Advaita *maṭhas* are vague and flexible and a householder can become a *sanyāsi* by renouncing his family.[11] Even the number of requirements and rules of the monastic traditions vary. Advaita *maṭhas* hardly contain any rules except an implicit renunciation of worldly desires, while Jain *maṭhas* have elaborate rules and regulations. Furthermore, the Dvaita *maṭhas* contain an icon of the Guru which is the form of a memorial/tomb called *vṛndāvana*, that contains the deceased body of the Guru. These are living icons and almost a hundred is found in the Dvaita *maṭhas* of South India.

HISTORIOGRAPHY

Although Hindu monasteries have been popular from past seven hundred years in South India, scholars have not paid sufficient attention to them in comparison to their focus on Hindu temples.[12] While numerous studies on Buddhist monasteries have been published, Hindu monasteries remain nearly as obscure to the western scholar today as they did years ago.[13] Studies on the monastery have tended to focus on the philosophical commentaries that are written by monastic heads of Vedānta *maṭhas*, namely the Advaita, Viśiṣṭādvaita, and Dvaita *maṭhas*. Among them, are some significant publications, such as by Cenkner in 1983, *The Teaching Tradition* which focuses on Ādi Śaṅkarācārya.[14] In 1992 Yoshitsugu Sawai elaborated on the doctrines of Ādi Śaṅkarācārya in his book *The Faith of Ascetics and Lay Smartas*, and provided a detailed discourse on the date of the founder. Works on Rāmānujācārya (the founder of Viśiṣṭādvaita system) include those by Harold Coward that provides details about his life and philosophical teachings.[15] Studies on the life and philosophy of Madhvācārya (the architect of the Dvaita system) have been examined by B. N. K. Sharma,[16] in his *History of the Dvaita School of Vedānta and its Literature* and *Philosophy of Śri Madhvacarya*. Subsequent brief descriptions of the life of Gurus have been published by C. M. Padmanabhachar, Hayavadana Rao, and Acharya Bannanje Govindacarya.[17]

The study of Hindu monasteries has been extended to include the traditions of asceticism and education that laid the foundation for the rise of monasteries. A comprehensive investigation about these two traditions (*sāmpradayas*) has been conducted by Patrick Olivelle, in the *Saṃnyāsa Upaniṣad* and the *The Āśrama System*, from a socioreligious context.[18] Publications on ancient Indian education system by Hartmut Scharfe and on asceticism by Haripada Chakraborti provide significant insight into the nature of learning and teaching.[19] Leela Shantakumari's book on *agrahāras* has valuable information on early formal educational institutions between 400–1300 CE.[20] Publications that have dealt with the social organization of the monastery are however very few. A. K. Shastry examines the records of the Śringeri *maṭha* relating to Keladi Nayakas. Vasudeva Rao in his book *The Living Traditions in Contemporary Texts: The Madhva Matha of Udipi* deals with the organization and architecture of Udipi *maṭha* apart from the divisions within the Dualist order. The history of Śri Vaiṣṇava *maṭhas* has been described by S. Kumara on *maṭhas* in Kanchipuram, Śrirangam, Tirupati, and Melkote.[21]

Although there have been studies about lives of individual gurus,[22] their philosophical theories, ascetic (*āśrama*) and teaching (*ācārya*) traditions, there has not been any critical or detailed investigation of the institution. The publication by Tamara I. Sears on early monastic architecture of Śaiva monasteries deals largely with institutions in Central India under the Kakatiyas between the eleventh and thirteenth centuries CE.[23] Anila Verghese has investigated into various types of monasteries at the Vijayanagara capital, Hampi, based on archaeological and inscriptional evidences.[24] Studies on patronage of monasteries, particularly regarding Dvaita *maṭhas*, have been conducted by Valerie Stoker, in 2006, in her publication *Polemics and Patronage in the City of Victory: Vyasatirtha, Hindu Sectarianism, and the Sixteenth-Century Vijayanagara Court*. But, none of these books deal with a comprehensive account of the historical rise of the monastery from a leadership and institutional perspective. Some Kannada works describe the lineage of Gurus, their holy sites, and a contextual history of the life of the Guru.[25]

In regard to relic worship, a comprehensive research has been done by Gregory Schopen into Buddhist relics in his book *Bones, Stones and Buddhist Monks* and by John S. Strong in *Relics of the Buddha*.[26] Till now, the only available literature on *vṛndāvanas* along with pilgrimage sites, icons, and teachings can be found in the monthly Kannada journal *Sudha*, but they have been dealt very briefly. Research on the *vṛndāvana* from a literary perspective has been conducted by Maura Corcoran in 1995, but she does not mention the icon of the Guru.[27]

Individual studies do little justice to the complexity of the subject or to the sheer length of its history. There is no scholarly book that has dealt with the growth of Hindu monasteries and particularly on the icon of the Guru. Studies on the visual, historical, and religious dimension of the *vṛndāvana* have yet to be conducted. This study will rectify the situation by a comprehensive study of the *maṭha* as a dynamic institution of the "living" Guru and within a sectarian monastery, as that of a living as well as the "dead" Guru. The study reveals the importance of the Guru and the integral system of education in medieval India within Hindu monasteries. It explains the reasons for the decline of Buddhism in India and the rise of the dynamic multifaceted monastery as an institution of the Guru. The research brings to light a paradoxical existing phenomenon of mummification and veneration of "whole-body relics" of the Guru within Hinduism that considers death as polluting.

Problems of Study

The rise of the Guru and that of a monastery in a historical context is a complex topic and is replete with varied problems. This is particularly the case in regard to literary and historical evidences. There are no textual descriptions or writings about the *vṛndāvana*s. There are uncommonly scant textual records and inscriptions to cast any light on these sacred objects. As mentioned above, books have been written from the standpoint of extolling the Guru in a monastery, and one can hardly find information about the aims of the organization or of its art or architecture, or even about the funerary rituals of monks. Due to lack of written historical sources, the study about the evolution of the monastery as well as that of *vṛndāvana* has been a conundrum. A lack of historical evidences, and a deliberate absence of the meaning of the term in many scriptures, calls for intensive research.

Furthermore, the simplicity of architecture and sculpture, as well as its subordinate status to a Hindu temple, have led to the relegation of this institution into the background, despite its significant role in historical times and the fact that the living Guru is still very popular, powerful, and revered. In addition, architectural and ritual manipulation and additions to the built environment at monastic sites around *vṛndāvanas* have recontextualized the monastic and popular practices from past few decades. Examples of such sites are Mantralaya, Udipi, Mulbagal, Sode, Anegondi, Kolar, Hampi, Malkhed, and Pajakshetra in the state of modern Karnataka. The art historian's task is further complicated by the fact that religious sanctuaries do not keep detailed reports about conservation and new constructions at these sites and one has to rely largely on cultic memory, oral tradition, and interviews with staff members and Gurus. The task has been rendered difficult by the reluctance of few institutions to provide access to manuscripts in the monasteries. Moreover, *vṛndāvanas* are considered extremely sacred, and a close examination and photography of these objects is normally prohibited.

The lack of predecessors in this field has led me to rely on my own sources of investigation. I do not claim to have answers to all the questions, and hope future studies might be able to contribute. The study is more of a discourse and is the first of its kind that investigates into the iconography of the icon in connection to the growth and development of monasteries, and particularly the Guru. It is indeed a mine full of anomalies that deserves an in-depth study. This book is an attempt to unlock the long tradition of the icon, and the institution that has survived for hundreds of years. This study will provide an insight into the icon and the rationale for its sacredness, form, and meaning that bridges various seemingly outward denominations of the cults of God and Guru with convincing evidences.

HISTORICAL SOURCES

The method of study followed in this book is dictated by the nature of direct and indirect sources available, for both the institution and the icon. There is a dual aim for the publication: to provide a holistic understanding of the monastery in relation to the Guru and to investigate into the form and meaning of the icon. If we are to capture the multifaceted nature of the *vṛndāvana* and the *maṭha*, it is essential to bridge disciplinary boundaries and focus on issues overlooked by past scholarship. The study breaks from typical studies of religious or art historical studies of religious phenomena that originate from a single tradition. It encompasses a multiplicity of practices that have a common cultural fabric. I use multiple sources, such as literary, archaeological, artistic, and epigraphical in addition to oral tradition and discussions with Gurus. Some of the monastic sites where fieldwork was conducted are Udipi, Hampi, Kanchipuram, Hampi, Śringeri, Mantralaya, Mysore, Tumkur, Kaladi, Kolar, Mulbagal, Melkote, Sannati, Malkhed, and Gokarna in South India, particularly Karnataka.

After a careful collection of historical, literary, and archaeological evidences, I examine the primary sources, in the form of commentaries on the *Upaniṣads* written by various Gurus, as well as secondary sources, such as biographical narratives of Gurus and the miracle stories that provide a narrative to the spread of the *bhakti* movement. Secondary sources in the form of publications, both in English and Kannada, throw an important light on aspects of *guruparamparā* (lineage), educational principles, philosophy, and nature of knowledge imparted in the institutions. The *Purāṇas* (such as the *Padma Purāṇa*, *Bhāgavat Purāṇa*, *Viṣṇu Purāṇa and Harivaṃśa*) have been particularly useful in comprehending the relation between God and Guru. More importantly, rituals, oral traditions, Kannada poetry and songs composed by *haridāsas* (devotees of God), interviews with living Gurus who are heads of *maṭhas*, their assistants and students have been crucial in gaining insight into the importance of the *vṛndāvana* and the workings of these institutions. This book is based on tangible artistic, literary, archaeological, and epigraphical evidences and provides a framework for the arguments.

SCOPE

The area of reference covers a major part of South India, namely the Deccan Plateau, south of the Vindhya Mountains. It deals with a wide expanse of historic land in peninsular India that stretched from the Sahyadri Mountains with the rivers Mahanadi and Godavari in the north and the Krishna and the Tungabhadra in the south and from the Arabian Sea in the west to the Bay of Bengal in the east. The Deccan plateau, which has an elevation of 300 to 1000 feet above sea level, lies within this as a triangular space enclosed by the Satmala Hills in the north and the Western and Eastern Ghats that stretch in long lines nearly parallel to the coast.[28]

The plateau is a rich area, diverse with many languages and religious practices. In the north Marathi is spoken while in the east Telugu speaking population predominate. The southwest part of the plateau is marked by Dharwar, while a third area is Karnata or Karnataka, where the prevailing language is Kannada. The river which watered the land was fittingly termed *kṛṣṇa*, the black, *kṛṣṇavarṇa*, of black hue, or *kṛṣṇaveṇi* with a braid of black hair.[29] The area of investigation is within the modern state of Karnataka, particularly the districts of Mangalore, Hampi, Bellary, Golcunda, Bijapur, Dharwar, Mysore, Mangalore, and Shimoga. The geography and history of Karnataka has been a conducive area for the growth of Hindu (and Jain and some Buddhist) monasteries from about fourth century CE till the present. The state is enriched by the tributaries, of rivers, Krishna, Bhima, Tungabhadra and the entire area is rich in agricultural and mineral resources.[30] The celebrated doab of Raichur is formed by the junction of River Bhima with Krishna which was the site of early monasteries. The area has a distinct social, ethnic, and cultural trait, evidenced in language and literature.[31]

However, Karnataka was not impervious to northern influences from the north; monks and ascetics arrived and migrated, carrying their messages of peace and righteousness. Waves of invasions took place at times. Islamic forces penetrated the forest barriers and the valleys of river Narmada and Godavari and ultimately reached the Raichur *doab* (land between two rivers). Contending forces on either side of the rivers, Tungabhadra and the Krishna, were locked in deadly combat in centers such as Koppal, Anegundi, Mudgal, Raichur, Devarakonda, and Nalgonda.

The rulers of *dakṣiṇapathapati* (sovereign of the Deccan) considered themselves as the most magnificent rulers of the world.[32] Between the seventh and fourteenth centuries CE, powerful empires of Western Chalukyas, Gangas, Eastern Chalukyas, Rashtrakutas, Hoysalas, Vijayanagara dynasties, Wodeyars, and Keladi Nayakas ruled Karnataka, although neighboring empires, such as the Pallavas, Pandyas, and Cholas often had a hold over part of its territories. The fragmentation of kingdoms, and fluidity of political boundaries, led to dispersal and movement of social groups. The threat of Islam marked the late medieval era. This was a crucial period in South Indian history, when there was a proliferation of religious and social traditions. Karnataka grew to be the home of the *Śaiva* and *Vedānta* ascetic philosophers who played an important role in the renaissance of monasticism—the renewal of ancient Upanisadic tradition. The flexibility of political boundaries and concomitant language, and economics, allowed a vigorous exchange of philosophic and religious traditions that was substantiated in the institution of the monastery and in its visual culture.

Book Chapters

This book is divided into six chapters each of which focuses on a particular aspect with considerable elaboration. These include the Hindu monastic system and its historical growth and development in chapters 2 and 3 and the origin, form, and meaning of the *vṛndāvana* in chapters 4 and 5.

For about fifteen hundred years, Hindu monastic organization, underwent a growth in function, form, and practice. The growth of *maṭhas* can be roughly divided into regional types while maintaining a rough chronological order, and religious differences, as well as recognizing their parallel expansion. These include the following: (1) An evolutionary period (ninth to twelfth centuries CE) when they grew to be independent institutions, in three different regions—the Śaiva Siddhānta *maṭhas* in Central India and Tamil Nadu and of Pāśupata and Kālamukha *maṭhas* in Karnataka; and (2) a mature period with the rise of the multifaceted Vedānta *maṭhas* (ninth to fourteenth centuries CE). They based their doctrines on the Upanisadic theistic philosophy, rooted in the authority of the *Vedas*. These include the Advaita Vedānta *maṭhas* (that arose in the ninth century CE), Viśiṣṭādvaita *maṭhas* (between eleventh and twelfth centuries CE), and Dvaita *maṭhas* (between the thirteenth and fourteenth centuries CE). However, all *maṭhas* (except the Pāśupata, Kapālika, and Kālamukha monasteries) continued to develop and divide and are still popular religious institutions in South India.[33]

Chapter 2 examines the vexing problem of the beginnings of the monastic system mainly through inscriptional evidences and traces its subsequent history during the early medieval period (ninth to twelfth centuries CE). From my preliminary study of epigraphical sources, I have found that they can be traced to traditions of teaching and asceticism that continued to play a predominant role in monastic and pre-monastic centers. However, the influence of Buddhist order cannot be neglected; it inspired the Hindu Gurus to establish their own orders. I compare the educational systems within the two religious systems. The foundations of the monastic system can be said to have been laid between the fifth and ninth centuries CE, while their growth as multifaceted institutions occurred between the ninth and twelfth centuries CE, particularly of the Śaiva Siddhānta, Pāśupata, and Kālamukha orders. They flourished as semi-independent institutions, in the context of the decline of Buddhism and the rise of militant Śaiva kings. *Maṭhas* differed from other formal educational institutions in many ways. Historical evidences prove that they were nonsectarian in important centers where Buddhist, Jain, and Hindu monasteries flourished together.

The rise of the independent monastery as a seminal institution began with Vedānta monasteries, particularly the Advaita monasteries (that believed in monism) established by Ādi Śaṅkarācārya, while their proliferation into various denominations/divisions occurred with the rise of Viśiṣṭādvaita (qualified non-dualist *mąthas*) of Rāmānujācārya and of Dvaita (dualist/realist) *maṭhas* of Madhvācārya. Chapter 3 examines the identity of each Vedantic order, and aspects of patronage as well as their community oriented architectural system. It aims to comprehend the process of crystallization of the monastic system, through the traditions of asceticism, Guru lineage, philosophical theories, icons, identity, architecture, and religious practices. A brief description of the architecture of *maṭhas* and its relation to the Hindu temple both in form and function illuminates the larger social processes of the two institutions, the monastery and the temple, as well as the role of the Guru and the priest.

With the development of Vedānta Dvaita (Dualist) order and its divisions into twenty four denominations (each under a founder Guru), monasticism takes a unique turn with its powerful symbolic form of the icon of the Guru, the *vṛndāvana*. Worship of an "embalmed body" within the *vṛndāvana* invites comparative exploration along multiple trajectories and raises important questions: Why do relics assume such a prominent role in the tradition when Hinduism considers relics as polluting? Is there something distinctively Buddhist or Hindu about the treatment of relics? Why are there so many apparent parallels—superficial or otherwise—between Buddhist *stupa* and Hindu *vṛndāvanas* and its relic cults? These queries have guided my multidisciplinary investigation in order to explain the principal historical forces that might have led to the 'reinvention' of the *vṛndāvana*.

I begin by a discussion into the terminology of these special types of "relics" and their tombs/memorials by comparing them to early Buddhist traditions. Pre-Buddhist and medieval Hindu burial and enshrinement practices have been a neglected field, but archaeological and literary evidences can provide an insight into the origins of whole-body relic cult. This study is more a discussion on the possible origins of the icon/relic, its unusual material structure, and its role and function within Hindu monastic culture. Chapter 4 probes into the tradition of relic enshrinement, funerary practices, memorials, and commemorative monuments within Buddhist, Jain, and Hindu traditions. It finally reveals the paradoxical phenomena of worship of the embalmed body of the Guru in Hinduism which considers death as polluting. The study consequently presents a new hypothesis that whole-body relic worship in Hinduism, was the result of multiple factors and a product of the institutionalization of the Guru.

As *maṭhas* gained in popularity, they continued all the elements of organized learning, feeding, living, and worship. Indirectly, the *vṛndāvana* acquired a more powerful symbolism, sacredness, and status. Chapter 5 discusses the anomaly of the *vṛndāvana* in terms of various levels of meaning. A discussion into the issues of iconic and "aniconic"/non-figural forms in Indian art, the transformation of the relic into icon and portrait, throws light on the iconographical connotations of the *vṛndāvana*. A particular attentiveness has been paid to etymological, mythological, and ontological import of the term *vṛndāvana* in order to comprehend the relation between Tulsi *vṛndāvana* by relating it to Lord Kṛṣṇa and Viṣṇu. Its multileveled meaning as a death marker, symbol of *ānanda* (bliss), the garden of Kṛṣṇa, elucidates the theory of Hindu aesthetics between true and eternal form, *avatāra* (manifestation) and non-manifestation, thereby forming a link between ancient and medieval beliefs. The visual, historical, and religious dimensions of the powerful premodern monastery are revealed for the first time where exchanges between death and sacredness, God and Guru are enacted.

In chapter 6, I conclude that the Hindu monastery was an institution of the Guru and that the relation between the living and the deceased Guru was particularly close in the Dvaita *maṭhas*. I have attempted to prove that the Hindu monastery was a flexible, multifaceted institution that could adapt to changing historical circumstances, while the *vṛndāvana* in a monastery was a form of religious symbolism strategies to mediate de facto sociocultural changes that sustained traditional education and order during a critical period of Indian history. Gurus were able to rephrase/reinvent traditions, interpret philosophy, rituals, iconography, and ideals, and yet maintain a sense of continuity, echoing Vedic and Upanisadic thoughts, across time and space.

The importance of the *maṭha* as an ecclesiastical system with an integral function can be attributed to the leadership of the ascetic Guru, who shaped the trajectory of its development between the ninth and seventeenth centuries CE. The growth of the multifaceted institution from an educational establishment to organized centers of socioreligious power sustained the growth of intellectual thought while the Guru provided a structure to Hinduism. The efficacy of the *vṛndāvana* was not in the connotations of death or the embalmed body or relic, but in the eternal and "true" biography of the life of the Guru that can be transmitted to the devotee and community. Here the boundaries between the dead and living, sacred and unholy, aniconic and iconic, relic and icon were flexible.

I have explored a relatively uncharted territory. Identifying the importance of the Guru within the institution of the *maṭha*, in the icon and relics, the book addresses the role of the bodily remains in the devotional practices of the community. It fills the lacuna in our understanding of the social history of India during the medieval period. Essentially, it bridges the disciplinary boundaries in terms of interwoven artistic, religious, archaeological, and literary contexts that are crucial for an in-depth comprehension of the rich heritage of Hindu monasteries.

NOTES

1. Sanskrit diacritics have been used for Sanskrit and Kannada words, see note and abbreviations.

2. The term is used in Advaita *maṭhas* founded by Ādi Śaṅkarācārya.

3. Vedānta *maṭhas* are the Advaita, Viśiṣṭādvaita, and Dvaita *maṭhas* that uphold the authority of the *Vedas* and *Upaniṣads*. *Vedānta* developed into a major philosophical system in the medieval period. They consist of Advaita (monistic) order, the Viśiṣṭādvaita (qualified monistic), and Dvaita (Dualist) systems all of which believed in the concepts of *brahman*, *ātman*, *dharma*, *karma*, and other *tattvas* (realities) and adhered to the *Vedas* and *Upaniṣads*.

4. Sircar, D.C. *Studies in the Religious Life of Ancient and Medieval India*. Delhi: Motilal Banarsidass, 1971, pp. 29, 302–3.

According to the *Encyclopædia Britannica* the term monasticism is derived from the Greek word *monachos* living. http://academic.eb.com/levels/collegiate/article/109510

5. Leclercq, Jean O.S.B. *The Love of Learning and the Desire for God: A Study of Monastic Culture*, translated by Catharine Misrahi. New York: Fordham University Press, 1961, pp. 21, 74, 82.

6. Sawai, Yoshitsugau. *The Faith of Ascetics and Lay Smartas: A Study of the Sankaran Traditin of Srngeri*. Vol. XIX. Publications of the De Nobili Research Library. Edited by Gerhard Oberhammer. Vienna: Institute for Indology, University of Vienna, 1992, p. 22.

7. Apte, Vaman Shivram. *Sanskrit-English Dictionary*. Delhi: Motilal Banarsidass. 1963, p. 417.

8. Cenkner, William. *A Tradition of Teachers: Śankara and the Jagadgurus Today*. Columbia, MO: South Asia Books, 1983, p. 8; Bhadri, K.M. *A Cultural History of Northern India: Based on Epigraphical Sources from the 3rd Century. B.C. to 700 A.D.* Delhi: Book India Publishing Co., 2006, p. 167

9. In the west, one is familiar with the Rāmakṛṣṇa *math*, whose founder was Vivekānanda. His guru was Śri Rāmakṛṣṇa Paramahamsa.

Considering the nature of Christian and Hindu monasteries, I retain the term "monastery" as closest that translates the term in English. According to Glenn Yocum a *maṭha* cannot be translated as a monastery, and the term is misleading. Yocum, Glenn E. "A Non-Brahman Tamil Shaiva Mutt: A Field Study of the Thiruvavduthurai Adheenam." In *Monastic Life in the Christian and Hindu Traditions*, ed. Austin Creel and Vasudha Narayanan. NY: Edwin Mellen, 1990, p. 250.

The term "*maṭha*" is defined as a college, hut of an ascetic or student.

Monier Williams, *Sanskrit-English Dictionary*. New Delhi: Munshiram Manoharlal, 2002.

It can also mean an institute and an extended meaning—as a residence or institute of an ascetic or saint. (It should not be confused with the word '*mata*' that means reflection or understanding.)

10. There are approximately ninety-five monastic orders in Hinduism, and about seventy-five adhere to celibacy.

11. This is also the case in Śri Vaiṣṇava *maṭhas*.

12. Huntington, Susan L. *The Art of Ancient India: Buddhist, Hindu, Jain*. New York: Weather Hill, 1985.

Granoff, Phyllis, and Koichi Shinohara. *Monks and Magicians: Religious Biographies in Asia*. Mosaic Press, NY: Motilal Banarsidass, 1994.

13. Schopen, Gregory. *Bones, Stones, and Buddhist Monks: Collected Papers on the Archaeology, Epigraphy, and Texts of Monastic Buddhism in India*. Honolulu: University of Hawai'i Press, 1997, 2004;

Dutt, Sukumar. *Early Buddhist Monasticism: 600 B.C.–100 B.C.* Bombay: Routledge, 1960.

14. Cenkner. *A Tradition of Teachers*.

Sears, Tamara I. *Worldly Gurus and Spiritual Kings: Architecture and Asceticism in Medieval India*. New Haven: Yale University Press, 2014.

15. Coward, Harold. *The Perfectibility of Human Nature in Eastern and Western Thought*. Albany, NY: State University of New York Press, 2008.

16. Sharma, B.N.K. *History of the Dvaita School of Vedānta and its Literature*. Delhi: Motilal Banarsidass, 2008.

Sharma, B.N.K. *Philosophy of Śri Madhvacarya*. Delhi: Motilal Banarsidass, 2008.

17. Padmanabhacharya, C.M. *Life and Teachings of Śri Madhvachariar*, 2nd ed., Bombay, (n.d.) 1983.

Rao, Hayavadana. *Poornaprajna Vijaya: Life and Teachings of Madhvacarya*, translated from Kannada by Dhadra Krishnamoorthy. Chennai: Śri Krishna Śri Raghavendra Trust, 2010.

Govindacarya, Bannanje. *Acharya Madhwa: Life and Works*, translated into English by Upadhyaya, U.P. Udipi: Isavasya Pratishanam, 2011.

18. Olivelle, Patrick. *Samnyasa Upaniṣads: Hindu Scriptures on Asceticism and Renunciation*. New York: Oxford University Press, 1992. Olivelle, Patrick. *The Asrama System: The History and Hermeneutics of a Religious Institution*. New York: Oxford University Press, 1993.

19. Scharfe, Hartmut. *Education in Ancient India*. Leiden: Brill, 2002.

Chakraborti, Haripada. *Asceticism in Ancient India: In Brahmanical, Buddhist, Jaina and Ajivika Societies: from the Earliest Times to the Period of Śaṅkarāchārya*. Calcutta: Punthi Pustak, 1993.

Chatterjee, Mitali. *Education in Ancient India: From Literary Sources of the Gupta Age*. New Delhi: D.K. Printworld, 1999.

20. Shantakumari, S. Leela *History of the Agraharas, Karnataka, 400–1300*. Madras: New Era Publications, 1986.

21. Shastry, A. K. *A History of Sringeri*. Dharwad: Prasaranga, Karnatak University, 1982.

Rao, Vasudeva. *Living Traditions in Contemporary Contexts: The Madhva Matha of Udupi*. New Delhi: Orient Longman, 2002.

Kumara, S, and others. Ed. *Bhagavad Sri Ramanuja's Contribution to Four Swayamvyakta Kshetra—Kanchipuram, Srirangam, Tirupati and Melkote*. Melkote: Academy of Sanskrit Research, 2015.

22. Works in Kannada: Malagi, Jayatirthacharya. Ed. *Shri Suddha Vishesh Sanchike*. Dharwad: Shri Suddha Karyalaya, 1989.

Kulkarni, Kolhara Krsna. *Madhva Mathagalu*. Bangalore: Bhagyalakshmi Prakashana, 1996.

Gururajachar, Rajashree. *Kaliyuga Kalpaturu*. Mysore: Sri Parimala Samshodhana Mandir, 2007.

Badrinath, S K. *Shri Raghottama Tirtharu*. Bangalore: Susheela Prakashana, 1998.

23. Sears. *Worldly Gurus and Spiritual Kings Architecture and Asceticism in Medieval India*. New Haven: Yale University Press, 2014.

24. Verghese, Anila. *Religious Traditions at Vijayanagara: As Revealed through Its Monuments*. New Delhi: Manohar, 1995.

Verghese, Anila and Dieter Eigner. *A Monastic Complex in Vithalpura*. Hampi: Vijayanagra. South Asian Studies: *Journal of the Society for South Asian Studies* (incorporating the Society for Afghan Studies) 14, 4. (1998): 127–140.

25. Gopalcharya, Agnihotri (Kannada). *Sri Uttradi Mathada Guru Pramparеya Samkshipta Charitre*. Hubli: Raghavendra Swami Matha, 1972.

Balagaru, Ruchiracharya (Kannada). *Pajakakshetra Vaibhava*. Bangalore: Pajaka Seva Trust, 1999. Vedavyasachar. (Kannada) *Shri Madvadhiraja Guru Sambhavagalu*. Dharwad: P. S. Desai, 1998.

26. Strong, John. *Relics of the Buddha*. Delhi: Motilal Banarasidass, 2007. Schopen. *Bones, Stones, and Buddhist Monks*.

Schopen, Gregory A. On the Buddha and His Bones: The Conception of a Relic in the Inscriptions of Nagarjunakoṇḍa. *Journal of the American Oriental Society* 108, no. 4 (1998): 527–537.

Schopen, Gregory. Ritual Rights and Bones of Contention: More on Monastic Funerals and Relics in the Mulasarvastivada-Vinaya. *Journal of Indian Philosophy* 22, 1 (1994): 31–80.

Sharf, Robert H. "The Idolization of Enlightenment: On the Mummification of Chan Masters in Medieval China." *History of Religions* 32, no. 1 (1992): 1–31.

27. *Sudha*. Bangalore: Uttaradi Math, n.d. (Monthly journal). Corcoran, Maura. *Vrndavana in Vaisnava Literature: History, Mythology, Symbolism*. Delhi: KKPW, 1995.

28. Yazdani, Ghulam. *The Early History of the Deccan*. London: Oxford University Press, 1960, p. 4.

29. The name of the region is probably derived from *Kari* or black and *nadu* country that aptly designates the black cotton soil, or *Krishnabhumikshetra*.

30. IA, V, 319.

Yazdani. *The Early History of the Deccan*, 11.

31. Nilakanta Sastri K. and Radha Champakalakshmi. *A History of South India: From Prehistoric Times to the Fall of Vijayanagar*. New Delhi: Oxford University Press, 1958, p. 102.

32. Yazdani. *The Early History of the Deccan*, 40.

33. The Liṅgāyat *maṭhas* are Śaiva *maṭhas* and have a large number of disciples and adherents.

Chapter 2

Beginnings and Growth of Śaiva Monasteries in South India

South India is the home of innumerable types of ancient and living Hindu ascetics, who have renounced worldly life. But the origins of institutionalized renunciation are relatively obscure. This is partly due to the paucity of literary and historical evidences about their organizational structure and multifarious role. In addition, there is a lack of literary evidences, an absence of the term *maṭha*, ambiguity of architectural ramifications, details about the life of the ascetic Guru (head pontiff), and complex concepts in Sanskrit that evade complete translation.

This chapter attempts to uncover its origins as an organization of the Guru and trace its subsequent history during the early medieval period (ninth to twelfth centuries CE) mainly in South India. *Maṭhas* were educational and ascetic institutions headed by a Guru. The word *maṭha* comes from the root *mạth* (to dwell) and this may mean the residence of ascetic, a monastic school,[1] but it usually indicates a monastery in a town and often associated with a temple.[2]

ORIGINS OF HINDU MONASTIC SYSTEM

A history of Hindu monasteries can begin only with an introduction about Buddhist *saṅghas* (monasteries) which have been known to exist from as early as second century BCE, and flourished in almost all parts of India till ninth to eleventh centuries CE. Supported by powerful kings, monasteries were wealthy, popular, and powerful, particularly in Andhra Pradesh[3] and Tamil Nadu. Unlike the large Buddhist institutions, Jain monasteries (also known as *maṭhas*) were small and largely in remote areas. Although the beginnings of Hindu monasteries go back to third century CE, it is only between the ninth and twelfth centuries that they developed into seminal institutions.

The earliest reference to the term *maṭha* has been found in stray Jain texts of second and fifth centuries CE. They were educational organizations of gurus who moved from place to place[4] as evidenced in the inscriptions from Paharpur in Bengal.[5] With the migration of the Jain saint Bhadrabahu with his disciple Chandragupta Maurya, the theater of Jain monasteries shifted to the Deccan.[6] It then flourished in Karnataka under the Ganga kings, Eastern Chalukyas, and Hoysalas (fifth to tenth centuries CE).[7] An early reference to a Hindu *maṭha* can be found in the inscription of Samudragupta, which stated that it was a hostel for students. They were rest houses, where food might or might not have been given to travelers or for mendicants and ascetics. Numerous inscriptions provide interesting aspects about the early functions of a *maṭha* during the Gupta and post-Gupta periods (fourth to seventh centuries CE). A *maṭha* of Maninaga Bhattarak of Ekambaka (599–600 CE) has been described as an institution of Vedic studies.[8] According to the Aphsad inscription of Adityasena of seventh century CE it was a religious college,[9] while the Mundesvari inscription of Udayasena records that it was a religious building attached to the temple of Śrī Nārāyaṇa.[10] In South India, inscriptional evidence from the Cola and Pandyan domains dates them to seventh century CE.

Although the early history of Hindu monasteries has been difficult to trace, it is reasonable to assume that by seventh century CE they functioned as a hostel for students, and a residential college. In addition, they grew to be a place of Vedic studies, devoted to a particular school of the Vedas. Later medieval inscriptions came to refer to them as an academic institution.[11] Although they were situated near temples, there has been no reference to a deity or to an ascetic as the founder of a *maṭha*. Miller contends that *maṭhas* were loosely organized religious schools, and can be termed as "quasi monastic institutions, before the ninth century CE, and even predating Buddhist and Jain orders."[12] However, after the decline of Buddhism, Hindu *maṭhas* became formidable institutions particularly with the rise of the earliest Śaiva monasteries.

The growth of *maṭhas* can be roughly divided into regional types, while keeping in mind their rough chronological order, religious differences, and at the same time recognizing their parallel expansion. There was

1. A foundational period between the fourth and ninth centuries CE;
2. A period of growth with multiple functions between the ninth and twelfth centuries CE. They were in three regions—the Śaiva Siddhānta *maṭhas* in Central India and Tamil Nadu and *Pāśupata* and *Kālāmukha maṭhas* in Karnataka;
3. A period of proliferation of *maṭhas* as independent, powerful institutions between the twelfth and fifteenth centuries CE. The rise of Vedānta *maṭhas* in Karnataka and their spread was based on their philosophical orientation. These include the Advaita *maṭhas* (ninth century CE onward), Viśiṣṭādvaita *maṭhas* (twelfth century CE onward), and Dvaita *maṭhas* (thirteenth century CE onward).
4. Viraśaiva *maṭhas* flourished in Karnataka (twelfth century CE onward) and they still continue to play a major role in society.

The Ascetic Tradition

In order to uncover the origins of monasteries, inscriptional evidences are insufficient by themselves. Two relevant sources that are often overlooked are the socioreligious *sāmpradāyas* (traditions) of *sanyāsa* (asceticism) and *ācārya* (teaching) that provided inspiration, and were a raison d'être for their continuous expansion as a public organization.

Asceticism flourished in India from about 2500 BCE particularly in the Indo-Gangetic doab. The Jains attached the highest importance to it and Buddha resorted to the golden middle path of avoiding self-indulgence and practicing self-denial. Numerous Vedic seers practiced *sanyāsa* which was passed down through oral tradition and eulogized in texts such as *Dharmasūtras*, *Bhagavad Gīta*, *Āśrama Upaniṣad*, and *Sanyāsa Upaniṣad*. Olivelle rightly observes that *vairāgya* (renunciation) was an established way of life. He explains that renunciation, essentially, is a negative state: one is a renouncer not because one performs certain distinctive actions or conforms to certain characteristic habits and customs but because one does not perform actions and does not conform to customs that characterizes life—in society.[13] The ascetic shaves his head, cuts the sacrificial string,[14] performs the *sāvitrī* rite, sacrifice, and deposits the fires in the self, and takes the vows of celibacy and nonattachment. He is now a *sanyāsi* and continues to practice these values, by internalizing them. The orange robe is one of the most powerful symbols of asceticism, of the triumph of virtue, discipline, life of continence, renunciation, liberation, physical control, order, vigilant striving for divinity, spiritual strength—the characteristics of a yogi. He is not attached to a site or place and hence is considered a *parivrajaka* (wandering monk), except for the rainy season when he lives in a fixed place.[15] Renunciation implied the ritual death of the renouncer, discarding the sacrificial thread, plucking the hair of the top knot, ritual death, holding a staff, loop, water strainer, water pot, and begging bowl.[16] The ascetic nature of a guru was helpful in cultivating and teaching discipline, love, dedication, passion for knowledge, and service to society. *Sanyāsa* was not a mask for escapism, nor an order that sheltered parasites of society, but for the liberation of the individual soul and also for the good of the world.[17]

The ascetic was known by various names, such as *sant*, *ṛṣi*, *sanyāsi*, *sādhu*, *bhikku*, *sanyāsin*, *muni*, *yati*, *ācārya*, *sādhu*, *mahāpūruṣa*, *yogi*, *bābā*, or *mahārāja*.[18] These terms specifically applied to the varieties of saints/monks/gurus who maintained the continuous ascetic tradition.[19] Seventeen out of eighteen *Upaniṣads* deal with *sanyāsa* practiced under different names: *bhikṣu*, *sanyāsin*, *parivrajaka*, *avadhūta*, and *paramahamsa*.[20] It viewed the ascetic and hermit life as an essential part of its system which prescribed the path of four *āśramas*, namely *brahmacārin* (student-hood), *gṛhastha* (householder), *vānaprasthya* (retired), and *sanyāsi* (renunciate).[21] It was a remarkable system headed by *sanyāsis* or married *ācāryas* and *paṇḍitas*.[22]

The Teaching Tradition

Being an ascetic did not appear to be contradictory to the function of teaching. Ancient India had a teaching tradition that goes back to the Vedic and Epic periods, with *gurukulas* and individual teachers. Many *sanyāsis* were teachers or gurus, which might appear as an anomaly. Both ascetics and householders were teachers.[23] There were a number of categories of teachers, and the titles used for a teacher were *ācārya*, *guru*, *sadguru*, *śāstrī*, *paṇḍita*, *adhyāpaka*, who spread or taught philosophy and religious studies. An *ācārya* was one who taught the *Vedas*, although Yaska defined *ācārya* as one who imparted traditional precepts, or one who systematically arranged the various objects of knowledge, or one who developed the intellectual faculty.[24] An *upādhyāya* was one who taught only a specialized part of the *Vedas* or the auxiliary sciences—the *Vedāngas*; the *paṇḍita* meant scholars whose profession was teaching or who acquired a great intellectual mastery through Sanskrit,[25] or a specialist in traditional knowledge, with no pride or jealously.[26] The title of guru was the most popular and seen as one who was an authority on the knowledge of the *Vedas* (Books of knowledge), *Purāṇas* (quasi-historical texts), and *śāstras*.[27] Although the titles, *śāstrī*, *ācārya* were all related to education, teaching, and learning, it is the *paṇḍita* that was most strongly identified with the figure of the guru.[28]

The most commonly used term for the teacher was guru. He has been described as one who brings light, meaning divine reality. There is actually no English word that can be used to translate the word guru, which has been connected only to Hindu/Buddhist and Jain traditions. The guru in the *Maṇḍukya Upaniṣad* is defined as one who is well versed in the *Vedas* and one who is absorbed in the *brahman*.[29] The guru in the *Upanisadic* tradition was a realized individual, while in the epic tradition it meant ascetics, and householders with *āśramas*. In the *Bhagavad Gīta* (2.54) it is mentioned that gurus were those who were steeped in *brahmavidyā* (science of understanding *brahman*);[30] they were illuminators who had the power to change others.[31] The guru was a realized being, who occupied a special place and became indispensable for the attainment of spiritual knowledge of *brahman*.[32] Thus the grace of the guru became invaluable for learning.[33]

All the scriptural traditions agreed that the term guru was one who imparted *vidya* (knowledge), particularly spiritual knowledge. Imparting knowledge to a pupil (*vidyopadāna*), so as to make him/her a *śikṣita*, a learned person,[34] was given great importance. *Vidyā* was accorded a high place and regarded as a third eye that gave insight into life.[35] The number of *vidyās* that were translated as subjects varied: they included *anvīkṣikī* (science of inquiry), logic, metaphysics, *daṇḍanīti* (science of governance), and four *vidyās*, namely *Rgveda*, *Yajurveda*, *Sāmaveda*, and *Atharvaveda* while Manu adds a fifth *Veda*, namely *ātmavidyā* or knowledge of the soul or spirituality.[36] It is well known that ancient India had a comprehensive system of educational philosophy, theory, and classification along with steps of learning, and complexity of subjects; to put it in modern terminology, a method, approach, theory, and a way of inquiry.[37]

The ritual of commencement of studies (*vidyārambha* or *akṣara abhyāsa*) was (and is still) performed at the beginning or commencement of primary education in the fifth year.[38] The first stage of student life was that of the *brahmacārin* which demarcated the period of education from the fifth or sixth year, from the period of *vidyārambha* (commencement of education) till the sixteenth year, the *samartha*. This was generally followed by specialization in arts and sciences.[39] In this system, *vidyā*[40] and guru were both considered sacred. The importance of a guru was so great that he was accorded a high place in society and his status equaled that of the gods.[41]

The teaching and ascetic traditions came together in the traditional school system of *gurukula* and later during the medieval period, in the monastic culture. According to Miller,[42] the system was established prior to Ādi *Śankarācārya* (788–820 CE) who systematized the Hindu monastic system. However, Buddhist and Jain systems had a constant stream of varied ranks of ascetics, which were organized into fraternities, and these developed their own doctrines, disciplines, individual teaching, and learning units. Thus the amalgamation of the two systems of asceticism and teaching can also be seen in the rise of the Buddha, who was an ascetic and teacher, which was synthesized in the institution of the Buddhist *saṅgha.* It may be added that the Hindu monastic system was an institution that was largely influenced by the earlier order of the Buddhist *saṅgha*,[43] although the traditions of asceticism and teaching were pre-Buddhist.

BUDDHIST AND HINDU MONASTIC EDUCATION SYSTEMS

The Buddhist Monastery

In everyday language, *saṅgha* connoted the nomadic community of monks. In the language of *dhamma*, *saṅgha* also referred to those who followed the truth and was the highest mental quality of a monk or nun. If the Buddha was the first refuge or jewel of Buddhism, *dharma* and *saṅgha* constituted the other two jewels. The Buddha, *saṅgha*, and *dharma* were the *triśaraṇa* (refuges) which marked the evolution of Buddhism.[44] Thus both the Buddhist and Hindu systems had a common root denominator in the tradition of monks, learning, and studentship. The Buddhist *saṅgha* was not a new phenomenon but positively a greater development upon the Hindu monastic tradition.[45] The Buddhist *saṅgha* emerged spontaneously from reverence for the Buddha, with its basis in earlier systems, communities, and organizations. However, due to reverence for the ascetic teacher, the Buddha, the tradition of residential monks in *saṅghas* became stronger. Thus the Buddhist monastery as a place for congregational life, study, and meditation became a major institution of education.

The rules of Buddhist monastic education system of initiation closely followed the line of the Hindu initiation of studentship (*brahmacārya*), ordination, responsibility of the teacher for students training, and conduct. The *pabbaja* (*pravrajya*) or going out of home into the order resembles *sanyāsa* (renunciation) in Hinduism. In both systems, the minimum period of studentship was twelve years, there was an age restriction, and admission to the order was permitted only with the consent of the parents—a feature that reflects the tradition of respect to the home and family. In addition, *sanyāsa* was not for one with physical defects or times of sickness, or because of a serious moral defect.[46] Kern points out that Buddhist *bhikkus* and Hindu *sanyāsis* each formed the nucleus of a different sect, each following the doctrines of its masters.[47]

The Buddhist *saṅgha* was a preaching institution as well, but the Dhamma of the *saṅgha* pertained to moral qualities of the *bhikkus* (monks) and *bhikkunis* (nuns).[48] The *saṅgha* of *bhikkus* lived under the guardianship of a common teacher—the *upajjhaya* or *ācārya*. It is interesting to find that each individual group was known by a teacher and his students were organized around him. However, these groups or schools did not exist as isolated and independent unit or institution in the Buddhist world. They lived in *vihāras* (monasteries) and each school (or subschool) of Buddhism had its own code of discipline and regulations that was binding upon all. In the Hindu monastery, the individual schools were isolated, and the ideal was the successions of teachers and disciples. The differences between the Buddhist and Hindu education system played a vital role in the decline of the former and the rise of the Hindu monastery.

The Buddhist *saṅgha* was the only system of education and there were no educational opportunities outside of monasteries. All education, religious and secular, were in the hands of the monks, who were custodians and bearers of Buddhist culture.[49] While the Hindu system was predominantly a domestic system of education, with fathers as teachers in *pāthśālās* (local schools), *gurukulas*, and individual homes (or even where the schools and homes were often next to each other as in *agrahāras*), in the Buddhist system the home was superseded by the monastery. The Hindu system did not supplant a formal system that produced en masse monks. Although the Buddhist system was a wonderful liberal system of brotherhood, that promoted intellectual progress, and helped to resolve the problem of poverty, the relationship between the teacher and student was not so deep as in the Hindu one. The Buddhist system abolished differences in the ranks of monks, but this republican or democratic type of administration (with all having equal voting power, including the unworthy) was different than the Hindu monarchical principle. The *saṅgha* was loosely knit, in the sense that there was no common authority to reconcile the differences that arose among monastic life or discipline.[50]

The Buddhist *saṅghā* depended on the laity for its support, and it did not admit day scholars to its school. For those outside the *saṅghā*, the discourses in the *saṅghā* were the only recourse; monasteries were the exclusive centers of education and monks alone were experts in the sacred lore. Thus, the laity sought other centers of education outside the Buddhist monasteries. There were centers of education in medicine, surgery, and solitary Buddhist centers in forests, as in the Hindu model of hermitages. *Vedas* were taught in the universities at Takshasila and Nalanda, where *yogaśāstra*, *nyāya*, *hetuvidyā* were taught. Hindu and Buddhist teachings were taught and students were free to learn the type of *vidyā* they desired—sciences, arts, or crafts.[51]

The accounts of Hieun Tsang in seventh century CE refer to education that was centered around Hindu temples and Buddhist *vihāras*. One of the oldest universities was Takshasila, which specialized in archery, warfare, and medicine, a proponent being Jivaka, a well known medical authority. At Ayodhya, Jain works were taught, while Rajagriha was a Jain center for education of women.[52] Fa Hsien records that Nalanda was the most illustrious university, where 80,000 disciples and 10,000 teachers lived (fourth to eighth centuries CE). Other centers included Vallabhi, the capital of Maitraka kings (fifth to eighth century CE), Vikramasila (in tenth century CE), and Odantapuru Mahavihara (700–1200 ACE), each being a residential university with a library of books and manuscripts written in Ardhamagadhi and Pali. Mithila was known for studies on *kāvya* (poetry) and music; Nadia or Navadvipa (on the confluence of rivers Jalangi and Bhagirath in East Bengal) and Kundinapura near Pataliputra were famous centers.[53] Thus with the coming of *saṅghas*, important Buddhist centers grew up which were supported by both Buddhist and non-Buddhist kings, such as the Satavahanas. Important centers were Kanheri (Krshnagiri)—whose cave inscriptions between the first and eighth centuries CE consisted of numerous donative inscriptions to Buddhist monasteries. Hindu, Buddhist, and Jain institutions were patronized by ministers, and laity, as well as by Hindu kings, such as the Guptas, Vakatakas, Chalukyas, and Rashtrakutas. In North India, the seven cities of Ayodhya, Mathura, Maya, Kasi, Kanci, Avantika as well as Dvaravati (Dvaraka) were known for imparting excellent education.[54] Thus specialized institutions were not divided into purely Buddhist or Hindu religious systems.[55]

The above evidence throws ample light on the importance of education outside and within the Hindu system. However the context for the incorporation of the ascetic titular head during the post-Buddhist period (ninth century CE onward) is intriguing. Can this be attributed to the influence of the ascetic heads within the *saṅgha*? Although the ascetic tradition was rooted in ancient Indian culture, it was practiced largely by individuals. Moreover, no parallel Hindu *maṭha* arose in the early centuries despite the presence of Buddhist and Jain *saṅghas*. This widens the scope of our inquiry into the beginnings of the Hindu monastery as a continuation of the preexisting Hindu formal/informal education systems from pre-Buddhist and post-Buddhist eras.

The Hindu Educational System and the *Maṭha*

After the gradual waning of Buddhist *saṅghas*, various types of educational institutions arose. Hindu education was in the ascendancy around seventh century CE (and many Hindus consecrated their lives to a life of celibate study). However, it was only after the decline of Buddhist *saṅgha* that Hindu monasticism arose as an institution with an ascetic as the head of the order. Before we examine the origins of the Hindu *maṭha* system as a formal educational center, it may be pointed out that an informal educational system was also prevalent among the Hindus. The informal education system imparted knowledge outside the walls of a formal school. Family and other social institutions played a vital role in making the individual a holistic and creative personality.

The informal system of education comprised of *āśramas* and in homes. But there was a formal traditional Vedic educational system that existed as *gurukulas*, *ghaṭikās*, *brahmapuris*, and *agrahāras* in South India (fourth century CE to ninth century CE). The earliest educational institution was the *gurukula* (or the house of the Guru) where the celibate student (*brahmacāri*) lived with his teacher *ācārya/upādhyāya*, in a *gurukula/āśrama*.[56] But there is not much evidence of the existence of *gurukulas* after tenth century CE. Instead there is evidence of numerous *agrahāras* (a community of *brāhmins*). They flourished in large numbers in the South between the Godavari and Kaveri rivers in Tamil Nadu under Pandyas, Pallavas, and Colas; in Karnataka under the Kadambas, Chalukyas of Badami, the Gangas, the Rashtrakutas, Chalukyas of Kalyana, the Sunas, and the Hoysalas (fourth and thirteenth centuries CE).[57] Inscriptions praise the *agrahāras* at Balligame and Kuppatur (Shimoga District)[58] as comparable to Amravati and Alakapuri, which prospered because of the presence of the learned versed in *Vedas*, Vedānta, and *śāstras*.[59] Another institution of great antiquity in first century CE was the *ghaṭikāsthana*, which scholars defined as religious center, an educational establishment, and a place for discourse.[60] In South India, the most famous *ghaṭikā* was in Kanchipuram. There were *ghaṭikās* in Karnataka, particularly Mysore (fourth–twelfth centuries CE),[61] in Polliyur (Dharwad district), Kadalevada (Bijapur district), and Shikaripur (Shimoga district) in twelfth century CE.[62] A record dated 1181 CE from Teridal (Bijapur district) states that *ghaṭikās* were attached to temples.

Equally important were colleges called *vidyāsthānas*,[63] particularly in Kanchipuram (200–900 CE), where teams of learned men were responsible for the maintenance of the organizations, received patronage from the king, and were exempted from paying taxes. The *vidyāsthāna* had fourteen *gaṇas* identified with fourteen divisions of literature—four *Vedas*, six *Angas*, *Mīmāṃsā*, *Nyāya*, *Purāṇa*, and *Dharmaśāstra*—and fourteen divisions of musical science. It is said that even the Kadamba king, Mayur Sharma (345–365 CE), who ruled Northern Karnataka from Banavasi, went to Kanchipuram accompanied by his guru to complete the full course of his studies.[64] The pavilions of the temples in Chidambaram and Tanjavur were named as *vyākaraṇa dāna maṇḍapa* (*maṇḍapa* exclusively for the study of grammar) that contained innumerable manuscripts.[65] Temple schools played a significant role during the Cola period (eighth to twelfth centuries CE) in Kanchipuram, Srirangam, Melkote, and Tirupati thus influencing the rise of *maṭhas*.

In addition, there were the *vidyāpīṭhas* (seats of learning or centers of knowledge).[66] There is also a reference to *ācārya pīṭhas*, or *pancāryās*, such as those of Sri Renukacārya of Rambhapuri at Mysore, Sri Darukacārya at Ujjain, Sri Ekoramaradhya at Himavatkedar in Himalayas, Paditharadhya at Śrisaila in Andhra Pradesh, and Sri Viswaradhya at Kasi who founded five pontifical thrones which are still living institutions.[67]

There was not much difference between the early medieval *vidyālaya*, *vidyāpīṭha*, *agrahāra*, *ghaṭikā* and the *maṭha* regarding the teacher or teaching methods, subject matter, and recital of *Vedas* (or specific *śāstras* specialized by some); and even the practice of *gurudakshina* in the form of *dāna* (gifts). All educational institutions appear to have been attached to some temple or had some temple attached to them. There were various levels of teaching in Hindu educational institutions. The teaching in *brahmapuris* and *ghaṭikās* was at the school level, while *vidyālayas* and *mahavidyālays* were academies similar to undergraduation or postgraduation, and *maṭhas* could be schools or academies with a specialized branch of teaching of *Vedas* (and even *Āgamas*).

However, there was a difference between the *maṭha* and another educational institution, largely in regard to the type of students. There were two kinds of celibate students in a *maṭha*: the temporary celibate, contemplating a family life and his training called *upakurvāṇa*, and the perpetual celibate, called *naiṣṭhika brahmacāri*, who chose to live with his teacher lifelong (figure 2.1).[68] An epigraph of 1055 CE from Dharwar records that the village of Pallavura was turned into a *naiṣṭhika-sthānam*, and gifted to the temple of Kadambesvaradeva into the hands of Somesvara Paṇḍitadeva.[69] Another support comes from a record of 1077 CE, from Yevur (Gulbarga district), that mentions that the *mạtha* was not open to any except those who observed perpetual celibacy to abide in the monastery "(*naiṣṭhika-bhramacārigalg-allāde maṭhadol-iral-sallādu*)".[70] It was stipulated that those who did not observe celibacy would be expelled.

Figure 2.1 Students in a *maṭha*.

In addition, *maṭhas* were headed by a *sanyāsi* or ascetic and they were his residences which led to the introduction of new norms. There also existed the Guru-disciple lineage (*guru-śiṣya paramparā*) in a *mạtha*. The *śiṣya* (or disciple) would be selected and he would ascend the *pīṭha* or throne of the particular *maṭha*.[71] The lineage within a *maṭha* was parallel to the royal patrilineal system which allowed wisdom to be passed on from the male teacher to the male disciple and later became a part of *maṭha* organizational structure.

It cannot be said with certainty that *maṭhas* originated from any one particular type of formal educational system.[72] However a convincing evidence for the transformation or renaming of an *agrahāra* as a *maṭha* can be found in the city of Bengaluru, where the Sitapati *agrahāra* in Chamrajpete is a fully functional *maṭha*. In addition, the Pejawar *maṭha* and the Advaita *maṭhas* are known as *vidyāpīṭhas*. Evidences offer a compelling argument that *maṭhas* had their origins within the *sāmpradāyas* of asceticism and education and had their origins as educational institutions—either as *vidyālayas*, *vidyāpīṭhas*, or *agrahāras*[73]—depending on the region. They were integral institutions that were later adopted as residences by wandering ascetics, which led to the introduction of certain norms/principles in a *maṭha*. In addition were the traditional practices of asceticism and teaching, not to discount the influences of the Buddhist *saṅgha* and the Jain *maṭha*. In order to uncover the origins of the institution, and to trace their subsequent history, it is crucial to understand the influencing factors, namely the Śaiva religious movement and the socio-historical circumstances.

EARLY SAIVITE MONASTERIES

A marked factor for the growth of *maṭhas* was the political influence of Gupta-Vakataka kings who patronized Hindu Sanskritic culture.[74] The rise of a sovereign monarchical kingdom and prosperity provided a conceptual unity of vassal/feudatory kings in the post-Gupta period (seventh to twelfth centuries CE).With the successive reigns of warring kingdoms in Central and South India in the neighboring domains of the Gurjara Pratiharas, Candellas, Kalachuris, Paramaras, Chalukyas of Badami, and Pallavas of Kanchipuram, contestations for land and resources were inevitable. This was also the period when Buddhism was on the decline, although it flourished in pockets in Andhra and Tamil Nadu.[75] Another significant phenomenon was the rise of Saivism, particularly of Pāśupata, Kālamukha, and Śaiva Siddhānta *sanyāsis* who traveled to the countryside. Between the seventh and twelfth centuries they developed as independent institutions in four major areas: (a) Saivite *maṭhas* in Central India, under the Kalachuris; (b) Cola and Pandyan domains in Tamil Nadu; (c) in Andhra (under the Kakatiyas); and (d) in Karnataka under the Chalukyas of Badami, Chalukyas of Kalyani, Rashtrakutas, and Hoysalas.[76]

Regional Monasteries

In South India, Saivism flourished around Śaiva temples in centers such as Aihole, Pattadakal, Mahabalipuram, and Kanchipuram and received patronage from almost every dynasty that ruled South India. The Śaiva *maṭhas*, unlike other educational institutions such as *agrahāras* and *ghaṭikās*, aligned themselves with the worship of Śiva[77] and as mentioned, divisions within Saivism played a role in the division of *Śaiva maṭhas*. A brief description of Saivism is a prelude to the discussion of role of Śaiva Siddhānta *maṭhas*. Saivism is divided into Puranic and non-Puranic Saivism. While the Puranic form continued as popular worship of Śiva, the non-Puranic ones were divided into *atimārga* and *mantramārga*. The *atimārga* tradition was followed by Pāśupatas, Lakulas, Kālamukhas, and Lingāyats, while the *mantramārga* tradition was revered by Kapālika and Śaiva Siddhāntas. Kapālika Saivism is again divided into Kaula and Trika schools. From the Kapālika tradition arose the Aghorīs, while the Śaiva Siddhānta that began in Central India gave rise to Tamil Śaiva Siddhānta.[78] The Śaiva Siddhānta school are listed under *Purāṇas* and *Āgamas*, and considered a *mahātantra*, with belief in *paśu* (*jeeva* or soul), *pati* (Śiva or lord), and *pāśa* (bondage). The foundation of the system was *jñāna* (knowledge), *kriya* (ritual practices), yoga, and *caryā* (discipline). It was based upon the doctrine of Vaiśeṣika philosophy and Agamic theism and although God and soul are separated, a mystic union between the two is recognized. Innumerable Śaiva Siddhānta, Pāśupata, and Kālamukha *maṭhas* appear in the forests of Central India and river valleys in South India.

Maṭhas in Central India

In Central India, the Vindhya forest lands stretched across vast lands from south of river Yamuna from Mathura to Allahabad. In the forest lands of Gopacala or modern Gwalior (seventh to fourteenth centuries CE) and the Dahala region, between Yamuna and Narmada rivers (tenth to thirteenth centuries CE),[79] lived Śaiva ascetics in *āśramas* (in *ātvikas*, woodland communities) that grew into *maṭhas* affiliated to Śaiva Siddhānta doctrine.[80] Known as *śivacāryas*, ascetics, such as Vimalaśiva I, Rudra Śiva, Paraśiva, Śaktiśiva built *maṭhas* near temples, such as in Chandrehe and Chunari[81] (near Rewa) on the *dakṣiṇapatha* road.[82] The ascetics who practiced Śaiva Siddhānta lived in monasteries and administered the Śaiva temples nearby. The *maṭhas* consisted of *vyākhyānaśālās* (lecture halls), *sattras* (charitable feeding houses), gardens, temples, colleges, maternity homes, and hospitals.[83] They promoted a distinct economic agenda among woodland and forest communities and marginalized groups. Lands were granted to forest-dwelling individual ascetic gurus, who helped extend cultivable land, and ascetics benefited from rights over revenue as well as status. The rigors of geographical and tribal environment led the ascetics to be warrior-type monks, and live in fortress-type monasteries. As they took care of the requirements of subsistence of the woodland communities, they earned their allegiance, promoted Saivism, and soon grew to be the leaders of the *maṭhas* and the community. They promoted religious fervor by patronizing temples. Even rulers acknowledged the Gurus, and voluntarily sought their help.[84] Patronized by kings with large land and money grants, the *maṭhas* grew wealthy as seats of authority, such as the Chandrehe and Kodal *maṭhas* that had even hidden vaults for storing wealth.[85] Equipped with elephants and horses, they offered training and manufactured weapons, thereby, augmenting the kingdom's war machine even as the king recruited them as officers. Kings revered and depended on them and soon they became *rājagurus* (gurus to kings).[86] By twelfth century CE they even carved an independent kingdom.[87] With the rise of political power, ascetics took over power when rulers waged wars in distant lands. The *munis* (ascetics) were regarded higher than *brāhmaṇas*, while *kshatiryas* were relegated to a subservient status. A new monastic system was created, where the pontiffs had no caste, but had combined the role of *brāhmaṇas* and *kshatiryas*.[88]

Guruparamparā or lineage of Gurus provided another support for their legitimacy. The lineage of Mattamayuras and its branches were widespread in Northern, Eastern, and Central Madhya Pradesh, Rajasthan, Bengal, Orissa, Maharashtra, Andhra, and Tamil Nadu between the seventh and thirteenth centuries CE.[89] The Golaki *maṭha* was particularly famous and its ascetics were *rājagurus* to the Kalachuri kings.[90] Visvesvara Śiva was the *rājaguru* of Ganapatideva as well as his *diksha* guru.[91] The Golaki *maṭha ācāryas* exerted great influence on the Kalachuri kings of Chedi, the Kakatiya kings of Warangal, kings of Malava as well as in the Cola domain.[92] Interestingly, the identity of kings with a particular *maṭha* begins from this period on. The Kakatiya kings, such as Kakati Ganpatideva of the Pāśupata Śaivas, belonged to the Golaki *maṭha*. In Central India, Visvesvara Śiva was guru to the Kakatiya king Ganapati between 1247 and 1252 CE. He is said to have obtained the headship of the lineage and was known by the epithet "*tri–laksha-grāma-Golakki-mahāmaṭha-sāmrājya-patta baddha* (the bearer of the crown of the empire of the great Golaki *maṭha* of three lakh villages)".[93]

The ascetics of the Śaiva Siddhānta *maṭhas* in Central India have been described as "worldly" by Sears.[94] It is important to note that the ascetics were patronized by the kings and the heads of *maṭhas* did not seek the help of kings. The ascetics valued meditational pursuits, study of texts *svādhyāya* and *anushthana* (practice of religious rites, self-discipline),[95] and disseminated Siddhata theology and *Śaiva Āgamas*.[96] They exercised authority that was built upon discipline, religious doctrines, and propagation of theological concepts.

Maṭhas in Tamil Nadu

Like the *maṭhas* in Central India, the ascetic Guru in the Śaiva Siddhānta *maṭhas*, in Tamil Nadu (ninth century CE), were caretakers of temples.[97] They were known as *mudaliars* in Saivite institutions and *mahamunigal* and *brahmavidvans* or (*brāhmiṇ* ascetics) in Vaisnavite *maṭhas*. Important Śaiva Siddhānta *maṭhas* existed as philosophical schools at Mayuram in Tanjore District which subscribed to the Vedic concepts and followed the Saivite vows of renunciation. The Gurus managed and regulated temple rituals and established ways of worshipping Śiva[98]. In Pandyan towns, they were assigned with the responsibility of watching over temple rituals and procedures.[99] The *maṭhas* functioned as feeding houses for pilgrims, provided shelter, trained disciples, and organized Śaiva recitals.[100] They acted as an adjunct of the temple as well as an independent organization that received grants from the king that were tax free. *Maṭhas* in Tamil Nadu can be described as large, full-fledged, independent, multifaceted, dynamic[101] and formidable institutions.[102]

Maṭhas in Deccan and Karnataka

The early medieval Saivite *maṭhas* in Karnataka were influenced by Pāśupata beliefs.[103] Here, Pāśupatas,[104] Kālamukhas,[105] and Kapālikas were followers of Lakulisa Siddhānta and followed the popular text *Lakulāgama* or *Pāśupatadarśana.*[106] Kālāmukha temples[107] existed in Hassan, Kadur, Chitradurga, Mysore, Bengaluru, Tumkur, Kolar, and Shimoga districts, as well as in Ablur, Hangal, Gadag, Sri-Parvata (Śrisaila) in Kurnool District, and generally all over Kannada-speaking country as well as in parts of Andhra.[108] Although there were four classes of Śaivaism—Śaivas, Pāśupatas, Karunika Siddhantins, and Kapālikas—there are no records about clashes between these denominations.

The Pāśupata and Kālamukha *maṭhas* were established near temples each with their own personnel who were caretakers of temples, resembling those in Tamil Nadu.[109] From inscriptional evidences it can be deduced that they were responsible for proper ritualistic maintenance of the deity.[110] An epigraph from Begur refers to the *maṭha* attached to the temple of Mallikarjuna.[111]

It is striking to find that Kālamukha *maṭhas* and temples attained fame primarily due to the pivotal role of Gurus, whose names characteristically ended in *śakti*, such as Śivasakti, Rudrasakti, Isvarasakti, Isanasakti, Tribhuvanasakti, or *śiva*, such as Kumaraśiva, Jñānaśiva, or *rasi*, such as Sumarasi, Nagarasi, Vamarasi, or *ābharaṇa*, such as Vidyābharaṇa, Surābharaṇa.[112]

Many of the Śaiva Gurus who headed the *mạthas*, acted as *sthanādhipatis* of temples. Ramesvara *paṇḍita*, the guru of Kakati Prola II, was the *sthanādhipati* of the temple of Bhimesvra Mahadeva at Dakṣaramam and a contemporary of Tribhuvanamalladeva, Vikramaditya VI.[113] The innumerable Kālamukha temples, such as the Kallesvara temple and the Sambhulinga temple at Chadurugola and Kasargod in Jagalur Taluk (Devangere district), had *maṭhas* attached to them, and were presided over by the Kālamukha Gurus.[114]

An important contribution of Saivite *maṭhas* was the adherence to the ancient system of guru lineage that provided additional legitimacy to the institution. We also find that Kālamukha *maṭhas* were presided over by a line of *chaturanana paṇḍitas*, one of whom has been described in an inscription of the Rashtrakuta king Krishna III.[115] In addition, they aligned themselves with royal houses, and were *rājagurus* to powerful kings. With the spread and construction of large temple complexes patronized by royalty, *maṭhas* began to play a central role in Karnataka.

A significant note that can be added is that although Hindu Tantrism was popular during this period, Kālamukhas were not Tantric sects which is attested by an inscription of 806 CE in Nandi Hill in Kolar district in Karnataka.[116] According to Lorenzen, the Kālamukha temples were not Tantric and the imagery in the temples in Belagave are not sexual but semi-secular entertainment provided by the temple.[117] He continues,

> It is hard to consider them (Kāpālikas and Kālamukhas) as sects. In a Christian context the concept of a "sect" embodies three essential features: a specific doctrine (including a prescribed mode of worship), a priesthood, and a well-defined and exclusive laity. The structure of Hindu "sects" is in general much more amorphous than that of Christian ones. In most cases more emphasis is placed on the doctrine and modes of worship than on organization.[118]

Golaki Maṭha

The Saivite Golaki *maṭha*, which originated in the Jabalpur region of Madhya Pradesh (1234–1291 CE), had an extensive network of monastic institutions in Tamil Nadu and Karnataka as well.[119] It was based on the *Āgamas* and although they were not Pāśupata *maṭhas*, they emphasized the role of the Guru and his lineage. The *maṭhas* were located near temples and functioned as feeding centers. In Tamil Nadu there were both *brāhmin* and non-*brāhmin maṭhas* as in Tenkarai and Tirupparankunram.[120] The celibate heads of these *maṭhas*, called Śivacarayas, belonged to the Govamsa (a religious lineage) and were known as *bhiksha maṭha santāna* (descendants) of gurus supported by a monastery endowed with a *bhiksha* or maintenance gift. These multifaceted institutions with functions of feeding, teaching, boarding, and lodging, (consisting of a pluralistic community, and headed by Gurus who were ascetic, scholarly, and charismatic), played a key role in society.[121]

IMPORTANT MAṬHAS IN KARNATAKA

Unlike the Śaiva Siddhānta *maṭhas* in Central India, *maṭhas* in Karnataka were distinguished by their role as learning and teaching institutions. A significant center of Kālamukha *maṭha* (and temple) system in Karnataka was at Balligame (in Shimoga district), capital of the kingdom of Banavasi.[122] It was a well-known seat of learning and known for its prestigious university town between the eleventh and thirteenth centuries

CE.[123] It is interesting to note that while the Śaiva *maṭhas* in Central India and the five Śaiva *maṭhas* in Sriparvata (Andhra Pradesh) were headed by Saivite ascetic Gurus,[124] those in Balligame were headed by learned scholars. Here, various philosophies were taught, including Buddhist and Jain. A record from Shikaripur Taluk, extols the heads of the *maṭha* at Balligame: the *ācārya* of Kodiya *maṭha* was proficient in Siddhanta, Tarka, Vyakarana, Kavya, Nataka, Bharata *Śāstra*, and other sciences connected with Sahitya as well as in Jainism, in Lokayata, Buddhism, and Lakula Siddhānta.[125] The Balligame *maṭha* also trained gurus, *ācārya* and priests, and other temple functionaries.

Clear differentiation existed within the *maṭhas* in regard to the status of students and the purpose of their religious training. Here *naiṣṭhika* (celibate) and *śāstrikā*-(married non-celibate) *brahmacārin* students were separated. Hence Kālamukha priests had sons and daughters and were referred to as *naiṣṭhika tapomārga nirata* as well as *naiṣṭhika brahmacāri* in many inscriptions.[126]

Among the educational *maṭhas* at Belligame, the Kodiya *mạtha* (or Koti *maṭha*), also known as the Kedaresvara *maṭha* (abode of Kedara of the South), was a great center of learning from about 1094 CE onward and described as an abode of Goddess Sarasvati.[127] The heads of the *maṭha* produced commentaries on the six systems of philosophy, *śad darśanas*, *yogaśāstras*, and Lakula Siddhānta.[128] It was an institution for the study of the *Purāṇas*, where Jain and Buddhist mendicants—*ksapanakas, brāhmaṇas, ekadandins*—lived.[129] Here, students studied both the *Vedas* and the Lakula Siddhānta.

Royal grants were made to teachers proficient in *Vedas* and *Vedāṅgas* and not merely to ascetics. The rise in status of the heads of the Kālāmukha *maṭhas* in Balligame was also due to their being *rājagurus* to Kakatiya, Hoysala, and Vijayanagara kings. The Ablur inscriptions mention names such as Ramesvara *paṇḍita* and Somesvara *paṇḍita*[130] who acted as *rājagurus* of Kakatiya kings. Among the Kālamukha priests, many had the prefix *rājaguru* (teacher to the king), such as *rājaguru* Sarvesvarasakti[131] (1071 CE), *rājaguru* Rudrasakti[132] *rājaguru* Vāmasambhu of Yuvarajadeva,[133] *rājaguru* Rudrasakti[134] of Dvarasamudra (1255 CE), *rājaguru* Kriyasakti[135] of Asandi (1206 CE), and *rājaguru* Kriyasakti (1368 CE)[136] who was also the preceptor of the Vijayanagar kings, Harihara and Bukka.[137] The prestige of the Balligame *maṭha* was great during the reign of Gautama, and his successor Vamasakti II, during the Kalacuris, Bijjala, Somesvara Deva and Ahavamalla Deva as well as the Hoysala king,

ViraBallala II. Kālāmukha Gurus were advisors to villagers as well. A Hoysala record of Viraballala I from Kudatini in Bellary district states that the Mummuridandas and others assembled together and resolved disputes in the village, and stated that the local officials should act according to the advice of the *tapodhana* named Visnukara *brahmacāri*.[138] However, it is not known as to what happened to Kālāmukha heads. Unfortunately, many of them disappeared from Mysore, whether due to Moslem invasions or loss of patronage or even due to the Pāśupatas of Golaki *maṭha* or were incorporated into Virasaivism.[139]

Multireligious *Maṭhas* in Karnataka

Inscriptional evidences clearly support the fact that the twelfth-century *maṭhas* were not sectarian institutions, particularly those in Balligame and Golaki. Here apart from Hindu *maṭhas*, Jain *basadis*, and Buddhist *vihāras*, there were many temples, such as Dakshina Kedaresvara, Tripurantakesva, Panchalingesvara, Nakharesvara, and Kesava. The five original *maṭhas* in Balligame were dedicated to Śiva, Viṣṇu, Brahma, Jina, and Buddha respectively. Panch *maṭha* (referred to as Panchamaṭha Hiriyamaṭha dated 1099 CE), was dedicated to a Chaturmukha temple of Śiva, Viṣṇu, Brahma, Jina, and Buddha in eleventh century.[140] Although we do not know what temples were attached to Viṣṇu, Jina, and Buddha (*maṭhas*), we do know that the Chadresvara and Panchamaṭha were referred to as "old *maṭha*" and were attached to Śiva *maṭha*. We also know that Nandikesvara was referred to as *mūla sthāna maṭha* (original/earliest *maṭha)* in the old inscription of 1017 CE. Perhaps this was the Śaiva *maṭha* which was included in the five original *maṭhas*. But the temples which are most frequently mentioned in the Balligame inscriptions of eleventh and twelfth centuries namely, the Kedaresvara temple, the Panchalinga temple, Tripurantaka temple, Nakharesvara, Sarvesvara, Kusumesvara temples are not included in the five original temples. They must therefore have been later in time than these *maṭhas*. According to Lorenzen, the head priest of the Pancha *maṭha*, according to the record of 1129, comprised the temples of Harihara, Kamalasana, Brahma, Vitaraga, Jina, and Bauddha. This attests to the cooperation between different religious groups.[141] In addition, all of these *maṭhas* were administered by a Saivite priest. Among the five original *maṭhas* of Balliagame, one was dedicated to Jina and other to Buddha. Thus it is possible to infer that the *maṭhas* were multi-faith institutions.

Among the five original *maṭhas* (*panchamaṭha mūla sthāna*) at Balipura, Jaina and Baudhist *maṭhas* prominently figure in the records.[142] At Balligame, Jain and Buddhist *maṭhas* imparted their respective doctrines. An inscription of 1165 CE from Soraba (Shimoga district) specifically mentions that the five *maṭhas* at Balipura were practicing the rites of their own respective creeds.[143] Jain *maṭha ācāryas* were learned,[144] such as the *ācārya* Bhanukriti Siddhanti of the temple at Bandhavapur.[145] A record from Shikaripur states that a Jaina teacher, Munichandra, published commentaries, made the science of grammar his own, adopted the rule of logic, and explained poems."[146]

Thus, in the eleventh and twelfth centuries CE, Balligame was the seat of various philosophical and religious studies, including Hindu, Buddhist, and Jain, and divisions within Kālamukha *maṭhas* in Balligame were not religious in nature but organizational.[147] It is interesting to find that Buddhist teachers and goddesses are mentioned along with Hindu gods, and it may be conjectured that these were not different systems in this part of the Deccan. An inscription dated 1065 CE records that the *dandanāyaka* Rupabhattaya had a *vihāra* named Jayatipra. Bauddha-*vihāra* constructed and made some gifts to the temples of Tara-Bhagavati, Bauddha Deva, and Lokesvara Deva Buddhist temple. In 1067 CE, a Nagiyakka is said to have built a temple for the goddess Tara Bhagavati at Balligave, and granted some land to the Buddhist teacher (Jayani) Prabha Bauddha Balara.[148]

Viraśaiva Maṭhas

During the twelfth century CE Viraśaiva *maṭhas* took shape under the guidance of Basaveshwara (1105–1167 CE). He was a chief minister to king Bijjala and despite not being a *sanyāsi*, became the sole organizer of a monastic order and religious system that brought various creeds under a single religious banner, Virasaivism.[149] Basaveshwara was a socioreligious reformer who emaphasized *kāyaka* (manual labor). He attracted adherents from the commoners of the Andhra country and became popular in Karnataka. Virasaivism/Lingayatism is an offshoot of Saivism, and its philosophy grew out of the twenty-eight Śaiva *Āgamas*. Lingāyats venerate the *liṅga* as a symbol of *chaitanya* (consciousness), and is equated with the *parabrahman* of the *Upaniṣads*, source of the universe.[150] Particularly important for the Liṅgāyat community is the Guru in the *maṭha*, who activates the power of *liṅga*/consciousness.[151] The Lingāyat Guru is a realized individual who believes in the equality of all men, rejection of caste, the norm of four *āśramas*, plurality of gods, and even rituals. He had a broad ideology of equality and social justice that provided the *maṭha* with an identity and grew to gain status and power. Due to the intimate relation between the laity and the *maṭha*, its institution has rendered great social service.

HISTORICAL CONTEXT OF *MAṬHAS* IN SOUTH INDIA

The rise of Śaiva *maṭhas* was the result of a complex number of political, social, and religious forces in medieval South India. After the decline of the Guptas in the north, various kingdoms were constantly waging wars. The Pallavas (third to ninth centuries CE) in Tamil Nadu fought with the Western Chalukyas of Badami (sixth to ninth ceturies); the Colas who had ruled from about first century CE grew to be powerful warrior kingdom till thirteenth century CE; in the Deccan were Kadambas (third to sixth centuries), Gangas of Talakad (fourth to sixth centuries), Rashtrakutas (eighth to tenth centuries), Hoysalas (twelfth to fourteenth centuries), Kakatiyas and Eastern Chalukyas of Kalyani (eleventh to fourteenth centuries).

Apart from the rise of militant kings, there was the decline of Buddhist monasticism and the rise of Saivism. While Buddhists were losing their privileged position of patronage, Pāśupata *sanyāsis* and *brāhmins* traveled to the countryside. While *brāhmins* were given bad lands as well as land near the temples, Buddhists lived in small scattered communities. The Pāśupatas were groups of *sanyāsins* who could be compared to the zealous Buddhist proselytizers. They were successful in temple building and obtained royal patronage for their construction.[152] Pāśupatas even appropriated Buddhist iconography, as was in the case of Lakulisa, who is represented in the form of turning a wheel and is represented with a *usnisa* (top knot).[153]

In addition, kings favored Śaiva values as Śiva represented a militant quality; he was a destroyer of forces, unlike Buddha. Saivism represented the activities and qualities of the kings. The Bilhari Inscription of Kalachuri Yuvarajadeva II, the Aihole (*praśasti*) by Ravikirti to the Chalukyan king Jayasimha Vallabha, and the Aihole stone inscription of Pulakesin II on the Jain temple on Meguti hill, idealize warfare by the kings.[154] Although we should not conclude that the evidence represents what really happened, the early medieval times were militaristic. It is not that the Buddhist kings were less militaristic; Hieun Tsang justifies Harsa's campaign against Sasanka in seventh century CE. However, a comparison of Buddhist inscriptions with Saivite ones leads us to conclude that descriptions of Śaiva royal inscriptions were described in terms of military heroism and had a more religious fervor while Buddhist kings were represented as compassionate kings.[155] Patronage to Śaiva institutions was on the rise, particularly in the Krishna and Godavari river valleys. The area between Mukhalingam, Kanchipuram, and Badami was dominated by aggressive Śaiva kings, such as the Western Chalukyas, Pallavas, Gangas, and Rashtrakutas. The Krishna river valley was the site of Buddhists (with Nagarjunakonda, Gutapalli, Amravati, Gubhaktada, Jaggayyapeta between the sixth–seventh centuries CE), while Badami had only one Buddhist site (which was abandoned). Overall, it might be added that Buddhist monasteries could not compete with Śaiva monasteries for royal patronage from Saivite kings in South India.

Saivite kings displaced Buddhists in the Decccan, Bhaumakaras, and Kadgas were yet to declare Buddhist affinities in Eastern India, while Kalachuris became stronger in Central India. Moreover, the Maitrikas in Western India were fearful of Islamic armies. Movement of population from north and west to South India further contributed to the complete collapse of Buddhist monasteries (seventh to fourteenth centuries), which had relied on great kings for land grants, maintenance of land, and generous funding. Instead, kings made land grants to *agrahāras*, and when the *brāhmins* settled near forested areas, or in villages, there might have been tensions due to the different observances by *brāhmins*. The Puranic sects became mediators between Vedic Brahmanism and the religions of the local peoples.[156] *Brāhmins*, as religious beneficiaries of land grants from kings, in return legitimized and validated the royal dynasty or averted a misfortune through the performance of rituals. Often the status of kings as gods was enhanced either by *brāhmins* according to *jāti* and *varna* status or composing poetic compositions. Royal patronage had repercussions on *maṭhas*, Vedic teaching, and learning.

The post-Gupta period also witnessed the lessening of donations to Buddhist monasteries. Trading guilds were crippled due to internal military situation. The search for new kinds of patronage placed monasteries (and temples) in a position of assuming many of the characteristics of the society around them. "They gained stature as landed feudal lords, such as collection of rents and taxes and exercising judicial powers in their domains of Buddhism."[157] There was also the demarcation of a sacred religious space for Śaiva monasteries (in Central India and Tamil Nadu) near temples, and in towns were monks, townspeople, head men, and all groups could live together.[158] In addition, Buddhist monasteries were not required to provide troops for the kings who granted them patronage although they provided other labor services, ritual, and educative. Śaiva monks, in addition to providing them ritual services, provided them with cultural services, such as securing scholars, learned priests, personnel for temple and other ceremonies, and even served as *rājagurus*—advisors to kings. The religious conditions of the eleventh and twelfth centuries CE reveal a strange mixture of apparent religious catholicity on the one hand (as manifested by Hoysala kings) and subtle rivalries on the other.[159] There were few Buddhist vestiges, while Jainism was gaining importance.

The ascent of Saivism with the Pāśupatas and the Kālamukhas taking the lead, protection of the good and suppression of the evil, was the ideal: *śiṣṭa parigraha and duṣṭa nigraha* became important. The twelve *saṃhāra* (destroying) forms of Śiva and the six *anugraha* (boon bestowing) forms of Śiva with twenty-four miscellaneous forms were enunciated by the different *Āgamas*.[160] In addition, highly evolved spiritual ideas and religious beliefs and rites in the Tantras, brought Śaktism of the Śaiva Kapālikas to the forefront. Thus the rise of Śaiva *maṭhas* was the result of a complex number of medieval forces, including the influence and ultimate decline of Buddhism, the rise of Saivism, Saivite temples, and kings along with their patronage, and the leadership of the Guru in the *maṭha*, whose pivotal role would lead to higher status in late medieval period in Karnataka between the twelfth and seventeenth centuries. Whatever be the circumstances of their evolution, the growth of Saivite *maṭhas* as centers of both secular and religious education laid a solid foundation for the growth of Vedānta *maṭhas* that institutionalized the system of monasticism.

NOTES

1. Leclercq, Jean. *The Love of Learning and the Desire for God: A Study of Monastic Culture*. New York: Fordham University Press, 1961, pp. 74, 82.

2. Miller, David M. and Dorothy C. Wertz. *Hindu Monastic Life: The Monks and Monasteries of Bhubaneswar*. Montreal: McGill-Queens University Press, 1976, pp. 6–7.

3. Dutt, Nalinaksha. Notes on the Nagarjunikonda Inscriptions. *Indian Historical Quarterly* 7.3 (1931): 633–53.

4. Personal interview with Jagadguru Karmayogi Charukeerty Bhattarak Swamiji, head of the Jain monastery in Sravana Belagola.

5. The inscription (dated 159–479 CE) records that a *brāhmaṇa* pair donated land for worship with sandalwood, incense, flowers, lamps etc. of divine *Arhats* in a Jaina *vihāra* at Vatahohali, the original site of the present temple at Paharpur. The disciples of Guhanandin dwelt here and the names of the Digambara *ācāryas* included Yasonandin, Jayanandin, Kumaranandin, and others.

EI XX, 1894, 61–62.

In the ninth and tenth centuries CE Paharpur was known as the great Buddhist *vihāra* of King Dharmapala at Somapura.

6. The Bawa Pyara caves at Junagadh contain many Jaina symbols such as *svāstika, bhadrāsana, nandipada, mīnayugala.*

7. Ravivarman is said to have granted a village of Pumkhetaka for the celebration of the festival of Jinendra and for the maintenance of ascetics during the rains.

8. The Kanas plate of Lokavigraha Bhattarak dated 599–600 CE records the grant of a village for the purpose of the institution of *bali*, *charu*, and *sattra* at the *maṭha* of Maninagabhattaraka of Chaikamaka or Ekambaka and for the maintenance of the *brāhmaṇas* belonging to different *gotras*, who were the students of the Maitrayaniya school of the *Yajurveda. EI* XXVIII, 332 ff. 1, Mentioned by Bhadri, K.M. *A Cultural History of Northern India: Based on Epigraphical Sources form the 3rd Century. B.C. to 700 A.D.* Delhi: Book India Publishing Co, 2006, p. 166.

9. The Aphsad stone inscription of Adityasena, of seventh century CE records the name of Mahadevi Srimati, the mother of the king, who constructed a *maṭha* or religious college, meaning Vedic scholars and students. *CII* III, No. 42.

10. *Maṭhametat karitakam Nārāyaṇa-devakulasya.* The inscription records the construction of a *maṭha* of the devakula of Nārāyaṇa by the *kulapati* Bhagudalana (text 1.6). *EI* IX, 289 ff. Refer to Bhadri, *A Cultural History of Northern India*, 167.

According to Bhadri, Bhagudalana is described as a *kulapati* who caused its construction. Normally *kulapati* meant the head of a family. But technically *kulapati* means a sage who feeds and teaches 10,000 pupils. Delhi: Bharatiya Vidya Bhavan, 1951.

11. *QJMS* VII, 170.

12. Miller and Wertz. *Hindu Monastic Life*, p. 4.

13. Olivelle, Patrick. *Vasudevsrama Yatidharmaprakasa: A Treatise on World Renunciation.* Part 2. Translation. Vienna: Publications of the de Nobili Research Library Gerold & Co. in Komm, Delhi: Motilal Banarsidass. 1976–77, pp. 74–79.

14. Olivelle, Patrick. *Samnyasa Upanisads: Hindu Scriptures on Asceticism and Renunciation*. Oxford: Oxford University Press, 1992, p. 4.

15. Chakraborti, Haripada. *Asceticism in Ancient India: In Brahmanical, Buddhist, Jaina and Ajivika Societies from the Earliest Times to the Period of Sankaracharya*. Calcutta: Punthi Pustak, 1973, p. 4.

16. Olivelle. *Vasudevsrama Yatidharmaprakasa*, 40.

17. Swahananda, Swami. *ātmano mokshartam jagaddhitaya cha*. Monasteries in South India. Hollywood, CA: Vedanta Society of Southern California, 1989, p. 29.

18. In fact, the *Sanyāsa Upaniṣad* provides details of different types and classes of ascetics—*turiyatita*, *vairāgya sanyāsin*, *jñāna sanyāsin*, *jñāna vairāgyam*, *karma sanyāsin*.

There are regional variations and terminological differences as well. Chakraborti. *Asceticism in Ancient India*. 42.

19. For instance, *kutcichakas* were those who remained in hermitages, eating eight morsels of food; *bahudakas* were those bearing a water jar, wearing ocher colored clothes, begging food; *hamsas* were those who stayed for one night in a village, *paramahamsas* stayed under a tree, they wore an ocher garment or remained naked, and are above *dharma* and *adharma*; *turaiyatitas* lived only on fruits and ate without using hands, and lived with no consciousness of the body; *avadhutas* took food from all *varnas*, and are deeply absorbed in meditation; *ṛṣis* lived with their wives, performed *yajna*, and they wear *yajnopavita*, while *sanyāsins* did not perform *yajnas* nor wore the sacred thread.

20. Dikshit, T.R.C. *Sannyasa Upanishad*. Madras: Adyar Library, 1929.

There are different types of *sanyāsins*: *vairāgya sanyāsīn* is one who is free from all desires; *jñāna sanyāsin* renounces the sensual enjoyments for knowledge; *jñāna vairāgyam* realizes the self and is indifferent to everything; and *karmana sanyāsin* passes through first three *aśrama* in due order and enters *sanyāsīn*-hood.

21. Olivelle. *Samnyasa Upanisads*, p. 4.

However according to Dumont, the heart of Hinduism is in the interaction between the renouncer and the man in the world. Dumont, Louis. World Renunciation Indian Religions. *Contributions to Indian Sociology* 4 (1960): 37.

22. Exceptions, were the right to renunciation by non-*brāhmaṇas*, learned disputations at the courts of kings, where scholars of different classes and castes participated including *kshatriyas* and women. None were debarred from the right to renounce home; a mendicant monk, lead a life of purity and these exceptions became the rule with the Buddhist order or community.

23. Uddalaka Aruni and Svetaketu in *Chāndogyopaniṣad*, VI. 11–2.3. Bedekar, Vijay. Ed. *Vidya, Veda—their Genesis*, Scope and Illustration by Sudarshan Kumar Sharma in Education in Ancient India. Bombay: Itihaas Patrika Prakarshan, 1996, 51.

24. Bedekar, *Vidya, Veda—their Genesis*, p. 44.

25. The equation between *brāhmaṇa* and *paṇḍita* is not an implicit one; *Brāhmaṇa* is defined by birth, *jati*, and *dharmic* duties, while a *paṇḍita* is characterized by one's own intellectual path.

Aklujkar, Ashok. Pandita and Pandits in History. In *The Pandit: Traditional Scholarship in India*. Ed. Michaels, Axel. New Delhi: Manohar, 2001, pp. 17–38.

26. According to Aklujkar, a *paṇḍita* is a *vidvan*, a well-educated scholar, also characterized by wisdom, a great skill for memorization, with an oral knowledge of the Vedas.

27. The *Mānavadharmaśāstra* (2.140–142) calls the *brāhmin* (who acts as a teacher) an *ācārya* who teaches him the *Vedas*, the sacrificial rules and the *Upaniṣads*.

28. Rigopoulos, Antonio. *Guru: The Spiritual Master in Eastern and Western Traditions*. Venetian Academy of Indian Studies Series, No. 4. New Delhi: DKPW, 2007, p. 314.

29. *Maṇḍukya Upaniṣad* 1.212.

30. Cenkner, William. *A Tradition of Teachers: Śankara and the Jagadgurus Today*. Delhi: Motilal Banarsidass, 1983, p. 9.

31. Guru would have the same etymology as Latin gravis and gravitas and thus in origin it meant "heavy," "ponderous," grave, efficacious, powerful, and influential. Gonda, J. *Change and Continuity in Indian Religion*. The Hague: Mouton & Co., 1965, pp. 238 ff.

32. Rigopoulos, Antonio. Ed. *Guru: The Spiritual Master in Eastern and Western Traditions*. 2007.

33. Earlier, the *Upanisadic* guru transcended caste. Janaka was a king, Yajnavalkaya was a householder, Gargi was a woman. Torcinovich, Giovanni. "The Custodians of Truth." In *Guru: The Spiritual Master in Eastern and Western Traditions. Edited by Rigopoulos, Antonio.* Delhi: DKPW. 2007, pp. 137–156. *Chāndogya Upaniṣad* 8.15.1.

34. Pellegrini, Gianni. " Figure of Pandita as Guru." In *The Spiritual Master in Eastern and Western Traditions*, pp. 305–26.

35. *Vidya* comes from the root *vid* (to know) or to receive. It has been used in a broad sense, meaning knowledge, a science, learning, subject, method, education, scholarship, and philosophy. Bedekar. *Vidya, Veda—their Genesis*, 23.

36. Scharfe, Hartmutt. *Education in Ancient India*. Leiden: Brill, 2002, pp. 46, 53.

37. Cenkner. *A Tradition of Teachers*, 8.

38. The traditional manner of beginning one's education or learning is by reciting the Sanskrit *slaka, Gurur Brahma, Gurur Viṣṇu, Gurur devo Maheśwaraha, Guru sākshāt para Brahma, tasmai Śri Guruve namah.* Guru is the representative of Brahma, Viṣṇu and Śiva. He is truly nearby and beyond. I salute to that Guru.

39. The *samartana or snāna* ceremony was performed at the end of the Brahmacārya period to make the termination of the education course.

40. But acquiring *vidyā* connotes a process and makes use of five perceptions: knowledge, reality, attainment, discrimination, and sublime emotion.

41. Cenkner. *A Tradition of Teachers*, 250. Gonda. *Change and Continuity in Indian Religion*, 238 ff.

42. Miller and Wertz. *Hindu Monastic Life*, 4.

43. According to Satkari Mookerji, "The greatest genius of the Buddha lay in the organization of the ascetic order and the creation of a code of rules and regulations for the conduct of monastic life." Mookerji, Satkari. *Buddhist Philosophy of Universal Flux*. Delhi: Motilal Banarsidass, 1935. Orient Book Distributors, 1975.

44. *Buddham śaraṇam gacchāmi, Dhammam śaraṇam gacchāmi and saṅgham śaraṇam gacchāmi.*

45. Chakraborti. *Asceticism in Ancient India*. 199.

46. However, there were few differences, such as *pravrājya*, or outgoing from home into homelessness, was final in Buddhism, but *brahmacāris* were given the option to live with his teacher's family.

47. Kern, H. *Manual of Indian Buddhism*, 1896. Reprint Delhi: Indological Book House, 1972, pp. 74, 399.

48. Beggiora, Stefano. "The Subtle Teacher. Typologies of Shamanic Initiation: Trance and Dream Among the Lanjia Saoras of Orissa." In *Guru: The Spiritual Master in Eastern and Western Traditions,* p. 348.

49. Aklujkar. "Pandita and Pandits in History". In *The Pandit*, 394.

50. Oldenberg, Hermann. *The Grihya Sutras: Rules of Vedic Domestic Ceremonies*. Delhi: Motilal Banarsidass, 1886, 1981, pp. 337–345.

51. One of the reasons that the monastic order in Hinduism did not appear till the post-Buddhist is because of the ascetic tradition that the mendicant should wander and then live in a fixed place in the season. Hence no monastic organization (or order) appeared until the post-Buddhist period.

52. Bedekar. *Vidya, Veda—their Genesis*, 114.

53. Bedekar. *Vidya, Veda—their Genesis*, 110–120.

54. Although Kasi might not have been known as an illustrious university center like those of Taksasila, Vikramasila, Vallabhi, and Kanchi.

55. Religion was only one of the subjects, and these were not purely religious schools.

56. Bedekar. *Vidya, Veda—their Genesis*, 31.

57. Kadamba kings from Goa were known to have given grants to an *agrahāra*. JBBRAS IX, 216; Bedekar. *Vidya, Veda—their Genesis*, 101.

58. *EC* VIII, Sorab Inscriptions, 250.

59. Gururajachar, S. *Some Aspects of Economic and Social Life in Karnaṭaka*. (A.D. 1000–1300) Mysore: University of Mysore, 1974, p. 190.

60. Shantakumari, Leela, S. *History of the Agraharas Karnaaka, 400–1300*. Madras: New Era Publications, 1986, p. 107.

61. Kalas Inscription, 929–30 CE. *EI* XIII, 33.

62. Gurujachar, *Some Aspects of Economic and Social Life*, 195–96.

63. Nagaswamy, R. *Studies in South Indian History and Culture. Professor V.R. Ramacandra Dikshitar Centenary Volume*. Delhi: DKPW, 1997, p. 164.

64. *El* VIII, 24.

65. Karashima, N., Subbarayalu, Y., and P. Shanmugam, P. Mathas and Medieval Religious Movements in Tamil Nadu: An Epigraphical Study. *IHR* 37.2 (2011). 217–34. Srinivasan, C.R. *Kanchipuram the Ages*. Delhi: Agam Kala Prakashan. 1979. p. 10 ff.

66. According to Gangadharan, there were currents passing—the Vedic and the Agamic and Tantric. Gangadharan, H. *Glimpses of Suttur Mutt*. Mysore: Sri Shivarthreswara Granthamala, 2001, p. 8.

67. In the *Swayambhuvāgama* there is a reference to the origin of the five *ācāryas* and in *Suprabhedāgama*, the five *ācāryas* are called *jagadgurus*. Gururajachar. *Some Aspects of Economic and Social Life in Karnaṭaka,* 9.

68. Gururajachar. *Some Aspects of Economic and Social Life in Karnaṭaka*, 180.

69. *KI*, Vol. I, 23.

70. *EI*, Vol. XII, 284. See Gururajachar. *Some Aspects of Economic and Social Life in Karnaṭaka*, 185.

71. There are only stray evidences regarding this phenomenon in early medieval Śaiva *maṭhas*. The lineage known as Tirukailasa-*paramparā* in Tamil Nadu was traced from Dakshinamurti (teaching form of Śiva), Sanatkumar, and Nandi and the canonical literature of the poets that was compiled in the eleventh century by Namiandar-Nambi in Twelve Tirumurais.

72. *EI* IV, 63 ff.

73. The Sitapati *agrahāra* in Bengaluru is a *matha*, which throws some light on some sort of transformation of an earlier institution, and its renaming as a *maṭha*.

74. The Gupta kings also patronized Buddhism.

75. Beal, Samuel. *The Life of Hiuen-Tsiang by the Shaman Hwui Li with an Introduction Containing an Account of the Works of I-Tsing*. London: Trübner, 1914.

76. The Rashtrakuta Empire extended to Maharashtra.

77. Saivism played an active role in the assimilation of communities, and a social unity that included all groups.

78. Flood, Gavin D. *The Blackwell Companion to Hinduism*. Oxford: Blackwell, 2003, p. 152.

These denominations of the institution arose as a continuation of Tantric sects. Chakraborti. *Asceticism in Ancient India*. p. 154

According to Lorenzen, Kapālikas were Tantric, but Pāśupatas and Kālāmukhas were not Tantric. Lorenzen, David N. Early Evidence for Tantric Religion. In *The Roots of Tantra*. Ed. Katherine Anne Harper and Brown, Robert L. Albany: State University of NY Press, 2002, p. 34. Pathak, V. S. *History of Saiva Cults in Northern India from Inscriptions (700 AD to 1200 AD)*. Allahabad:

Abinash Prakashan, 1960, pp. 3, 4. Pathak distinguishes four major ones, *Śaiva Siddhānta*, Karuka, Pāśupata, and Kāpālika.

79. Misra, R.N. *Ascetics, Piety and Power. Saiva Siddhanta Monastic Art in the Woodlands of Central India.* New Delhi: Aryan Books International, 2018, p. 8.

80. Misra, *Ascetics, Piety and Power*, 61.

81. Singh, Pritam. *Saints and Sages of India.* New Delhi: New Book Society of India, 1948, pp. 47–52. Pathak, V.S. *Saiva Cults in Northern India, from inscriptions, 700 A.D. to 1200.* A.D. Varanasi: Ram Naresh Varma,1960, pp. 49–50.

82. Cunningham, A., *ASI Report* XIII, p. 9.

83. Sears, Tamara I. *Worldly Gurus and Spiritual Kings: Architecture and Asceticism in Medieval India.* New Haven, CT: Yale University Press, 2014, p. 121.

84. Misra, R.N. *Ascetics, Piety and Power*, 63.

85. Misra, R.N. *Ascetics, Piety and Power*, 55, 101, 113.

86. A Śaiva *ācārya* is said to have erected temples, *maṭhas*, charitable feeding houses—*sattras*, dwellings for the *brāhmaṇas.* Misra, R.N. *Ascetics, Piety and Power*, 28, 64–7, 73.

87. Misra, R.N. *Ascetics, Piety and Power.* 69.

88. Misra. *Ascetics, Piety and Power*, 74; Mirashi, V.V. "Inscriptions of the Kalachuri Chedi Era," *Corpus Inscriptionum Indicarum*, Vol. 7, no. 7, Parts I–II, Ootacamund, 1955, p. 372.

89. See Ranod inscription, Misra. *Ascetics, Piety and Power*, 40, 41.

90. Misra, *Ascetics, Piety and Power*, 73, 126 ff.

91. Malkapuram inscription of Rudramadevi, daughter of Ganapatideva, mentions how Sadbhava Sambhu received from the Kalachuri monarch, three lakh provinces as a *bhiksha* (maintenance gift) and founded the Glolaki *maṭha* and gave away that province as the *vritti* for the maintenance of the teachers of the *maṭha*.

92. According to Glenn Yocum, Pāśupata Saivism of the Golaki *matha* flourished almost up to the end of reign of Prataparudra, the last Kakatiya monarch of Warangal, who was himself a *parama* Maheśwara. Yocum, Glenn E. A Non-Brahman Tamil Shaiva Mutt: A Field Study of the Thiruvavduthurai Adheenam. In *Monastic Life in the Christian and Hindu traditions A Comparative Study.* Ed. Creel, Austin and Narayanan, Vasudha. Leweiston: NY: Edwin Mellen Press, 1990, p. 710.

93. Talbot, Cynthia. Golaki Matha Inscriptions form Andhra Pradesh: A Study of a Saiva Monastic Lineage in Vajapeya. In *Essays on Evolution of Indian Art and Culture. K.D. Bajpai Felicitation Vol.* Vol. 1, ed. A. M. Shastri and R. K. Sharma, Agam Prasad. Delhi: Agam Kala Prakashan, 1987, pp. 135–136.

94. Sears. *Worldly Gurus and Spiritual Kings*, 59.

95. Misra. *Ascetics, Piety and Power*, 56.

96. Mirashi. *Inscriptions of the Kalachuri–Chedi Era*, p. 200.

97. In the eleventh century, the Tiranda *maṭha* was near a temple.

Tirumalai, R. The Maṭhas in Pandyan Townships in 395-407. In *Vajapeya: Essays on Evolution of Indain art and Culture. K.D. Bajpai Felicitation Volume. Vol 1.* Ed. Shastri, A. M, Sharma R.K., and Prasad, Agam. Delhi: Agam Prasad, Agam Kala Prakashan, 1987, pp. 395–407.

98. Prasoon, Shrikant. *Indian Saints and Sages: From before Shankaracharya to Vivekanand.* New Delhi; Delhi: Hindoology Books; 2009, p. 80.

99. Tirulamai, R. The Maṭhas in Pandyan Townships, 395.

100. Tirulamai, The Maṭhas in Pandyan Townships, 395.

101. Karashima, N., L. Subbarayalu, and P. Shanmugam. Maṭhas and Medieval Religious Movements in Tamil Nadu: An Epigrahical Study. *Indian Historical Review* 37, 2 (n.d.): 217–34.

102. The term "*maṭha*" can be found in the Tamil inscriptions from ninth century, and occur more frequently later in the eleventh century and continued to grow between eighth to twelfth centuries. According to Karashima this might have been due to the increase of Śaiva sects from North India. Karashima, Mathas and Medieval Religious Movements, 217–34.

103. There were four classes, Śaivas, Pāśupatas, Karunika Siddhantins, and the Kāpālikas, and according to Chakraborti, all were Tantric. Chakraborti. *Asceticism in Ancient India*, 162.

104. The Pāśupatas were known as Kālāmukhas ninth to eleventh century, according to Chakraborti, *Asceticism in Ancient India*, p. 312.

They were followers of *Naiyayika and Vaiseshika* philosophy. Yocum, Glenn E. A Non-Brahman Tamil Shaiva Mutt: A Field study of the Thiruvavduthurai Adheenam. In *Monastic Life in the Christian and Hindu Traditions.* Ed. Creel, B. Austin and Narayanan, Vasudha. Lewiston, NY: Edwin Mellen Press. 1990, pp. 250–252.

They were followers of Lakulisa and displayed hostility to caste consciousness. Lorenzen, David. *The Kapalikas and Kalamukhas: Two Lost Saiva Sects.* Berkeley: University of California Press, 1972, p. 6.

105. Kālamukha *sanyāsins* were believed to eat food from a skull, besmear their bodies with ashes, hold a club, wear a garland of *rudraksha*, and wear a string of matted hair on the head.

106. The Lakula or Pāśupata *darśana* is described in ch. 349; *Sāntiparva, Mahābhārata*; in the *Vāyu*, *Liṅga* and *Kurma Purāṇas,* in the Suta Samhita of the *Skanda Purāṇa*, and in the *Sarvadarśana Saṅgraha*. It is also noticed in the commentaries of Śankara, Rāmānuja, in II. 2, 36, 37 of the *Brahma Sutras*.

Saivites are divided into four sects: Kālāmukhas, Pāśupatas, Śaivas, Mahavratadharas, recognized by their staff. These four are mentioned in Ramanujacārya's *Śri Bhashya* on II. 2, 36 where it is said that that *laguda-dharana* or carrying a staff was one of their characteristic practices. *EC* VII, Sk. 114, 96, 107, 123.

107. Shantakumari, *History of the Agraharas*, p. 107 ff.

108. Shantakumari, *History of the Agraharas*, 114, 137, 153.

109. From an inscription dated 1051 ACE, from Dharwad district, is a reference to a *maṭha* attached to the temple of Jogabesvara of Moebennur, in Ranebennur taluk, while in Bjapur district there was the Marasanahalli *maṭha* attached to temple of Uttaresvara, which has been mentioned by Chalukya Somesvara I, 1066 CE.

110. Shantakumari, *History of the Agraharas*, pp. 107–115.

111. *EC* VII, Sk. 16.

112. Pathak, V.S. *Saiva Cults in Northern India from Inscriptions from 700 A.D. to 1200 A.D.* Varanasi: Ram Naresh Varma, 1960, pp 49–50.

113. *SII* IV, No. 1229.

114. Shantakumari, *History of the Agraharas*, 77. *EC* XI, Sb. 8, 10.

115. This sect of Bhairava Yogis flourished in the Deccan even after the introduction of Advaita by Ādi Sankaracārya, who suppressed some nasty practices, as evidenced by an inscription of the twelfth century CE in Baligame in Mysore area. Chakraborti, *Asceticism in Ancient India.* In *Brahmanical, Buddhist, Jaina and Ajivika Societies from the Earliest Times to the Period of Sankaracharya*, Calcutta: Punthi Pustak, p. 166.

116. Lorenzen. *The Kapalikas and Kalamukhas*, 16–23, 54–55.

117. Lorenzen. *The Kapalikas and Kalamukhas*, 139.

118. Lorenzen. *The Kapalikas and Kalamukhas*, 99, 104.

119. Talbot. Golaki Matha Inscriptions from Andhra Pradesh, 133.

120. Yocum. A Non-Brahman Tamil Shaiva Mutt.

121. *SII* XX. N. 40 In fact, they flourished even during the time of Ādi Śankarācārya as well.

122. B.L. Rice in EC, Vol. VII; J. F. Fleet, Inscriptions at Ablur. In EI. Ed. Hultzsch. Epigraphia Indica and Record of the Archaological Survey of India, Vol. 5 (1898–99), pp. 213–65.

Lorenzen. *The Kapalikas and Kalamukhas*, 98 ff.

Kālamukhas are said to have migrated from Kashmir, were worshippers of Lakulisa, and followed the *Black Yajurveda El* VII, Sk. 114; 19, 20.

123. It was similar to Takshasila in Northwest India and Varanasi. Fleet, J.F and Venkata Subbiah, A. "Venkata: A Twelfth Century University in Mysore," *The Quarterly Journal of the Mythic Society*. Vol. VII, April, 1917, pp. 157–196.

It has been described as a *vidyaśāstra*—an educational institution. *SII* XX, No. 40.

124. QJMS Vol. VII, 183.

125. *EC* VII, Sk. 94. Shantakumari, *History of the Agraharas*, 182–83.

126. *Vidyārthi-tapodhanas SII* XV III, No. 62.

In addition the students in *tapodhanas* were required to study properly during their stay in the *maṭha*, or else they would be expelled. Kannada inscription 1060 CE. *EI* VI, p. 90.

127. *El* VII Sk. 100 (1129 CE).

128. Other centers included, Ablur, Gadag, Sudi, although the *maṭha* lineage was different from those in Balligame.

129. Fleet. Ed, Tr., EI, V 22; Lorenzen. *The Kapalikas and Kalamukhas*, p. 104.

130. Yocum. A Non-Brahman Tamil Shaiva Mutt, 705, 112.

131. *EC* VIII, Sb, 276.

132. *EC* VIII, Sb, 275.

133. *EC* VII, Sk, 96, 101, 105.

134. *EC* V, Sb, 108, 8.

135. *EC* VI, Kd. 154.

136. *EC* VII, Sk. 281.

137. *EC* XI, Dg. 23.

138. *SII* IX (i), no. 101 (11.56.59).

139. There is no information about them. Shantakumari, *History of the Agraharas,* 176.

140. Shantakumari, *History of the Agraharas*, 181; Subbiah, A. Venkata: A Twelfth Century University in Mysore". *QJMS* Vol. VII. No. 3 (April 1917): 115.

141. Lorenzen calls these as rival creeds. Lorenzen, *The Kapalikas and Kalamukhas*, 124.

142. Subbiah, A Twelfth Century University, 175, 193.

143. The Jain and Buddhist institutions provided instructions on subjects such as logic, grammar, philosophy, and literature while Hindu *maṭhas* also taught all castes including Sudra students in Balligame. *EC* VII. Sk. 277. See Shantakumari, 1986, p. 108.

144. *EC* VII, Sb. 262.

145. *EC* VII, Sk. 197.

146. *EC* VII, Sk. 197.

147. Shantakumari, *History of the Agraharas*, 111. The area is said to have been plundered in the thirteenth century.

148. Gururajachar, S. *Some Aspects of Economic and Social Life in Karnataka (A.D. 1000–1300).* Perasaranga. Mysore: University of Mysore.1974, p. 205.

149. Lorenzen. *The Kapalikas and Kalamukhas*, 167 ff.

150. It has other connotations as well. Also Guhai Namaśivaya had spent time in Arunachala, where he had a vision of a brilliant light.

151. The Gurus of the Lingāyat *maṭha* perform a long initiation ceremony and a long period of continuous following.

152. Davidson, M. Ronald. *Indina Esoteric Buddhism: A Social History of the Tantric Movement.* NY: Columbia University Press. 2002, p 86.

153. This can be seen in the images of Viśṇu and Kṛṣṇa.

Shah, U. P. "Lakulisa: Saivite Saint." In *Discourses on Siva: Proceedings of a Symposium on the Nature of Religious Imagery.* Edited by Michael Meister, Philadelphia: University of Pennsylvania Press and Delhi: Oxford University Press, pp. 92–102. 1984.

154. Shah, U.P. Lakulisa, 1984, p. 88.

155. Davidson, Ronald M. *Indian Esoteric Buddhism: A Social History of the Tantric Movement.* NY: Columbia University Press. 2002, pp, 68–71, 87–91, 177.

156. Thapar, Romila. *Early India: from the Origins to AD 1300.* Berkeley: University of California Press, 2004, p. 294.

157. Davidson, *Indian Esoteric Buddhism*, 111.

158. Sharma, R. S. *India's Ancient Past.* Delhi: Oxford University Press, 2005.

159. Misra, *Ascetics, Piety and Power*, 62–63, 147–151.

160. Vaisnavism, formulated the ten *avatāras* of Viṣṇu and by an interchange of the four main attributes—conch, disc, mace, and lotus—held by Viṣṇu used for the *chaturvimsati-murtis*—the twenty-four forms of Keśava.

Chapter 3

Vedānta Monasteries

Development, Identity, and Patronage

By twelfth century CE, Śaiva *maṭhas* had spread to various parts of South India and flourished particularly in Northern Karnataka and Tamil Nadu. However, there arose a parallel system in Karnataka, namely the Vedānta *maṭhas*. The three main Vedānta *maṭhas* were the Advaita *maṭha* that arose in ninth century CE, the Viśiṣṭādvaita *maṭha* in eleventh to twelfth centuries, and the Dvaita *maṭha* in the thirteenth to fourteenth centuries. They based their doctrines on the Upanisadic theistic philosophy, rooted in the authority of the *Vedas*. Their three main sources were the *Upaniṣads*, *Brahma Sutras*, and the *Bhagavad Gītā*—the three together known as the *prasthānatrayī* (sources of philosophy).[1] However, by eleventh century Śaiva *maṭhas* were educational institutions and performed multiple functions. But from the thirteenth century CE onwards, the Vedānta *maṭhas* grew to be formidable, independent institutions. They gave importance to philosophical theories, individual identity, and Guru lineage.

Unlike the Śaiva *maṭhas*, the Vedānta *maṭhas* were founded by individual *ācāryas*. The Advaita *maṭha* was established by Ādi Śankarācārya (788–820 CE), who began to articulate commentaries on the *Upaniṣads*. A few centuries later, Rāmānujācārya (1017–1137 CE) founded Viśiṣṭādvaita *maṭha* and in the thirteenth century CE, Dvaita *maṭha* was founded by Madhvācārya (1199–1278 CE).[2] The growth of Vedānta *maṭhas* was largely due to their interpretation and systematization of Vedic philosophy, royal patronage, and individual identity. The three large organizations were headed by charismatic ascetic Gurus whose lineage, ideology, and practices have continued to play a key role in socioreligious matters.

Advaita *Maṭhas*

Ādi Śankarācārya was born in Kalady (Kerala) and was the disciple of the ascetic, Gaudapada.[3] He was an eminent scholar, an ascetic and engaged in debates with Mandana Mishra, Bhatta Bhaskara, and Buddhist philosophers.[4] Within his short life of thirty-two years, he wrote exhaustive commentaries on the *Brahma Sūtras*, the *Bhāgavad Gītā*, and ten principal *Upaniṣads*. He is known for his philosophy of Advaita (nondualism/monism), the essence of which is the union of the *ātman* (individual soul) with the *brahmaṇ* (universal soul).[5] His major contribution lay in the establishment of *maṭhas* and the organization of ascetics. Thus, he organized the system of *sanyāsins* into ten branches or suborders of the Advaita School of *Saivism*, known as *dasanāmi sanyāsins* (ten names of *sanyāsins*) where the titles of ascetics indicate their section.[6] The ten titles included[7] *giri* (hill), *puri* (city), *bhārati* (learning), *vana* (wood), *araṇya* (forest), *parvata* (mountain), *sāgara* (ocean), *tīrtha* (ford), *aśrama* (hermitage), and *sarasvati* (true knowledge) forming the suffixes to the names taken by monks of these orders after their initiation, indicating that the Sankara school of monks cultivated complete renunciation.[8]

Ādi Śankarācārya's achievement lay in the establishment of four *maṭhas*, each headed by an ascetic philosopher,[9] where the philosophical and religious traditions could be preserved and practiced. Being influenced by Buddhist and Jain systems of organization, he was convinced of the necessity of building major monastic centers, in order to revitalize 'Vedism' and to preach Advaita. The monasteries were established in four different zones of the subcontinent—Śringeri,[10] Dvaraka, Puri, Badrinath (and in addition, Kanchipuram)—as principal seats of learning. Each *maṭha* was headed by an *ācārya*, titled Śankarācārya, and recognized as a *jagadguru*[11] (world teacher) who claimed direct lineage from the founder.[12] The appellation shows that the spirit of Śankara had been transmitted through the lineage of pontiffs. Śankarācārya posted his disciples on the basis of their affiliation to a particular *Veda*. Each *maṭha* was given a *gotra* (traditional lineage from a *ṛṣi*), presiding deities, and a special formula as the symbol of philosophical quintessence of pure monism.[13]

1. Padmapada was affiliated to the *Ṛgvedic* school, and head of the Govardhana *maṭha* of the eastern zone. The *maṭha* belonged to the Kasyapa *gotra* and was given a sacred formula, *prajñānam brahma* (true knowledge is in *brahmaṇ*).

2. Dvaraka was the seat of the Sarada center of the western region, and Suresvara was in charge. It belonged to the Avigata *gotra* and the formula of this *maṭha* was *tat tvam asi* or "that thou art." The institution had to take care of the teaching of *Sāmaveda*.
3. The Joshi (or Jyotir) *maṭha* at Badarikasrama in the north, was under Toṭakācārya. The center followed *Atharvaveda*; its sacred formula was *ayamātma brahma* or "I am *brahman*." The branches attached to this *maṭha* were *giri*, *parvata*, and *sāgara*.[14]
4. Hastamalaka was deputed to Sringeri and was in charge of the regions in the south-Andhra, Dravida, Kerala, and Karnataka. The center was concerned with the orders of *sarasvati*, *bhārati*, and *puri*.[15] The center was affiliated to *Yajurveda*[16] and the formula assigned was *aham brahmāsmi*, "I am *brahman*."

Ādi Śankarācārya institutionalized the tradition of *sanyāsā* and the teaching lineage in the *maṭha* thereby beginning an orderly way of spreading Vedānta throughout India.[17] He established the norm that only ascetics could be heads of *maṭhas*, and that Advaita branch identity was related to proficiency in a particular Vedic text.[18] Under the leadership of "Guru-*sanyāsis*," *maṭhas* became educational and philosophical institutions with their own system of pilgrimage sites, organization, ritual, and philosophy. These were distinct from heterodox traditions (Buddhism, Jainism) and earlier Śaiva *maṭhas*.[19]

Śankarācārya built the edifice of the *jagadguru* or world teacher on an ethical foundation. The *jagadguru* was to be in control of his senses, an expert in Vedic lore and proficient in yoga and *śāstras* (scriptures). He strictly enjoined that the head, short of learning and character, should be removed from the seat of a pontiff; he should wander in order to preach and administer his own realm. He must maintain the customs of the *varṇāśrama dharma*. Whenever the head ceased to be a spiritual leader, he should be replaced by another of similar characteristics. In addition, the head may live in the style of a god or a king, but all his riches should be for *dharmahetave* (for the sake of *dharma*) and he must remain indifferent to them.[20] *Dharma* should be the basis of all men and of the *ācārya* and the direction of the *ācārya* should always be carried out like those of a king. Thus, he raised the importance of the Guru[21] and under the leadership of the *jagadgurus*, the *maṭha* developed to be an integrated educational-philosophical system.[22]

During the post-Śankarācārya period, two developments occurred.[23] Advaita became a form of personal religion and philosophy and institutional aspects of monasteries took place in an unequaled fashion. When Vidyāranya became the head of the Advaita *maṭha* (1336 CE), the religious authority of the *jagadgurus* resembled that of royalty. The *maṭha* became a *vyākhyānasimhāsana* (throne of exposition) and it developed into a *saṃsthāna* (region under its jurisdiction) in Sringeri. During post-Vidyaranya period, it did not hesitate to hold lands as a trust intended for preservation and spread the ideals of Śankara *pīṭha* (pedestal).[24] From now on it was not merely an institution devoted to a particular philosophy, with worship in a temple within the premises or merely feeding pilgrims, but a large body of disciples to uphold the honor of the *maṭha*. Thus, Śankarācārya was able to revive Vedānta, which was propagated through songs, *mantras*, and philosophy (within the Vedic tradition), breaking down barriers between the Buddhist and Hindu systems.

Vaisnavism and Viśistādvaita *Maṭhas*

Four hundred years after Śankarācārya organized the monastic order, Rāmānujācārya (1017–1137) formulated the philosophy of qualified monism, by which he refuted Śankarācārya's doctrine of *māyā* (illusion), and incorporated the concept of *bhakti* (devotion) turning to Vaisnavism. The historical background and origin of Vaisnavism and Vaiṣṇava *maṭhas* is not clear. Vaisnavism had emerged by 750 CE as a popular religion in North India, particularly with the gradual decline of Buddhism and Jainism.[25] It had incorporated various religious streams of thought and centered around the cults of Viṣṇu, Nārāyaṇa, and Kṛṣṇa-Vāsudeva, as well as mythical and historical heroes. The composition of *Purāṇas*, such as *Viṣṇu Purāṇa*, *Padma Purāṇa*, *Harivamśa*, and the *Bhagavad Gītā*, had a mass appeal.[26]

However, it is difficult to say anything definite on Vaiṣṇava asceticism, whether it existed as a regular practice before the time of Ādi Śankarācārya.[27] But the flexibility and assimilative character of Vaisnavism and its popularity, contrasted with the rigidity of Vedic fire-worship, was largely due to the *avatāra* (incarnation) theory. The divine appearance of God in the form of living beings, both animal and human became a central feature of the Vaiṣṇava tradition. In addition, the doctrine of the Bhāgavata cult with Kṛṣṇa Vāsudeava held a unique place.[28] The theory assimilated various local gods/cults such as Narasiṃha, Varāha, Rāma, Kṛṣṇa, Buddha and narrowed the gulf between followers of Buddhism and orthodox Hinduism.[29]

Apart from the *avatāra* theory, Viṣṇu *bhakti* became a unifying force in society. *Bhakti* means a simple, sincere devotion to a deity and played a significant role in the transformation of Vaisnavism from a ritualistic and intellectual "Hinduism" to a highly devotional tradition between the tenth and twelfth centuries CE.[30] In South India, Vaisnavism that centered around *bhakti* and *puja* (worship), stories, deeds of gods, older Vedic mythology was expanded to a popular level (and articulated in the *Purāṇas*), while the Upanisadic philosophy and commentaries continued to be learnt.

Furthermore, the Ālvār Tamil saints[31] had given great impetus to the growth of Vaisnavism till eighth century.[32] They were known for their love for God over the physical form of *sat*, *cit*, *ānanda* (truth, consciousness, and bliss) and based their philosophy and spirituality on the *Bhagavad Gīta* and the *Upaniṣads*. The earliest three of the traditional list of Ālvārs (Saroyogin, Bhutoyogin, and Mahadyogin), were ascetics as well as lovers of God.[33] Saints, such as Srinath *muni*, composed verses which were later transformed into a path (*prapati mārga*) of *bhakti* by Rāmānujācārya. While in North India, Vaisnavism became more secularized, due to assimilation of immigrants and the Islamic community; the South hardened the tenets and principles. It became more conservative and distinct from Saivism, which was reflected in the doctrines of Viśiṣṭādvaita and Dvaita.

Rāmānujācārya

Rāmānujācārya was born in 1016 CE; he lived in Kanchipuram and later in Śrirangam. He was a pupil of Yādava Prakāśa who was an Advaita philosopher but separated from the doctrine and studied the *Prabandhas* of the Alvārs (legendary narratives of Vaiṣṇava saints). Due to persecution by the Chola prince (1096 CE), he migrated to Mysore, which was ruled by the Hoysala Yadava princes in Dvarasamudra. There he converted King Viṭhala Deva (Bitti Deva), who later came to be known as Viṣṇuvardhana (1104–1141 CE).[34]

Rāmānujācārya refuted Śankarācārya's doctrine of spiritual monism which had negated *bhaktivāda*, the doctrine of love and faith.[35] He argued that if there is only one universal sprit, there is no scope for love or devotion which necessarily postulated two separate entities—the lover and the beloved. Rāmānujācārya placed the *bhakti* cult on a firm philosophical basis by expounding the doctrine of qualified monism or Viśiṣṭādvaita which recognized three eternal principles, individual soul, the insensate world, and the supreme soul (the creator), thereby reconciling his philosophy of qualified nondualism with *bhakti*.[36] He also elaborated the system of worship in temples and propagated sixteen modes of worship to be practiced by the devotees of *Viṣṇu*.[37] He emphasized *bhakti*, *karmayoga*, and worship (by following the principle of Pacaratra, but also kept *Vaikhānasāgama*).[38]

After the death of Rāmānujācārya, the Viśiṣṭādvaita school divided into Vadagalai (Northern school) and Tengalai (Southern school) in the sixteenth century.[39] The essential difference between the two schools is the connection between God's grace and man's effort in bringing about final deliverance. Some of the important Viśiṣṭādvaita *maṭhas* are the Ahobala *maṭha* with its center in Andhra (founded in 1398 CE), Parakala *maṭha* in Mysore (patronized by the Wodeyar dynasty), Melkote *maṭha* (Tirunarayanapuram), all belonging to the Vadagalai denomination; while the Vanamamalai and the Yadugiri Yaturaja *maṭha* (established in 1103 CE by Rāmānujācārya) belong to the Tengalai school. He also established the tradition where a *sanyāsi* was thence forward to live and manage the affairs of temple and allowed the lower caste Hindus to enter the temple as in the Yatiraja *maṭha* in Melkote. It is interesting to note that the functions of the temple and *maṭha* were not as demarcated in these *maṭhas* as it was in Advaita *maṭhas*.

DVAITA *MAṬHAS*

With the coming of Madhvācārya (1238–1317 CE), the trajectory of *maṭhas* takes a different turn.[40] Madhvācārya was the historical founder of the Dvaita system of philosophy and was born in Pajakshetra, near Udipi, in South Kanara District, on the west coast of South India. He was originally called Vāsudeva, and in 1249 CE, in his sixteenth year, after taking initiation from Acyutapreksha, he was given the titles of Pūrnaprajna and Ānanda *Tīrtha* for his brilliance in *tarka* (logic).[41] Thus, all three names have been used in his works, although he is widely known by the last name of Madhvācārya.

The learned *ācārya* appears on the philosophical scene when the two systems, *Advaita* and *Viśiṣṭādvaita* had been well established. "Due to doctrinal differences and ideological dissatisfaction with contemporary trends and schools of thought,"[42] he founded a new school of thought, called *tattvavāda* or realism, popularly known as *Dvaita* or dualism. He postulated that Viṣṇu as *paramātma* (supreme soul) and *jeevātma* (individual soul) are independent realities; the latter is dependent on the former and that the *jeeva* cannot be absorbed in the universal soul.[43] His philosophy has not been considered as the main line of Upanisadic thought particularly in the west, but it is an integral part of Vedic and Upanisadic tradition.[44]

> Madhvācārya compiled thirty-seven works[45] that include *Dasa Prakarnas* (ten philosophical monographs expounding his doctrine and critiques of Advaita doctrines of *upādhi, māya and mithyātva*), commentaries on the *Bhagavad Gīta* and the *Brahmasūtras*, commentaries on the ten principal *Upaniṣads*, on the first forty *Suktas* of the *Rgveda*, an epitome of the Mahabharata verses, and notes on the *Bhāgavata*. He was a creative and charismatic Guru, and had a great (*upaya)* ability to attract followers.[46]

Although his philosophy was innovative, it relied on the authority of the *Vedas*, the *Upaniṣads*, the *Brahmasūtras*, the *Bhāgavad Gītā*, and the *Purāṇas* as they provided an index of authenticity.[47] The rise of Dvaita *maṭhas*, in a way, hardened the division between Advaita and Dvaita philosophies.

Division of Dvaita *Maṭhas*

Madhvācārya is said to have died on his way to the Himalayas.[48] In the post Madhvācārya period, a voluminous literature grew around his works. Later exponents of this school were Madhva *Tīrtha*, Jaya *Tīrtha*, Vyāsarāya *Tīrtha*, Vādirāja *Tīrtha*, Vijayīndra *Tīrtha* who were[49] interpreters, commentators, and dialecticians, and philosophers.[50] Vyāsarāya *Tīrtha* (1460–1539) who was a well known scholar, studied Madhva *śāstra* under Sripādaraja of Mulbagal and held the throne for sixty-one years. His *Vyāsatraya*, *Tātparya Candrika*, *Tarka Tāndava* and *Nyāyāmrta* are the last words on Dvaita philosophy. (In fact Bengal Vaisnava Gaudiya *maṭha* traces its origin to Vyāsa *Tīrtha* and regard him as the grand Guru of Caitanya). He was highly respected in the court of Vijayanagara and even ascended the Vijayanagara throne to ward off the evil for the Vijayanagara king.

Due to certain negligible philosophical differences between his disciples, the Dualist *maṭhas* (also known as Madhva *maṭhas*), began to get divided when ascetic disciples set up their own *maṭha*.[51] This led to the emergence of secondary (or branch) *maṭhas* from the two main groups, namely, Ashta *maṭhas* and Desastha *maṭhas* (However, before the emergence of Madhvācārya, there was no network of Vaiṣṇava *maṭhas* as there was of Śaiva *maṭhas*. Vaiṣṇava centers of education were affiliated with temples and Rāmanujacarya enhanced this idea). Madhvācārya had eight disciples who chose to stay in Udupi and each established his own *maṭha*, which came to be known as the Ashta *maṭhas* (Eight *maṭhas*). Hṛṣīkēśa *Tīrtha* was head of Palimar *maṭha*, Narasiṃha *Tīrtha* of Adamaru *maṭha*, Janardhana *Tirtha* of Kṛṣṇapura *maṭha*, Upendra *Tīrtha* of Puttige *maṭha*, Vāmana *Tīrtha* of Sirur *maṭha*, Viṣṇu *Tīrtha* of Sode *maṭha*, Rama *Tīrtha* of Kanayur *Matha*, Adhokṣaja *Tīrtha* of Pejavara *maṭha*. These were not sectarian *maṭhas* but can be described as denominations, as their philosophical thought, organization, and ideology were similar. However, each of the denominations had a different *guru paramparā* (Guru lineage) and *gotra*. They contain valuable manuscripts and idols of *avatāras* of Viṣṇu which are said to have been handed down by Madhvācārya. The Ashta *maṭhas* are located in Udipi, around a central courtyard near the main Udipi *maṭha*.

In Udipi, the eight *maṭhas* are as follows:

1. Palimar *maṭha*—established by Hrishikesh *Tīrtha*—with its deity Rāma. It houses original works with the handwriting of Madhvācārya; they have been copied by pontiffs, such as Rājarājeshwara and Raghuveer *Tīrtha*.
2. Admar *maṭha* with pontiffs Narasiṃha *Tīrtha* (original pontiff) and later Vibudha Priya *Tīrtha*. Its (*iṣṭa devatā*) favorite deity is Kalingamardhana.
3. Kṛṣṇapur *maṭha* with Janardhana *Tīrtha* as the original pontiff followed by Vidymurthy *Tīrtha*, Vidyadheeśa *Tīrtha*, and Vidyasagar *Tīrtha*. The main deity worshipped is Kṛṣṇa as Kaliyamardhana.
4. Puthige *maṭha* with Upendra *Tīrtha* as original pontiff. Panduranga Vitthala is the original deity (also called Upendra), who was the favorite disciple of Madhvācārya.
5. Sirur *maṭha* with Vaman *Tīrtha*, the direct disciple of Madhvācāya followed by Lakshmindra *Tīrtha*.
6. Sode *maṭha* with Viṣṇu *Tīrtha* (brother and disciple of Madhvācārya) followed by Vādirāja *Tīrtha*. After Vādirāja *Tīrtha*, Kumbhasi *maṭha* came to be called as Sodhe *maṭha*. Lord Bhuvaraha and Śrī Hayagriva are the principal deities.

7. Kaniyoor *maṭha* with Rāma *Tīrtha* and the favorite deity is Narasiṃha.
8. Pejawar *maṭha* with Adhokshaja *Tīrtha*, also a direct disciple of Madhvācārya.

While the Ashta *maṭhas* were located on the west coast (at Udipi, below the Western Ghats, or *Ghattada Kelage*), the early Desastha *maṭhas* were based in Northern Karnataka (over the Western Ghats, or *Ghattada Mele*). Madhvacarya's important disciple, Padmanābha *Tīrtha*, stepped into his shoes after his departure and occupied the seat for seven years after whom Narahari *Tīrtha* became its head. He is regarded as the first composer of devotional songs in Kannada on Śri Hari and was thus the inaugurator of the *haridāsakuta* in Karnataka. After Narahari *Tīrtha* came Madhva *Tīrtha* who became the head of Vedanta *sāmrājya*. He was succeeded by Aksobhya *Tīrtha* whose pillar inscription at Mulbagal, Kolar district stated that he encountered Vidyranya, the Advaita Guru, and defeated him in the interpretation of the Upanisadic passage *tat tvam asi* (that thou art).

After Akśobhya Tirtha, a powerful personality, Dhondo Raghunātha Deshpānde of Mangalwedhe ascended on the 'throne' (1350–1388). He took the name of Jaya *Tīrtha* after his *sanyāsa*, came to be called Teekācārya, implying his status of a critical philosopher and writer of commentaries. Among his commentaries, *Nyaya Sudha* is the most important and runs into 28,000 *granthas* (32 letters make a *grantha*).[52] In 1412, the main ascetic line descended from Jayatīrtha *Tīrtha* to Vidyādhiraja *Tīrtha* who climbed the 'throne' of Udipi. He ruled for sixty-four years and his successor was Rajendra *Tīrtha*. At the time of Vidyādhiraja's death, Rajendra *Tīrtha* was on a tour. In order to avoid the break in the worship of the image in the *samsthana*, he chose Kavindra *Tīrtha*.[53] Thus the two branches, one presented by Rajendra *Tīrtha* subsequently came to be known as Vyāsarāya *mạtha* (after the great Guru, Vyāsarāya) and the other by Kavindra *Tīrtha*. The Vyāsarāya *maṭha* established by Vyāsaraya *Tīrtha* (near at T. Narasimhapura) split into Kundapur Vyāsarāya *maṭha* (in South Canara district) and the Sosale Vyāsarāya *matha*.[54]

Kavindra *Tīrtha* was succeeded by Vagisa *Tīrtha*, whose successor was Ramancandra *Tīrtha*, who in turn gave *asrama* to Vibhudhendra *Tīrtha*. At the time of the death of Rāmacandra *Tīrtha*, Vibhudhendra *Tīrtha* was away and could not be present at the time. Hence Vidyānidhi *Tīrtha* tirtha took charge of the *maṭha*. Here again two branches came into existence: one was presented by the senior Vibhudhendra's branch (and was subsequently called as Rāghvendra Swāmi *maṭha* after the great philosopher saint, Rāghavendra Swāmi—who died in 1671. The saints that belong now to the Rāghāvendra Swāmi *maṭha* were Vidyādhiraja *Tīrtha*, Kvindra Tīrtha Vagisa *Tīrtha*, and Rāmachandra *Tīrtha*). The senior branch was embellished by several scholars; the most notable among them being Raghavendra Swami's works especially *Parimala*, a fine work on *Nyayasudha*, *Bhavadipa* a commentary on *Tatva Prakasika*, and the *Vadavati – Bhavadipika*. Another significant pontiff and writer of the eighteenth century is Sumatindra *Tīrtha*, and his *maṭha* was known as Sumantindra *maṭha* after him. The pontiff of the *samsthana* were Varadendra *Tīrtha* (who was honored by Peshwa Madhav Rao I), Dhirendra *Tīrtha*, and his successor Susilendra *Tīrtha*. Vidyanidhi *Tīrtha*'s branch is also adorned by great scholars and saints such as Raghottama *Tīrtha* who wrote the commentary, *Bhavabodha*. Vidyadhisa *Tīrtha*, author of *Vayyartha-Candrika*, wrote a voluminous commentary on *Nyayasudha*. Other prolific writers include Satyanath *Tīrtha* and Satyabodha *Tīrtha* (1744–1782), during whose period, the *maṭha* came to be known as Uttaradi *maṭha*. After Satyabodha *Tīrtha* it was Satyadhyana *Tīrtha*, who was an erudite scholar. Besides the several *maṭhas* and branches of pontifical seats, a large number of individual scholars flourished among the Vaisnavas, such as Sri Yadavarya, Srinivasa *Tīrtha*, Visnu *Tīrtha*, and Jaganntha *dasa*. Each of the *maṭhas* still continue to have their own lineage.

Thus, in conjunction with the eight Aṣṭa*mathas* in Udipi (8), the Desastha *matha*s included the following:

9. Uttaradi *maṭha*
10. Sosale Vyasarja *maṭha*
11. Kundapura *maṭha*
12. Raghvendra Swamy *maṭha*[55]
13. Sripadaraja *maṭha*[56]
14. Majjigehalli *maṭha*[57]
15. Kudli *maṭha*[58]
16. Balegaru *maṭha*.

In addition, there are four more *mathas* in the Tulu Region:

17. Subrahmanya *maṭha*[59]
18. Bhandarkeri *maṭha*
19. Bhimanakatte *maṭha*
20. Citrapura *maṭha*[60]

21. Gokarna Partagali Jivottama *maṭha*
22. Kasi *maṭha*[61]

Asceticism as A "Value" and "Practice"

It may be added that the Gurus of Desastha *maṭha* wrote numerous dialectical treatises and commentaries: the outstanding ones were by Viṣṇu *Tīrtha*, Padamanābha *Tīrtha*, Narahari *Tīrtha*, Trivikrama *paṇḍitācārya*, Nāryāna *paṇḍitācārya*, Vāmana *paṇḍitācārya*, Jaya *Tīrtha* (also known as Tikācārya), Vijaya *Tīrtha*, Rāghavendra Swāmi, and Yadupati *ācārya.*

Despite the many divisions centered at various sites, all denominations of Dvaita *maṭhas* adhere to the philosophy of Madhvacarya. There is a slight functional difference between the Ashta *maṭhas* and Desastha *maṭhas* regarding the head pontiff. The ascetic head of a Desastha *maṭha* is often a renunciate after he experiences the life of a householder (marriage), while in the Ashta *maṭhas* and Saṅkara Advaita mathas the ascetic remains a celibate and renounces worldly life. This elicits a brief discussion of the two *sāmpradayas* (traditions) of *gṛhastha* (householder) and *sanyāsa* (asceticism) that are rooted in Hindu culture. According to the Advaita order, the *sanyāsāśrama* is a necessary prerequisite before attaining *kaivalya* (salvation) and *moksha* is possible only to those celibates who are renunciates. Within the Madhva Dvaita Desastha order, celibacy was not a necessary stage for attaining *moksha* (liberation). Dvaita *sanyāsis* believe that the attitude of the householder and that of the renunciate, in regard to detachment, should be similar. Both share the same value of *vairagya* (detachment) and in Madhva *maṭha*s their status is the same.[62] Being a householder did not mean that he could not attain moksha (liberation).[63] The traditions of *gṛhastha* and *sanyāsi* are not contrary to each other, but consist of shared values, concepts, and attributes. *Vairagya* was the basis for *sanyāsa* and was also the aim of a householder.[64] Hence, many Dvaita ascetics were married and then renounced life. According to Heesterman, the true *brāhmaṇa* is "the renouncer or the individualised sarificer . . . the pre-eminence of the Brahmin is not based on his priesthood, but on his being the exponent of the values of renunciation."[65]

It is important to distinguish between *sanyāsa* within the *āśrama* order (as a formal renunciation) and *sanyāsa* as a value. *Vairagya*, as a value to the householder, is ambivalent; but *vairagya* to a *sanyāsin* is the foundation for his state, coupled with knowledge of *braman*. Hence the question arises as to what was so special about *sanyāśrama* (i.e., a *sannyāsin* within a *maṭha*) if *sanyāsa* or *vairagya* was open to all. It is said that a *sanyāsi* within the *āśrama* (state of renunciation or within a *maṭha*) had lesser obligations toward family and related matters; hence he could dedicate his life to realization of *brahman*, which is based on the teachings of the *Bhagavad Gīta*.[66] This meant abstaining from activities involving sense gratification and attachment to desires actively, by understanding the logic. Renunciation was to be toward the fruits of action, including resources, gifts, praise, status, and even ego. In addition, the practice of renunciation was a matter of degree between the *gṛhastha* (householder) and *sanyāsa*.[67] The interpretation by Madhvācārya was supported from the text *Satyasamhita* that stated that Brahma, Yagnyavalkya, and others had obtained *moksha* with the help of their wives. Hence to the *sanyāsin*, the *maṭha* (like the Buddhist *vihāra*) was a place where renunciation could be institutionally practiced.[68] Ascribing the same logic to *sanyāsis* who headed *maṭhas*, the Guru does not exclude the management of the *maṭha* resources or its organization to householders. A large number of householders (along with their families) live within the precincts of a *maṭha*.

IDENTITY OF *VEDĀNTA MAṬHAS*

Maṭhas, while continuing the self-defining ways as individual philosophical centers, also saw a need for individual identity that manifested in various ways, such as organization, lineage, body marks, and worship. Such a tradition of group identity was prevalent among early Śaiva *maṭhas* in South India as well. There were some common features between the two *maṭha* orders. They functioned as centers of learning, taught disciples in their respective doctrines, and were *sattras* (charitable feeding houses) for *tapasvins* and devotees.[69] They observed the practice of initiation (*diksha*),[70] were headed by ascetics who were *rājagurus* to kings, and were recipients of royal patronage. However, the Vedānta *maṭhas* had a more rigid order, with a hierarchy of organization, a large body of followers, and norms about celibacy, which were grounded in their individual philosophy. They were founded by one main Guru, and headed by ascetics who were also philosophers and learned scholars. The commentaries on the *Vedas* and *Upaniṣads*, written by the Gurus themselves became scriptures.

Each *maṭha* (whether Śaiva, Vaiṣṇava, Jain, or Liṅgāyat) was (and still is) an independent institution and is under the management of a Guru who offers worship to the God(s), and confers honorary titles to the learned or to those who grant endowments to the *maṭha*. The mode of succession within the Vedanta *maṭhas* is the *pattada* form when a guru selects one of his monastic disciples as his successor or from the community. The Viraśaiva *maṭha*, such as the Suttur *maṭha*, follows the *virakta* method of succession, in which the succeeding Guru is selected from among the family members of the current Guru. In addition, in these *maṭha*, the institution is managed by Pattadayyas (chiefs) who belong to a class of Jangamas, or Liṅgāyat priests. Jangamas are divided into *dhatāsthalas or viraktas* (who are unmarried) and *gurusthalas* (who are married) and conduct all religious ceremonies. Besides these are twelve Maris or junior assistants who bring flowers daily, and arrange the ritual vessels. In addition are *carantis* (movers) or chief assistants who are fundraisers, and look after the affairs of the *maṭha*.

The identity of *maṭhas* in the form of body markings of disciples was a natural growth from Śaiva and Vaiṣṇava religious movements. Followers of Advaita (known as *smartas*)[71] worship Śiva and are distinguished by horizontal marks. They characteristically wear on their forehead, triple white *vibhuti* or *tripundra* (formed from ashes). These marks are common to all Saivites. The Viraśaiva *maṭha* disciples (which are not Vedānta *maṭhas*) identify themselves with a *liṅga* tied around their neck.

Śrī Vaisnavites (followers of Rāmānujācārya's Viśiṣṭādvaita philosophy) wear *tilakas* which are vertical markings worn by Vaisnavites. The Vaiṣṇava *tilaka* consists of a long vertical marking starting from just below the hairline to almost the end of one's nose tip known as *urdhvapundra*. The followers of Madhvācārya adopt the marks worn by Vaisnavites, namely a mark on their forehead composed of two white perpendicular lines made with *gopicandana* (white or yellow clay) and a dark line in the middle with a spot in the center. The two white lines are joined by crossline on the bridge of the nose.[72] Body markings are applied on the torso, arms, neck, and face of men by both *sanyāsins* and non-*sanyāsins*, with *gopichandana* or yellow clay. The clay is rubbed on the palm of the left hand with water to form a watery paste and then applied in two vertical lines. Followers of Madhva Siddhanta also receive *mudradharane* (sort of tattoo, symbolic of fire ordeal). This consists of a type of branding on parts of the upper body with *mudras* or symbols: *śankha* (conch), *cakra* (disc), *gada* (mace), *padma* (lotus), that are symbols of *Nārāyaṇa*. These markings differentiate them from followers of *Śaiva* traditions.

There were differences between *maṭhas* in the ritual worship of Gods as well. Although all *maṭhas* performed the death ceremonies of the founder Gurus,[73] there were differences in the importance accorded to Gods. Advaita *mathas* worshipped five deities of the *panchayana* namely Ganesa, Śiva, Viṣṇu, Subramanya, and Devi with Śiva being regarded as *parabrahma*. In Śringeri, is a temple for Chandramoulishvara (*Śivaliṅga*) and a temple for Śri Saradamba (Sarasvati).[74] Dvaita *mathas* were worshippers of Viṣṇu and his *avatāras*, while Śri Vaiṣṇavas gave importance to Kṛṣṇa and Ranganatha.

Advaita *maṭhas* did not consider themselves as exclusively Śaiva or Vaiṣṇava or even Śākta (pertaining to the goddess) and hence worshipped all five deities.[75] However, there was a difference among the Ashta *mathas* and Desastha mathas regarding the worship of the icon of Kṛṣṇa in Udipi. The privilege of worshipping Kṛṣṇa remained with the heads of the Ashta *maṭhas*. Each of the Ashta *maṭhas* "manage" the Kṛṣṇa temple and worship the God for two years on a rotational basis.[76] It is also the time of succession when the new pontiff (*paryaya swamy*) of the *maṭha* takes over charge. The system of *paryaya* was established by Madhvācārya, who installed the idol in Udipi, in 1285 CE.[77] During the period of *paryaya*, the *paryaya swāmi* performs daily fourteen types of *puja* (ritual worship) to Udipi Kṛṣṇa. Such a democratic system of worship is rare in other *maṭhas* where the organization is more hierarchical.

GURU AND KING

The Guru, in early Śaiva and Vedānta *maṭha* played a central role, and his relation with the king was of great importance. In ancient India, it was the traditionally educated *brāhmin* who advised the king in matters of Hindu law, and interpreted the application of the law of *Dharmśastras*. He was the legal adviser, known as the royal *paṇḍita*, *rājaguru*, or *rājapurohita* (royal preceptor). "The relationship between the king, upholder of the *dharma* and his *purohita* (priest) was a marriage—like bond . . . and had an important role in the coronation rituals" observes Heestermann.[78] According to the *Dharmasūtras*, the king could not decide upon religious matters and had no legislative power. Hence, he formed an advisory board or council for socioreligious conflicts and ascetic heads, or Gurus who were advisers to the king.[79] However, being a *sanyāsi* (ascetic) and advising the king was not contradictory in Hindu traditional collective thinking. *Sanyāsis* practiced (*vairagya*) detachment and if they were fundraising for the *maṭha*, it was for a social cause and not for themselves and hence Vedānta ascetic heads cannot be considered "worldy" gurus.[80] In addition, religious gifting as an individual and social practice has been embedded in the ancient Indian religious traditions of Hinduism, Buddhism, and Jainism. As an intrinsic part of *dharma* (religious ethics), gifting was a part of *rājadharma* (royal obligation). Religious texts such as *Dharmaśastras Nibandha, Krityakalpataru* by Lakshmidhara were popular and in South India the ideology of *dana* was stated in *Caturvarga Cintamani.* Royal beneficence had immense symbolic, social, and economic implications within a network system as attested from inscriptional and archaeological evidences, which throw light on the complex relationship between kingly and religious institutions.[81]

The existence of numerous Advaita, Dvaita, Viśiṣṭādvaita, and Viraśaiva *maṭhas* in the city of Vijayanagara or modern Hampi has been attested by Anila Verghese.[82] There were the Vidyāranya Swāmi *maṭha*, Chintāmani *maṭha*, Hucchayappa *maṭha*, Hiriya *maṭha*, Parameśvara *maṭha*, and Kariyasiddapa *maṭha*. The Advaita branch *maṭha*, in Hampi, established a closer relation with Śringeri Advaita *maṭha*. The sage Vidyāranya, who was the head of Advaita *maṭha* from 1375–86 CE, was associated with Harihara and Bukka in the founding of the city. In fact, within the small *maṭha*, near Virupaksha temple is a small image of Vidyāranya.[83] There were the Kālamukha Gurus, such as Kriyasakti—the *kulaguru* and *rājaguru* of Harihara II during the fourteenth and fifteenth century.[84] The Kālamukha sect was incorporated into Virasaivism whose followers continued to be active in the region of Vijayanagara till the end of the sixteenth century CE. Their heads, known as *jangamas*, wielded considerable influence at Vijayanagara: Virupaksha *paṇḍita* and Sadāśiva were among those who lived in the capital city. Near the Matanga hill, there was the Kariya Siddappa *matha*.[85] There were Viśiṣṭādvaita *maṭhas*, as well at Hampi, between 1325 and 1623 CE.[86] During the Saluva and Tuluva periods, Śri Vaisnavism gained ground, and a number of Śri Vaiṣṇava families, such as the *tatācāryas* lived in Hampi. Tirumala Auku-Tiruvengalācārya, the Guru of Ramaraya, is said to have granted a village to the Vitthala temple in 1543 CE.

The Saints of the Dvaita Madhva *maṭhas* were extremely influential in the royal court. Among them was Vyāsarāya, contemporary of Saluva

Narasimha, who remained in the royal capital till the time of Achyutaraya. He attended their courts, and was like a minister from 1499 to 1539 till his death. He was the *rajaguru* to Krishnadeva Raya and assumed the throne during a "bad astrological" period, and was hence called Vyāsarāya. The inscription dated 1513 CE states that Krishandevaraya is said to have offered him large estates.[87] A painting in the *maṇḍapa* of the Virupaksha temple portrays Vyāsarāya in a procession.[88] Apart from Krishnadevaraya of Vijayanagara, Svadi Arasappa, Keladi Ramaraja Nayaka, and the Chauta chiefs of Puthige all vowed their veneration to Vādirāja by donating land and money for the maintenance of his services.[89] Other Gurus who were honored by Vijayanagara kings were Surrendra *Tīrtha*[90] and Vijayīndra *Tīrtha* by Rāmaraya with *ratnabhishekam* for his scholarship.[91] Near the royal capital of Vijayanagar (Hampi), in Anegondi, *vṛndāvanas* of eleven Gurus belonging to the *Dvaita maṭha* have been commemorated.

According to Valerie, the Vijayanagar patronage to various Vedānta *maṭhas* led to rivalry and alliances and ultimately to sectarian divisions.[92] All Gurus in a *maṭha* commanded respect and were accorded royal honors. Vyāsarāya was crowned and honored with a royal umbrella, taken in a procession, and his feet were worshipped. There is a painting in the Virupaksha temple in Hampi where the Guru (perhaps Vyāsarāya) is carried in a procession.[93] Such an institutionalization of the living Guru in a *maṭha* had significant impact during the late medieval period.

Gurus as Kings and *Maṭhas* as Kingdoms

The increase of royal patronage toward Vedānta *maṭhas*, in the form of land grants, led to a close contact between *mathas* and royal courts. With the growth of property, they had to look after the affairs of the *mathas* and keep the royal court well-informed about their conditions. Thus, a royal office *dhamādhikari* was appointed by the kings to supervise the affairs of religious organizations. Vikramaditya VI appointed Mahapradana Dandanayakam Srimad Ayyangalu Somesvarabhattopadhyaya as *dharmādhikari*, in charge of the administration of grants and gifts. Whenever a new *ācārya* ascended the throne of a *maṭha*, he had to be finally recognized by the king. It may be conjectured that the maintenance of the *maṭhas* and its development, became a matter of concern to royal courts. The Guru and the king grew to be interdependent institutions: the *ācāryas* also had a share in the administration, they were consulted in socioreligious matters, and their judgment was regarded as final. Furthermore, royal grants led to recognition of *maṭhas*, and to achieve extended sphere of influence in villages, many enlisted themselves as disciples. Free from economic worries, the *maṭha* was devoted wholly to propagation of religious education. Principal *maṭhas* appealed to their learned disciples to carry out their objectives at different sites which led to their growth.

The growth of the *maṭha* as a kingdom by itself can be found in the expansion of the Advaita *maṭhas* which were patronized by Vijayanagara kings. Land grants and monetary gifts to *maṭhas* took place even during the early medieval period in Central India, Tamil Nadu, and Karnataka (see chapter 2), and Saiva Gurus had exerted great influence on kings.[94] But there was now a marked increase in the number of donations accorded to *Vedānta maṭhas* and a drastic rise in the role of the Gurus in political affairs. Innumerable *maṭhas* were established in the Vijayanagara kingdom, particularly in the capital city (Hampi). Advaita *maṭhas* had significant links with the rulers of Vijayanagara. Two copper plate grants by Krishnadeva Raya mention the gifting of villages.[95] The political influence affected the internal administration of *maṭhas*, particularly in the fourteenth–fifteenth centuries CE. Heads of *maṭhas*, who were accorded kingly honors, began to run on hereditary lines of status. The powers of some *acāryas* increased, and they became owners of a *maṭhas*. Certain forms of the royal court crept into the functioning of some *maṭhas*. In Śankara *maṭhas*, the Gurus began to assume a number of titles and insignia. During festivals, the Guru is borne along in a *pallakki* or palanquin, attended upon by disciples chanting Vedic hymns. Thus, it became necessary to take the help of officials for such *maṭhas*. Hence *the Guru's* personal staff increased in number to keep track of movements of the Guru between villages and towns. These became formal and even pompous institutions, and were like an independent "estate" with its own territory.

Maṭhas and Royal Patronage

There are numerous inscriptional evidences about royal patronage to the Vedānta *maṭhas* by the Vijayanagara kings. However, it is important to place the kingdom and its capital city in a historical context. Details of the empire and city have been provided by Sewell,[96] and Michell, Fritz, and Nagaraj Rao.[97] The kingdom of Vijayanagara (1336–1565 CE) has been said to have been founded by the Advaita Guru, Vidyāranya, who reconverted Harihara and Bukka back to Hinduism. He is said to have inspired them to serve their ancestral country and to set up a kingdom for the defense of the Hindu religion. Thus, the two brothers never returned to Delhi but became the founders of the Vijayanagara kingdom. They established their sway over Kampili and founded the city of Vidyāranya (forest of learning) to commemorate the role of Vidyāranya[98] in the founding of a huge empire and gave it the name of Vijayanagara (the city of victory). "Here in the presence of God Virupaksha, Harihara I celebrated his coronation in proper Hindu style on 18 April 1336 A.D."[99] The most significant event during this period was the establishment of the Bahmani kingdom under Hasan Gangu, which was to remain as the chief enemy of Vijayanagara almost throughout its history.

The Vijayanagara kings styled themselves as *dharmarāya*, or kings of *dharma*. Their *rājadharma* (king's *dharma*) implied the king's obligation toward his subjects, which entailed almost every aspect of the social good. He was obligated to protect his subjects by defending them from enemies to maintain peace, promote prosperity, and support the moral order (through the caste system). Royal patronage thus entailed support for a broad range of gifting to religious institutions (including *maṭhas*), and thus the king could fulfill his dharmic obligations.

During the Vijayanagara period, the kings patronized saints, such as Purandara Dāsa and Kanaka Dāsa, whose influence largely spread through devotional poetry and music and were effective religious propaganda. The inscriptions at the capital city mention the name of Tondaradippodi Ālvār and Purandara Dāsa who were patronized by the kings, and the saints had considerable influence in the city of Vijayanagara.[100] Large gifts were made in the form of *mahādāna* (great gift),[101] such as the *tulāpurusadāna* (the weighing of king against gold)[102] and *hiranyagarbhadāna* (the birth from a golden embryo)[103] when *brāhmins* and Gurus (as well as temples) received gold, silver, and precious stones.[104]

This concept of the king as the most generous, who tried to bestow the good things in life to the people, also had a practical purpose: to gain the support of the people, as is very clearly revealed in the contemporary historical text, *Madhura Vijaya*, where Bukka Raya advises the prince to keep the people happy and to give gifts, as the people were the wealth of the state.[105] The large gifts to *brāhmins* had also a political motive. It was a means to sustain the group, accept their superior status, and once again maintain the caste system. In addition, it meant the recognition of the caste which sustained kingship. The *brāhmin* was the womb of kingly power, which was dependent on gifts and which upheld the ideas which the king valued.[106] The gifts to *maṭhas* indicate a linkage between kings, Gurus, and community which led to increased status, a sustenance of both the *maṭha* and the king, and articulated this close relationship.

MAṬHA AND TEMPLE

Hindu *maṭhas* were (and still are) scattered in various regions and their size depended on the multiplicity of functions and availability of land and finance. Unlike Hindu temples, they do not follow any architectural rules that are stipulated in the *Āgamas* or *Śilpaśāstras* (rules of architecture). However, all *mathas* display simplicity in elevation and a functional plan. There are hardly any visual images or sculptures either on the external or internal walls. It may be added that architecture was not the area of their greatest achievement, although it was an institution of seminal importance similar to the Hindu temple.

As mentioned in chapter 2, by the twelfth and thirteenth centuries CE, the functions of the monastery had been fused with those of the Hindu temple. Its personnel administered the proper functioning of the temple.[107] The *matha* maintained its influence and control over the management of the temples for well over two centuries and were a necessary and useful adjunct to the temple.[108] The Vaiśnava monasteries had similar functions as Śaiva *maṭhas* in temples devoted to the worship of Viṣṇu, but in addition, they looked after the shrines of Ālvārs when they were erected separately as in Rajendravinagar and Triukkurangudi. They laid down the code of conduct for the Vaiṣṇavas and performed the *samasrayana* (initiation) as disciples and gave *mantropadesa* and *dāsyanāma* to the Vaisnavite followers. A well-established *maṭha* belonging to Paramahamsa Parivrajaka Sripada Swāmi, wielded influence over the Venkatacalapati temple and its administration, organization, and managing properties, endowments, disciples, work, services of *maṭha*. The primary reason for the administrative function of the *maṭha* was that it ensured proper observance of rituals, kept watch over the temple treasury, ensured the recital of Tirujnanam, fed the mendicants and pilgrims, participated in the festivals of temples during procession, tended flower gardens, and supplied offerings for daily worship. Thus, *maṭhas* were a necessary and useful adjunct to the temple. It must be mentioned at the outset that like the Śaiva *maṭhas* in Central India and Tamil Nadu, all Vedānta *maṭhas* were in the proximity of temples or had a temple attached to it.

A study of Hindu monastic architecture is replete with difficulties. There are few structures that retain original architecture and many are largely dilapidated.[109] There is an ambiguity about their original identification largely due to its proximity with the temple. Furthermore, phases of structural expansion have occurred from past seven or ten decades, and there are scant records about these buildings. Furthermore, there have been no substantial studies on the architecture of *maṭhas* in South India, except for a descriptive account of the *maṭha* in Udipi. The following questions can be raised: How did the architecture of the *maṭha* substantiate the importance of the Guru? Was it an appropriation of the Buddhist tradition? How did its architecture relate to its functions or religious beliefs? The chapter examines architecture as a social institution related to its changing functions. There exists an immense variety of configuration of buildings in each *maṭha* complex that depends on the region, type, resources, functions, and social needs. This analysis of *maṭha* architecture is limited to a brief account of their commonality and differences between a temple and a *maṭha*. I deal with the architecture of Vedānta Dvaita *maṭhas*, as its architecture takes a unique turn with the introduction of secondary (branch) *maṭhas* and the icon of the Guru.[110]

There is a lack of archaeological evidences of early Saiva *maṭhas* in Balligame (probably due to vandalism), although there is ample evidence of *mathas* in the capital city of Vijayanagara. Dilapidated structures of many have been found in Hampi that reveal that *maṭhas* belonged to the Kalyani Chaluyan period.[111] However, there were numerous *mạthas* that arose around the city of Vijayanagara between the fourteenth and sixteenth centuries.[112] *Advaita matha* set up by Vidyāranya was situated to the west of the Virupaksha temple.[113] The Kālamukhas *maṭhas* and Viraśaiva *maṭhas* were the Kallu *matha* of ascetic Visvesvaranya and the *maṭha* was in Krishnapura, near Hiruya Kaluve, referred as Hiriya Chatra.[114] There were Śri Vaiṣṇava Gurus that had *maṭhas* there as well, such as Govindaraja, Tirumala Auku-Tiruvenglacharya, and Kandala Srirangacharya *maṭha*.[115]

Matha architecture consisted of some characteristic elements: an entrance (verandah)/courtyard that led to a central hall and rooms nearby or were surrounded by radiating rooms. The hall was either used for gathering or teaching or other ritual activities. *Maṭhas* are normally small, and

Figure 3.1 View of a Ashta *maṭha*, Udipi.

consist of a central courtyard around which can be either rooms for living or separate buildings for boarding for students. Large Vedānta *maṭhas* are normally divided into precincts, with a functional division between buildings, such as for learning, lectures, living quarters, kitchen, dining, and worship. Similarly, the large complex of Advaita *maṭha* in Sringeri or the Dvaita *maṭha* in Udipi and Mantralaya have separate buildings for dining, teaching, library, worship of Vrndavana, and so on. The Pejawar *maṭha* in Bengaluru, known as Pūrnaprajna/Vidyāpītha, contains structures for the *pāthaśala* (school) (figure 3.2), a sanctum for housing of the *vṛndāvana*(s), and a dining hall with a kitchen.

However, the *maṭha* has parallels with a Hindu temple as well, such as in the existence of the sanctum, a symmetrical plan, and an object of worship such as in Udipi. The sacred town is a major center of Dvaita *maṭha*, where Madhvācārya first installed the image of Kṛṣṇa in the temple. Its architecture displays an interconnected functional system between a temple and *maṭha* and may be termed *maṭha*/temple. The monastery in Udipi is near a large tank with various precincts within a large complex and in the center is the Udipi temple and *maṭha*.

Figure 3.2 Vidyāpītha, Pejawar *maṭha*, Bengaluru.

The continuous expansion of Udipi with a built environment has obscured much of what it was originally like. However, it is quite certain that there was the Ananteshwara (Śaiva) temple (that still exists) where Madhvācārya is said to have become *adrisya* (disappeared), the *sarovara* (lake) in front, and the *maṭha*/temple of Kṛṣṇa. The icon of Kṛṣṇa was housed in a large room (larger than a normal *garbhagriha* in a temple) with a *pradakshiṇapatha* (circumambulatory path).[116] Surrounding the *maṭha* is a large central square open space, around which are grouped the eight Ashta *maṭhas* (interspersed with modern buildings) (figure 3.1). Other precincts include the *pāthaśala* or school, the residence for students, a building devoted to *Bhagavad Gītā*, and so on. It is interesting to find that within the *maṭha* is a sacred private space for the Guru in the form of an enclosed bathing tank, a sacred room for him to meet the public, and even a separate private kitchen to cook his food separately.

The architecture of Dvaita monastery may be divided into two types: those that contained *mūla vṛndāvanas* (orginal *vṛndāvana* with whole-body relics of the Guru) and those with a *mritige vṛndāvana* (votive memorials). About fifty years ago, the original *vṛndāvana* of a deceased Dvaita Guru was near a river or a sacred site in the open and

Figure 3.3 Rāghvendra Swāmi *maṭha*, Mantralaya.

there was no structure around it. But from past few years, the original *vṛndāvana* is enclosed within a built structure particularly in Udipi, Bengaluru, Mantralaya (figure 3.3), Sode, and Malkhed.[117] In Udipi, the twenty-two votive *vṛndāvanas* were formerly at a distance from the main shrine of Kṛṣṇa.[118] But today the *vṛndāvanas* are completely enclosed and are interconnected with the main temple. Similarly, the *mūla* vṛndāvana of Rāghvendra Swāmi, which is a gigantic piece of sculpture, was not enclosed by built form, but today it is along with other *vṛndāvanas* as well.

The enclosures around a *vṛndāvana* in Mantralaya and Malkhed follow a certain pattern. They are normally on a raised platform and surrounded by a circumambulatory path used by devotees. Similarly, in a branch *maṭha* (where a votive *vṛndāvana* is installed) elements of a raised platform (in the form of a sanctum, with the *vṛndāvana*) and a circumambulatory path can be seen. This recalls the plan of the square *garbhagriha* and *pradakshiṇapatha* patha in a Hindu temple. If one were to compare this to the plan of a school in a *maṭha*, or the plan of one of the Ashta *maṭhas* or that of a branch *maṭha*, they followed the same plan. The former is a central courtyard surrounded by rooms. The rooms are on a raised platform in the form of a square open corridor with pillars. The corridor can be used either for feeding or teaching, or gathering or even for sleeping in times of festivals.

My examination of architectural evidences has revealed that both the Hindu *maṭha* and the Buddhist *vihāra* exhibit similarities especially in simplicity of external form: plan, arrangement of the living quarters around a courtyard, a central shrine (with a *stūpa/vṛndāvana*), and configuration of buildings. Furthermore, a comparison of the architecture of a *maṭha* and a *vihāra*, in a number of monastic centers such as Ajanta, Kanheri, Nagarjunakonda, Mantralaya, Kanchipuram, Sringeri, and Udipi, show significant parallels in the architectural layout, especially in the arrangement of the living quarters around a central courtyard, the form of the kitchen, storage, and well in the configuration of functional buildings in large monasteries. One might raise the question whether there existed a ubiquitous form of architecture and how far was this related to sacred and functional space.

Maṭha architecture was flexible due to the expansion of its functions. Its architecture was not governed by rules of *Śilpaśāstras* or *Āgamas, mandalas* or system of measurements or proportion. The multiple functions of Vedānta *maṭhas*, such as teaching, feeding, and lodging, necessitated a large precinct with separate yet interconnected buildings, with a place for the Guru and God. Secondly, it did not require trained architects for its buildings, and could be built of brick and mortar unlike a temple. Being an institution of an ascetic, it avoided visual imagery on its architecture, except for some symbolic ones, such as conch or trident.

Guru and Priest

The difference between the temple and *maṭha* architecture was also largely due to the dichotomy between the temple priest and Guru. The Hindu temple priest was (and still is) the caretaker of deities in a temple. He is responsible for their upkeep, comfort, and honor that includes bathing, clothing, and offering them food, incense, and prayers. The priest acts as the intermediary between the gods and the worshipper. But the Guru in the *maṭha* had a more expansive role. He was the *sthānādhipati* of a temple. Even today, for the consecration of an image in the *garbhagriha* of a temple, an ascetic head is invited and the eye-opening ceremony is performed. There were conflicts between the temple and *maṭha* as well. In the Śankara *maṭha* at Puri, in 1800 CE, the Mutt took care of the Jagannath (Vaiṣṇava) temple. But the image of Siva and that of Śankara had to be removed for renovation of the temple. After that there was an objection of the two being installed. The British chose not to interfere and ultimately the idols were never installed.[119]

Unlike the priest in a temple, the Guru in a Vedānta *maṭha* is a *sanyāsi* (renouncer). He is renowned and honored for his traditional learning; he is a scholar, teacher, proficient in the *Vedas* and *Upaniṣads*, and in the philosophy of the founder Guru. Although the priest studies the *Vedas*, and chants them for worship, he is not an interpreter of *sāstras*. Furthermore, the Guru has a long lineage which gives him legitimization in the eyes of the public. From the fifteenth century onward, it was not merely an institution devoted to a particular philosophy, with worship in a temple within the premises or merely feeding pilgrims, but a large body of disciples to uphold the honor of the *maṭha*.

Thus, the *maṭha* was not merely the residence of an ascetic but a community building, a full-fledged independent institution with an expansive multifarious function and a flexible built structure, under a respected Guru, all of which set the tone for its continued power in society. The activities of the Guru were focused primarily on the community. He inspired the public for the cultivation of devotion, morality, and values, giving examples from ancient mythology and epics to follow *dharma* and cultivate *vairagya*. Working within a complex tradition of education, asceticism, and devotion, he commanded a sacred status in the community. This chapter substantiates that the *maṭha* was an institution of the Guru. In the next chapter we will examine the institution of the deceased Guru.

NOTES

1. The *Prasthānatrayī* consists of the *Brahma Sūtras*, known as *Nyāya Prasthāna* (that included Badrayana's systematic commentary on the *Upaniṣad*s, fifth century BCE), the *Upaniṣad*s, known as *Upadesha Prasthāna*, and the *Bhagavad Gītā*, known as *Sādhana Prasthāna*. Cenkner, William. *A Tradition of Teachers: Śankara and the Jagadgurus Today*. Columbia, MO: South Asia Books, 1983, p. 108.

Glasenappu, Helmuth Von. *Madhva's Philosophy of the Vishnu Faith*. Translated by Shridhar B. Shrothriya. Edited by K.T. Pandurangi. Bangalore: Dvaita Vedanta Studies and Research Foundation (n.d.), p. 8.

2. Other Vedānta organizations include the *dvaitadvaita darśan* of Nimbarka (thirteenth century), the *shuddha-advaita* of Vallabhacharya (fifteenth to sixteenth century), the *achintya-bhedabheda* of Chaitanya Mahaprabhu (sixteenth century), and *akshar-puroshottam* of Bhagwan Swaminarayan (nineteenth century). The Ramakrishna *maṭha* founded by Swami Vivekananda (nineteenth century) belongs to the *advaita* tradition of Sankaracharya. The Siddharudha Swami *maṭha*, near Hubli, Northern Karnataka is one of the richest *maṭhas*, founded by Siddharudha Swami (late nineteenth century) and has several autonomous branches. Guggali, G. H. "The Siddharudha Swami Math". *In Monasteries in South India*. Edited by Swahananda. Hollywood, CA: Vedanta Society of Southern California, 1989, pp. 71–72.

In Chennai, are numerous *maṭhas*, such as Sri Sankaracharya *maṭha* of the Kanchi Kamakoti Pitha, Sankara *maṭha* in West Mambalam, *Śri Śankara* Gurukulam (Advaita *maṭha*) at Abhiramapuram, *Upaniṣad āśrama* (Yoga Vasistha) at Nungambakkam, Karapathra Sivaprakasa Swamigal *math* (based on Śankara's *Siddhānta*) at Vyasarpadi, Dharmasivachariar *maṭh* at Kachaleswarar Agraharam. *Maṭhas* propagating Śaiva Siddhānta philosophy in the city include Tiruporur Chidambaraswami and Appar Swami *maṭhas* in Mylapore, the Pamban Swami *maṭha* at Tiruvonmiyur near Adyar, and the Daksinamurti Swami *maṭha* at Mint.

There is also the Śaiva Siddhānta Ramalingaswamigal *maṭh* at Tiruvottriur, founded in honor of Ramalingaswamigal, in 1911, Jyoti *maṭh* in Truvottriyur founded by Arutprakasa Swāmigal, and the Arunagiri Narayana Desigar *maṭh* at Todiarpet.

The Sri Vaiṣṇava Ahobala *maṭha* in Triplicane belongs to the Vadagali denomination while in Triplicane belongs to the Vadagali denomination while the Ramanuja Kutam *maṭha* belongs to the Tengalai denomination. Other *maṭhas* include the DvaitaVyasaraya *maṭh* at Triplicane, the Dvaita Uttaradi Udipi *maṭha*, and Sri Gaudiya *maṭha* at Gopalapuram.

The Rāmakṛṣṇa *maṭha* has numerous branches throughout South India including Coimbatore, Chingleput, Kanchipuram, Nattarampatti, Ottacamund, Salem, Madurai; in Karnataka, at Bengaluru, Mangalore, Mysore, Ponampet; in Kerala at Trivandrum, Kalady, Trichur, Calicut, Tiruvalla, Palai, Quilandy and in Andhra at Vizagapatnam, Rajahmundry, and Hyderabad.

3. Śankarācārya has been called Ādi Śankara due to another great *ācārya* who became famous in the eighth century CE. He was the thirty-eighth *ācārya* of Kanchi *maṭha* and was known as Abhinav Śankara. Hence the earlier Śankara was called Ādi (original) Śankara. The dates of Ādi Śankarācārya have been ascribed to 788–820 CE. The traditional sources of accounts of his life are

from the *Sankara Vijayams*, which are essentially hagiographic. Madhavacharya's *Śaṅkaradigvijaya*—Manuscripts of Madhavas work entitled *Samksepa Śaṅkaravijaya*—and Ānandagiri's *Śaṅkaravijaya* are other important sources. Sawai, Yoshitsugau. *The Faith of Ascetics and Lay Smartas: A Study of the Sankaran Traditin of Srngeri*. Publications of the De Nobili Research Library, Vol. XIX. Edited by Gerhard Oberhammer. Vienna: Institute for Indology, University of Vienna, 1992, p. 17 ff.

Madugula, I.S. *The Acharya: Sankara of Kaladi*. Delhi: Motilal Banarsidass, 1985, p. 24.

4. Mandana Mishra was a protagonist of *Pūrva Mīmāṃsā* school, and had a ritualistic interpretation of the *Vedas*. Śankarācārya accepted few tenets of Buddhism, *Mīmāṃsā*, *Sāṃkhya*, and *Nyāya*, but transcended them by incorporating *jñāna* (knowledge). He relied on scriptural authority, mainly the *Upaniṣadic* texts, such as *Bṛhadāraṇyaka*, *Chāndogya*, *Taittirīya*, *Kena*, *Śvetaśvara*, *Aitreya*, *Isavasya*.

5. His four important utterances are *prajnānam brahma* (*brahman* is pure) *ayamātma brahma* (this *ātman* is *brahman*) *tat tvam asi* (you are that) *aham brahmāsmi* (I am *brahman*). Madugula, *The Acharya*, p. 26.

6. Miller, David M. and Dorothy C. Wertz. *Hindu Monastic Life the Monks and Monasteries of Bhubaneswar*. London: McGill-Queen's University Press, 1976, p. 5.

7. Chakraborti, Haripada. *Asceticism in Ancient India: In Brahmanical, Buddhist, Jaina and Ajivika Societies from the Earliest Times to the Period of Saṅkaracharya*. Calcutta: Punthi Pustak, 1973, p. 179.

8. Chakraborti. *Asceticism in Ancient India*, p. 180.

9. There is a slight discrepancy between the statements in the *Mathamnaya* and the *Śankara Digvijaya* of Madhvācārya.

10. Sringeri *maṭha* was the residence for *sanyāsis*, a center for philosophical study, and a site for worship of Goddess Sarada. Sawai. *The Faith of Ascetics and Lay Smartas*, p. 31.

Śankarācārya has been described as a Buddhist as well as a critic of Buddhism. Pande, Govind Chandra. *Life and Thought of Sankaracarya*. New Delhi: Motilal Banarsidass, 1994, Reprint 2004, pp. 255–273. The Guru lineage of the founder of Advaita *maṭha*, was Śankarācārya but the heads of the four/five regional *maṭhas* are also known as Śankarācāryas. The founder is distinguished by the title Ādi Śankarācārya.

11. Sawai. *The Faith of Ascetics and Lay Smartas*, p. 31.

12. Jyotir *maṭha* at Badri in the north, Sarada *pīṭha* at Dvaravati (Dwarka) in the west, Govardhan *maṭha* at Puri in the east.

13. Ānandagiri, an early biographer of Śankarācārya, confirms the fact that Śankarācārya had many disciples and the two headed many *maṭhas*, four of the five headed by his foremost pupils—Sureśvara, Padmapāda,

Totaka, Hastamalaka—from whom the lineage for the Śankarācāryas evolved. Chakraborti, *Asceticism in Ancient India*, pp. 81, 179.

14. Since the death of its head Rāmakṛṣṇa Swāmi, the head of Jyotir *maṭha*, the temple was in charge of nambudri *brāhmaṇas* and today the *maṭha* is headed by Swāmi Brahmānanda, a learned scholar of Benares.

15. Śankarācārya is said to have made Sureshwara in charge of Sringeri and Kanchi *mathas* too, as a guardian of the seven-year-old boy, Sarvagynatman.

16. Śringeri *mạtha* was affiliated with *Yajur Veda* according to *Mathamnaya*. Chakraborti. *Asceticism in Ancient India*, p. 182.

17. The tradition of lineage existed in the Buddhist monastery as well as in Saivite *mathas*. Cenkner. *A Tradition of Teachers*, pp. 36–41.

18. He gave them directions called *mahānushasana*. The heads were not merely *jagadgurus*, but were also Śankarācāryas in spirit. The basic tradition of *maṭhas* as *vidyāpīṭhas* (educational institutions/seats of learning) continued, but from now on, the Śankara *mathas* rested solely upon its teacher and his relationship to previous gurus. Although the tradition of lineage of gurus existed in the Śaivite *mathas*, the lineage of Guru to disciple (not Guru to son), who adhered to a particular philosophy was established.

19. Cenkner describes them as "new institutionalism," as a *maṭha* was organized around an ascetic Guru where Guru lineage could be maintained. Cenkner, *A Tradition of Teachers*, p. 40.

20. Chakraborti. *Asceticism in Ancient India*, p. 185.

21. Mandana Misra reduced the role of the guru to a minimum and left the individual responsible for his spiritual growth. Cenkner, *A Tradition of Teachers*, p. 30.

22. During the period of Śankarācārya, the monastery was probably not a fixed structure. There are no archaeological or literary evidences about the architecture of the *maṭha*.

23. Immediate successor of Ādi Śankarācārya was Sureśvarācārya. The *maṭha* gained prominence during fourteenth century CE with great pontiffs such as Vidya *Tīrtha*, Bharati *Tīrtha*, Vidyāranya, Narasimha Bharati. During Vidyāranya's time, Sringeri besides being a *maṭha*, became *saṃsthāna* owing to acquisition of lands. It collected revenue from lands in Santalige Nadu, Kikkunda Nadu, Gajanuru, Gavatur, Mukkara Nadu, Harakeri, Julligodu (as mentioned in the *maṭha's* records). Sastry, A.K. *History of Sringeri*. Dharwar: Prasaranga. Karnatak University. 1982, p. 62.

Among post Śankarācārya Gurus were Sureśvara in the twelfth century, known for his *Naiskarmya Siddhi*, and Madhusudana Sarasvati of fifteenth century.

24. Sawai. *The Faith of Ascetics and Lay Smartas*, p. 34.

25. Bhandarkar, R.G. *Vaisnavism, Saivism and Minor Religious Systems*. Collected Works of Sir R.G. Bhandarkar. Ed. Utgikar, Narayan. Vol. 4. Poona: Bhandarkar Oriental Research Institute, 1929.

26. Temples for Viṣṇu and some of his *avatāras* had been constructed in Besnagar and Mathura, such as those of Vārāha, Kurma, and Matsya in early first century CE.

Bhagowalia, Urmila. *Vaishnavism and Society in Northern India, 700–1200*. New Delhi: Intellectual Corner, 1980, p. 14 ff. Vaisnavism flourished in South India and remarkable temples were built, including the Kailasanatha temple in Kanchipuram attributed to Rajasimha Pallava (685–705 CE) and the Channa Kesava temple in Belur by Viṣṇuvardhana.

27. The *Arthaśastra* of Kautilya refers to "spies, disguised as ascetics with shaved head or braided hair and pretending to be the worshipper of God Sankarsana."

Chakraborti. *Asceticism in Ancient India*, p. 167.

28. Its practical teachings and doctrine of *karma yoga*, the theory of detachment bridged the gap between *sanyāsin* (giving up all action—as a *sanyāsi*) and living a materialist life. Gonda, J. *Visnuism and Sivaism*. Delhi: Munshiram Manoharlal Pub Pvt Ltd, 1977, pp. 23–24. Bhagowalia. *Vaishnavism and Society in Northern India*, p. 10.

29. The ten *avatāras* of Viṣṇu are Matsya (fish), Kurma (tortoise), Varāha (boar), Narasiṃha (man-lion), Vāmana (dwarf), Rāma, Kṛṣṇa, Buddha, and Kalki, among which Kṛṣṇa was the most complete, convincing, and emotionally satisfying of all the incarnations. Kṛṣṇa was a fully human and divine hero, who fought, married, loved, and died. The *Bhāgavata Purāṇa* had twenty-one *avatāras* for Viṣṇu to accommodate people of different shades.

Vaisnavism gave importance to Vasudeva in Western India, Purusottama and Upendra in Central India, Nārāyaṇa and Trivikrama in Eastern India, and in the Ganga valley, as Ādi-Deva and Chandra-Madhava by the Gahadavalas, which was to penetrate into South India.

30. *Bhakti* has been defined as "a structure of personal devotion which hegemonic groups as well as into the redefining of dominant classes, and is also central to the production of a syncretic vocabulary in accessible vernacular languages." Bhagowalia. *Vaishnavism and Society in Northern India*, p. 111.

31. R.G. Bhandarkar places them in fifth or sixth century. Bhandarkar. *Vaisnavism, Saivism and Minor Religious Systems*, pp. 49–50.

32. Ālvār means the person that has dived deep in the ocean of spirituality.

33. The twelve famous Ālvār saints were Visnu Chitta, Andala, Kulashekar, Vipra Narayan, Munwahan, Poyagai, Bhutatta, Peya, Bhaktisar, Neelan, Madhur, Namma. They were superior to ordinary folks and wandered from place to place addressing the people through songs of love.

34. Rāmānujacharya was the *rājaguru* of the Hoysala kings. He converted 790 Jain *basadis* to construct *Pañcanārāyaṇa* temples, that is, temples of Nambi Narayana at Tondanur, Kirti Naryana at Talakadu, Vijaya Narayana at Terakanambi (near Gundlupet), and Vira Narayana at Gadag and transferred all land grants belonging to *basadis* to these temples. Kumara, S. and others.

Ed. *Bhagavad Sri Rāmanuja's Contribution to Four Swayamvyakta Kshetras-Kanchipuram, Srirangam, Tirupati and Melkote*. Academy of Sanskrit Research, Melkote, 2015, pp. 20–22.

35. It is said that Śankara's Advaita had already been misinterpreted by his disciples, Sureśvarā, Padmapāda, and Vācaspati, by the time of the rival school. Rāmachandra Rao, S.K. *Sankara and Adhyasa Bhashya*. Bangalore: Abhijanana, 2002, p. 6.

36. The concept of Viśiṣṭādvaita of Śri Vaiṣṇava school is said to be Śankarācārya's *nirguna brahman* (*brahman* without qualities). *Brahman*, according to Rāmanujācārya, manifests as *Viṣṇu*. Pauranika, K. Hayavadana. *Poornaprajna Vijaya: Life and Teachings of Sri Madhwacharya*. Translated from Kanndada by Krishnamoorthy, Bhadra. Chennai: Sri Krishna Sri Raghvendra Trust, 2010. p. 16. Viśiṣṭādvaita tradition seen in the expositions of *Brahmasutura Bhasya* follows the traditions set by Tamil hymns. Rāmānujācārya composed *Vedānta Sara*, *Vedārtha Samgraha*, *Vedānta Silpa*, and *Bhasyas* (commentaries) on the *Brahmasūtras* and the *Bhagavadgītā*. Viśiṣṭādvaita stressed only one God (Vasudeva), liberation was the main goal and emphasized *ahimsa*, and the temples were open to all castes. He classified the *pujas* in the temples, such as *Nitya puja* or routine worship, *Naimitaika* or occasional *puja*, *Kāmya puja* or motivated worship, and added *utsavas*—social congregations, *tīrthayātra*, or pilgrimage.

37. Bhandarkar. *Vaisnavism, Saivism and Minor Religious Systems*, p. 55. The three most important Vaiṣṇava supporters of the Pancaratra tradition were Yamunācārya, Rāmānujachary, and Vedānta Desika. The four important centers or *kshetras* were Kanchipuram, Sringeri, Tirupati, and Melkote.

38. In 1110 CE, in his ninetieth year wrote *Niyamanappadi* a temple charter for Melkote which is still followed. He recruited fifty disciples to look after the services. Kumara and others. Ed. *Bhagavad Sri Rāmanuja's Contribution*, p. 24.

39. The Tengalai recognized Pillai Lokācārya and gave importance to *Divya Prabandhams*, while the Vadagalis followed Vedānta Desikachar and gave preference to the *Vedas*.

40. Rao, B.A. Krishnaswamy. *Outline of the Philosophy of Sri Madhwacharya*. Bangalore: Swetadweepa Publications, 2003, pp. 1–4.

41. Acyutapreksha, an ascetic of the *ekadandi* order belonging to the lineage of Śankarācārya.

Sharma, B.N.K. *Madhva's Teaching in His Own Words*. Ed. K. M. Munshi and R.R. Diwakar. Bombay: Bharatiya Vidya Bhavan, 1961, p. 4.

Madhvacarya's father was Madhyagehahatta and his mother was Vedavati.

42. Sharma, B.N.K. *Philosophy of Sri Madhvacarya*. Delhi: Motilal Banarsidass Publishers, 1962, p. xv.

43. Svatantram—asvatantram ca dvividham ātvamisyate
Svatantro bhagavān Viṣṇuh bhāvobhāvo dvidhetarat

'There are two realities in this world: independent and dependent. Only Lord Nārāyana is the independent reality. Everything else is dependent. The dependence also has two types: *bhāva and abhāva*, being and non-being.' Govindacharya, Bannanje. *Acharya Madhwa: Life and Works*. Translated into English by U. P. Upadhyaya. Udipi: Isavasya Pratishthanam, 2011. p. 67.

According to Madhvācārya's Siddhānta (philosophy), *jagat* (world) is real; it is dependent and the only independent entity is *paramātma* or *brahman*. Every *jeeva* (individual) is inherently different or *svarupatha*. God impels each *jeeva* into activity and converges benefits in conformity to the *karma* performed by the *jeeva*. This Siddhānta or belief system of mutual gradation is bitter truth and established by *Vedas*, *itihasa*, and *Purāṇas* (*vaidika dharma*). The cause of inequality between each *jeeva*, according to *Advaita*, is *māyā*, but according to *Madhvācārya*, it is *karma*. God is the creator of *jeeva*, he grants sorrow and joy, and discrimination between *jeevas* is due to one's *karmas*. Puranika, K. Hayavadana. *Poornaprajna Vijaya: Life and Teachings of Sri Madhwacharya*. Translated from Kannada, Krishnamoorthy, Bhadra. Chennai: Sri Krishna Sri Raghvendra Trust, 2010, p. 17. Sharma,1961, 76–80.

44. Glasenappu, Helmuth von, Pandurang, K. T. Madhva's Philosophy of the Vishnu faith (n.d).

The essential principles of Sri Madhvacarya's teachings—where they run parallel to the teachings of Sri Caitanya Mahaprabhu—have been summarized in ten points by Baladeva Vidyabhusana (who belonged to Gaudiya Vaisnavas) in his Prameya-Ratnavali that summarizes the following points about what Madhvacarya taught

"Shri Madhvacaharya taught that (1) Krishna, who is known as Hari is the Supreme Lord, the Absolute; (2) That Supreme Lord may be known through the Vedas; (3) The material world is real; (4) The *jeevas*, or souls, are different from the supreme Lord; (5) The *jeevas* are by nature servants of the Supreme Lord; (6) There are two categories of *jeevas*: liberated and illusioned; (7) Liberation means attaining the lotus feet of Kṛṣṇa, that is, entering into an eternal relationship of service to the supreme Lord; (8) Pure devotional service is the cause of this relationship; (9) The truth may be known through direct perception, inference, and Vedic authority. These very principles were taught by Shri Chaitanya Mahaprabhu. Vidyabhusana, Baladeva: *Prameya-Ratnavali*. Delhi: Ras Bihari Lal and Son, 2009, pp. 15–135.

45. He was a prolific writer, and is known as a *bhaṣyakāra*. Sharma B.N.K. *Madhva's Teaching in his own Words*,152–164.

46. Forsthoefel, Thomas A. and Humes, Cynthia Ann. *Gurus in America*. NY: State University of New York Press, 2005, pp. 1–14.

Rao, B.A. Krishnaswamy. *Outline of the Philosophy of Sri Madhwacharya*. Bangalore: Swetadweepa Publications, 2003, p. 92;

Stoker, Valerie, Conceiving the Canon in Dvaita Vedanta: Madva's Doctrine of "All Sacred Lore". *Numen*. Vol. 51. 47–77.

Madhvācārya did not agree with the monistic view of his teacher and opposed them by offering a different interpretation to the Vedic texts and the *Upaniṣads*. Govindacharya, Bannanje. Ed. *Madhva Rgbhasya in Sarvamula-grantha. Vol 4*. Udipi: Akhila Bharata Madhwa Mahamandala. 1973.

Sharma B.N. K. *History of the Dvaita School of Vedanta and its Literature from the earliest beginnings to our own times*. Delhi: Motilal Banarsidass, 2008, pp. 83–89.

47. Madhvācārya reconstructed the tradition of interpretation with the help of *itihasa* (history), *Purāṇa*, and *Pancarātras*. He was guided by the philosophical tradition behind *Upaniṣads*, *Brahmasūtras*, and *Bhāgavad Gītā*, which were the three *Prasthānatraya*: The *Upanishads*, known as *Upadesha Prasthāna* (injunctive texts), the principal *Upaniṣads* as *Śruti prasthāna* (the starting point or axiom of revelation), and the *Brahma Sūtras*, known as *Nyāya Prasthāna* or Yukti *Prasthāna* (logical text or axiom of logic).

48. His body was not found and hence he does not have a *vṛndāvana*.

49. For details about the many pontiffs of each of the Ashta *maṭhas* in Udipi, see Sharma. *History of the Dvaita School of Vedānta and Its Literature*. 1961, 201–210.

50. Vādiraja *Tīrtha* belonged to the Sode *maṭha*. He was an erudite scholar, critic, a poet, and mystic who wrote a number of polemical works, such as *Yukti Mallika* and *Rukminisa-Vijaya*.

51. Rao, Vasudeva. *Living Traditions in Contemporary Contexts: The Madhva Matha of Udupi*. New Delhi: Orient Longman, 2002, p. 34.

52. Sharma. *Philosophy of Sri Madhvacarya*, 1992, 255–256.

Sheridan, Daniel P. Jayatirtha. In *Great Thinkers of the Eastern World* ED. Ian McGready. New York: Harper Collins, 1995.

53. Sharma. *Philosophy of Sri Madhvacarya*, 1992, 255–256.

Another version of the story, is that, due to disputes between him and the pupils of Jaya *Tīrtha*, Rajendra *Tīrtha* was elected as their head.

54. While Advaita heads of *maṭhas* or *jagadgurus* do not have various denominations, and are known as Śankara *maṭhas*, all the heads of four (or five) branches are called *Śankarācāryas*. Dvaita *maṭhas*, came to be known by various names, depending on the site or founder.

55. Rāghvendra Swāmi, was the seventeenth pontiff of Śrī Madhvācārya Pīṭha (1623–71).

56. The *maṭha* is located in Mulabagal: founded by Padmanabha *Tīrtha* (1412–1504) Sripādarāja alias Śri Lakśminārāyana *Tīrtha* was one of the pioneers of *haridāsa* literature, and preceptor of Vyāsarāya *Tīrtha*.

57. The *maṭha* was established by Madhva *Tīrtha*. It split into Kudli and Balegaru *maṭha*.

58. The *maṭha* was established by Aksobhya *Tīrtha*.

59. The *maṭha* had branched from the line of Viṣṇu *Tīrtha*; it divided into two: Bhandarkere (in Udipi) and Bhimana Katte (in Tirthahalli).

60. The *maṭha* is located near Udupi and was a branch of Pejawar *maṭha*.

61. Dvaita *maṭhas* that belonged to the community of Gauda Sarasvata *brāhmaṇas* were the Gokarna Partagali Jivottama *maṭha* and the Kaśi *maṭha*.

62. Rao, Vasudeva. *Living Traditions in Contemporary Contexts*, 168.

63. In my discussion with the head of the Purnaprajna *Vidyāmatha* belonging to Pejawar *maṭha*, I gathered that this was an important difference between Advaita and Dvaita *maṭhas*.

64. The wife is not necessarily regarded as a temptress who will lead her husband astray but rather a partner on the path of spiritualiy.

65. Heesterman, J.C. *The Inner Conflict of Tradition: Essays in Indian Ritual, Kinship, and Society*. Chicago: University of Chicago Press, 1985, pp. 41, 44.

66. *Bhagavad Gītā* 18.2.

67. *Bhagavad Gītā* 5.19.

68. Rao, V. *Living Traditions in Contemporary Contexts*, 171.

69. See pages 29–34 in this book.

70. Pandey, R.B. *Hindu Samskaras: Socio-Religious Study of the Hindu Sacraments*. Delhi: Motilal Banarsidass. 1976, pp. 111–133.

Filippi, Gian Guisep. *Concept of Death in Indian Traditions*. New Delhi: D.K. Print World Ltd, 1996, pp. 70–76.

Diksha is the opening ritual to self-knowledge.

Filippi, Gian Giuseppe. "*The Guru and Death*." In Rigopoulos, Antonio. *Guru: The Spiritual Master*, 121–136.

71. The word *smarta* is a substantive derived from *smriti*, and denotes a strict performer of an action. Sawai. *The Faith of Ascetics and Lay Smartas*, 24.

72. Rao, V. *Living Traditions in Contemporary Contexts*, 54–55.

73. The *punyatithi* (annual death ceremony) of Rāghvendra Swāmi is performed for three days in all Rāghvendra Swāmi *maṭhas*, both in the original *maṭha* and its numerous branch *mathas*, and is termed *aradhana* in Kannada.

Dvaita *maṭhas* perform the following festivals as well: *Ugadi* (new year), *Matsay Jayanti*, *Rāma Navami*, *Hanuman Jayanti*, *Akshay Tritiya*, *Vasantotsava*, *Vasant Dvadasi*, *Narasiṃha Jayanti*, *Prathama Ekadashi*, *Jayatirtha's punyatithi*, *Upakarma*, *Hayagriva Jayanti*, Anniversary of Rāghvendra Swāmi, *Kṛṣṇa Jayanti*, *Ganesh Chaturthi*, *Vamana Jayanti*, *Ananta chaturashi*, and *Navaratri*.

74. Sawai. *The Faith of Ascetics and Lay Smartas*, 26.

75. Sawai. *The Faith of Ascetics and Lay Smartas*, 22, 147.

Śringeri tradition is neither Śaiva nor Vaiṣṇava but rather nonsectarian. It is interesting to find that although they cultivated Advaitism, they also worshipped different deities. Followers of the Smārta tradition that worships all five deities: Śiva, Viṣṇu, Devi, Ganesha, and Subramanya.

Chakraborti. *Asceticism in Ancient India*, 183.

76. The system is known as *paryaya*. In 1990s there was a controversy regarding the performance of *paryaya* by Sugenendra *Tīrtha*, head of Puthige

maṭha, who had crossed the ocean by coming to USA. According to tradition, if a *brāhmaṇa* were to cross the ocean, he was sort of ostracized and a *bahishkara* was performed. This angered the administration of the Kṛṣṇa *maṭha* and traditional Madhva community. The case went to court and he was granted the authority to perform the worship to Lord Kṛṣṇa, but ultimately an agreement was reached by which he could perform only six *pujas* that did not include touching the main sacred icon of Kṛṣṇa. However, the *paryaya* ceremony was boycotted by heads of seven *maṭhas*.

77. Madhvācārya entrusted the worship of Kṛṣṇa to eight ascetic disciples. Till the period of Vādirāja *Tīrtha* (1480–1600 CE), the *paryaya* took place once in two months, but Vādirāja (of Sode *maṭha*) changed the system to a two-year term. Each of the eight *maṭha* at Udupi get a chance once in sixteen years to manage the Kṛṣṇa temple and worship the icon for two years.

78. Heesterman, J. C. *The Ancient Indian Royal Consecrtion: The Rajasuya Described According to the Yajus Texts and Annotated.* La Haye: Mouton: 1957, 226.

79. Michaels, Axel "The Pandit as a Legal Adviser: *rajaguru, rajapurohita and dharmadhikarin.*" In *The Pandit: Traditional Scholarship in India.* Edited by Michaels, Axel Michaels. New Delhi: Manohar, 2001, pp. 61–77.

80. Sears, Tamara I. *Worldly Gurus and Spiritual Kings: Architecture and Asceticism in Medieval India.* New Haven: Yale University Press, 2014.

81. Rao, N. Navaratri in South India. Symbolism and Power in Royal Rituals. *Sagar: A South Asia Research Journal* XXIV (2016): 1–14.

82. Verghese, Anila and Eigner, Dieter. A Monastic Complex in Vithalpura, Hampi Vijayanagra. *South Asian Studies: Journal of the Society for South Asian Studies* (incorporating the Society for Afghan Studies) 14.4 (1998): 127–140.

83. Verghese and Eigner. A Monastic Complex, 127–140.

84. Verghese, Anila. *Religious Traditions at Vijayanagara: As Revealed Through its Monuments*, New Delhi: Manohar and the American Institute of Indian Studies, 1995, pp. 111–116

85. Verghese, *Religious Traditions at Vijayanagra*, 112, 116.

86. Kulke, Hermann. Maharajas, Mahants and Historians: Reflections on the Historiography of Early Vijayangara and Sringeri. In *Vijayanagara - City and Empire*: New Currents of Research. 2 Vols. Ed. Dallapiccola, Anna Libera and Lallemant, Stephanie Zingel-Ave. Stuttgart: Franz Steiner Verlag Wiesbaden GMBH, 1985, pp.130–33.

87. Stoker, Valerie. *Polemics and Patronage in the City of Victory*, Oakland, Ca: University of California Press, 2016, p. 32.

88. The image in the procession was earlier interpreted as that of Vidyāranya. However, the camel, green flag, and the drum were gifts accorded to him by Saluva Narasiṃha. Stoker. *Polemics and Patronage* 70–72.

89. Sharma B.N. K *History of the Dvaita School*, 413–16.

90. Sharma B.N. K *History of the Dvaita School*, 587.

91. Ayyangar, S. Krishnaswami. *Sources of Vijayanagar History*. Madras: University of Madras. 1919, p. 252.

92. Stoker. *Polemics and Patronage*, 44–71.

93. On the day the Guru takes up his *paryaya* (when the worship of the Kṛṣṇa *matha* is taken over by the new ascetic head of the paryaya *matha*, all the pontiffs of the Ashta *maṭha* partake of a grant procession toward the main Kṛṣṇa *maṭha* as thousands watch. Rao. *Living Traditions in Contemporary Contexts*, p. 37.

94. The leaders of Śaiva *maṭhas* such as the Vimala Śiva and Visvesvara Śiva were *diksha* Gurus of the Kalachuri kings (twelfth century). The Golaki *maṭha ācāryas* (teachers) exerted great influence on the Kalachuri kings of Chedi, the Kakatiya kings of Warangal, and the kings of Malava as well as in the Chola countries. In Tamil Nadu, Śaiva saints, particularly Manikka Wachaka, Sambandha, Wageesh, established ways of worshipping Śiva in the Pandyan kingdom and regulated temple rituals.

95. Shastri, A.K. *A History of Sringeri*. Dharwad: Prasaranga Karnatak University, 1982, p. 80.

96. Sewell, Robert. *A Forgotten Empire (Vijayanagar) A Contribution to the History of India*. London: Swan Sonnenschein & Co., 1900. Reprint, New Asian Educational Services New Delhi, 1983.

97. Fritz, Michell, and Rao, Nagaraja. *Where Kings and Gods Meet: The Royal Centre at Vijayanagara, India*. Tucson, Arizona: The University of Arizona Press, 1984, p. 9 ff.

98. Phillip Wagoner, *Tidings of the King: A Translation and Ethnohistorical Analysis of the Rayavacakamu*. Honolulu: University of Hawaii Press, 1993, p. 84.

99. Sastri, K.A. Nilakanta. *A History of South India from Prehistoric Times to the Fall of Vijayanagar*. London: Oxford University Press. 1955, p. 229.

100. The portrait of a saint has been found at Hampi. There is a controversy whether this is the image of Tondaradippodi Ālvār or of Purandaradāsa. There is also a *maṇḍapa* on the banks of the river, called the Purandaradāsa *maṇḍapa*, where the saint is said to have lived during his last days. Rajasekhara, Sindigi. Inscriptions at Vijayangara. In *Vijayanagara - City and Empire*: New Currents of Research. Vol. 1. Ed. Dallapiccola, Anna Libera and Lallemant, Stephanie Zingel-Ave. Wiesbaden GMBH, Stuttgart: Franz Steiner Verlag,1985, 109.

101. Rao, Nalini: *Royal Imagery and Networks of Power at Vijayanagara: A Study of Kingship in South India*. Delhi: Originals, 2010, p. 71.

102. Rao, Nalini :Royal Religious Beneficence in Pre-Modern India: Political and Social Implications. *International Journal of Dharma Studies*. 4. Article no: 7, (July 2016): 1–11.

103. There are many inscriptions all over Karnataka recording the *suvarnameru* and *ānandanidhi* gifts of Achyuta Raya. See Rajasekhara. Inscriptions at Vijayanagara, p. 110.

104. Rajasekhara, Inscriptions at Vijayanagara, p. 110.

105. Shanbhag, D.N. *Gangadeviya Madhura Vijaya*, Dharwar: Karnataka Viswavidyalaya, 1964, p. 5 ff.

106. Dumont, L. The Conception of Kingship in Ancient India. *Contributions to Indian Sociology* 1 (1957): 7–22.

107. In 1453 CE, Mukundnandapuri, a disciple of Amararaja Sripada, was pleased to declare that all property of the *maṭha* be amalgamated with those of the temple and that these together with the jewels of gold and silver vessels, coins, utensils, and valuable cloths of the *maṭha* be in the enjoyment of the temple. Tirumalai, R. *The Mathas in Pandyan Townships in Vaapeya: Essays on Evolution of Indian Art and Culture. K.D. Bajpai Felicitation*. Vol. 1. Ed. by Shastri, A.M, Sharma R.K, Prasad, Agam. Delhi: Agam Kala Prakashan, 1987, pp. 404–405.

108. See *Tirumalai, Mathas in Pandyan Townships*, 395–407.

109. For a study of their architecture, there are few archaeological evidences regarding early Śaiva *maṭhas* in Tamil Nadu, Śri Parvata in Andhra and Balligame.

110. Since the emphasis of this book is on the *vrndavana* in Dvaita *maṭhas*, I have accorded importance to the architecture of *Dvaita mathas* and not to the other Vedānta *maṭhas* or Viraśaiva *maṭhas*.

111. Verghese, *Religious Traditions at Vijayanagara*, p. 116. Further evidence stems from symbolic images of ascetics with a staff or rosary portrayed stereotypically on its pillars.

112. Stoker, Valerie. *Politics and Patronage in the City of Victory*, Oakland, Ca: University of California Press, 2016.

113. Stoker, *Polemics and Patronage*, 50–56.

114. The *Kriyasakti* Gurus were influential in the court of early Sangamas (mid-fourteenth century to early fifteenth century). A copper plate grant of 1378 CE indicates that Kriyasakti was the *kula* guru of king Harihara. Verghese, *Religious Traditions at Vijayanagara*, p. 112.

115. In addition, there were the Dvaita *mąthas* and the *vṛndāvanas* of Dvaita saints in Anegondi, near Hampi, from 1324–1623. Stoker, *Polemics and Patronage*, 59, 100–105.

116. It is said that when the great devotee, Kanakadāsa, could not obtain a *darṣan* of the Lord Kṛṣṇa, he approached the temple from a rear window (*kanakana kindi*), and the image is said to have turned around. But actually, the roof on the side of the entrance fell and it was never opened. Hence even today, the *darṣan* of the God can be had only through the small window that Kanakadāsa used. (Only the *paryaya* Guru can be inside the sacred space to worship Lord Kṛṣṇa).

117. This is largely due to the large number of pilgrims who visit the sacred site and to maintain an orderly way of providing *darṣan*. See Chapter 4 for *vṛndāvana.*

118. There might have been an injunction about installing *vṛndāvana* (even a votive one) within a temple as Madhvācārya had installed the icon of Krśṇa and the structure functioned as a temple. *Vṛndāvanas* of Gurus were installed only after the death of Madhvācārya by his disciples, following the example of Desastha *maṭhas*.

119. Krishnamani, M. N. *Shankara: The Revoltionary*. Rajan Publications. New Delhi. 2001, p. 350.

Chapter 4

The Icon and Relic of the Guru

By fourteenth century CE, Hindu monasticism was well established in the Deccan in the form of independent institutions headed by the ascetic pontiff, the Guru. The three well-known Vedānta monasteries encompassed the school of Monism (Advaita *maṭha*) established by Ādi Śankarācārya,[1] school of Qualified Non-Dualism (Viśiṣṭādvaita *maṭha*) of Rāmānujācārya, and of Dualist thought (Dvaita *maṭha*) of Madhvāchārya. Apart from these were the Viraśaiva/Liṅgāyat *maṭhas* known for their reformist program of equality. They had continually played a significant role in society from the rise of Basaveshwara in the twelfth century CE onward. Each of the *maṭhas* had branches at key centers in South India,[2] with the living Guru playing a central role in their maintenance and spread of religious doctrines.[3] They functioned as centers of ecclesiastical teaching, philosophical studies, boarding, training future priests, community feeding, and lodging, and grown to be an integral part of the community.

Within the Dvaita *maṭha* is a sacred icon which is worshipped daily with flowers, incense, lights, and chants. It is in the form of a rectangular non-anthropomorphic stone 'sculpture' called *vṛndāvana* (figure 4.1). But the *vṛndāvana* does not merely consist of post-cremation remains, like those of the Buddha. Below the hollow square sculpture, is a pit that contains the entire embalmed whole-body relic of the deceased Guru.[4] The immovable 'structure' along with the 'relics' may thus be called a sepulchral and mortuary icon. The *vṛndāvana* is housed and worshipped only within a Dvaita *maṭha* although all Vedānta monasteries respect the founder and living Guru. The practice of enshrinement, and veneration of whole-body relic, and the memorial above has continued from past seven

Figure 4.1 ***Vṛndāvana*** **of Raghuvarya** ***Tīrtha, Nava Vṛndāvana,*** **Anegondi.**

hundred years in the innumerable Vedānta Vaiṣṇava Dvaita (Madhva) *maṭhas*.[5] Sites that enshrine the *vṛndāvana* have grown to be popular and sacred pilgrimage centers.

The meaning and symbolism attributed to the *vṛndāvana* are numerous. Etymologically, *vṛndāvana* means the garden, forest, or orchard of Vṛndā, wife of Viṣṇu. In addition, here, Kṛṣṇa (the main deity of Vaisnavites),[6] is said to have danced with his female devotees, gopis. The term *vṛndāvana* is also related to Tulsi Vṛndāvana, which is a sacred pot with the Tulsi plant that is worshipped by women in almost every Hindu household. Tulsi is particularly sacred for Vaiṣṇavas and for the worship of Viṣṇu.[7] However, during the late medieval period (sometime between fourteenth and seventeenth centuries CE), the mortuary structures came to be known as *vṛndāvana*. The multileveled meaning of the *vṛndāvana* can be examined from various perspectives and the anomalous worship of a "mummified body" invites comparative exploration along multiple trajectories.

My principal aim in this chapter is to uncover its origins by an investigation into the the nature and history of whole-body relics, the form and shape of the memorial, the historical influences of Buddhism and pre-Buddhist as well as medieval Hindu practices. The literary, epigraphical, and archaeological evidences have been used along with oral tradition and enquiries from *paṇḍitas* (scholars), and heads of monasteries. The discussion that follows is not intended to be a final answer to the origins, rather, more to suggest the possibilities of its formation and origination. In chapter 5, I discuss its meaning from a symbolic, ontological, and metaphysical perspective.

Although enshrinement of the physical remains of a *sanyāsin* has been practiced in Dvaita Hindu monasteries for the past five hundred years, it has yet to spark scholarly interest. Until now studies on the *vṛndāvana*, such as those by Deepak Sarma, B. N. K. Sharma, Hayavadana Rao, and Bannanje Govindācārya have largely focused on the philosophy of Madhvācārya and on his teachings.[8] There have been serious scholarships on Buddhist relics and burial rites but a lack of studies on Hindu burials and memorials, except those by Settar.[9] There are no textual descriptions or writings about the *vṛndāvana*s.[10] There are uncommonly scant textual records and inscriptions to cast any light on these sacred objects. In addition, texts in the form of commentaries on *Vedas* and the *Upaniṣad*s do not mention or describe the *vṛndāvana* or even mention the funerary practices for ascetics. Even the popular musical works in Sanskrit and Kannada that are composed by disciples of Dvaita tradition extoll the former Gurus without mentioning any afterdeath practices.

Description of a *Vṛndāvana*

A *vṛndāvana* is an immovable, non-figural, stone sculpture in the form of a box or closed shrine ranging between 9 ft x 3 ft. The term refers both to the structure as well as the deceased body beneath. Thus it may be translated as a tomb, a dedicatory memorial, or a sepulchral "structure." *Vṛndāvanas* are normally installed on a stone platform and has a prescribed iconography: it is a closed cubical (or square) box with a hollow space in the center in which are placed *mritige* (soil), precious stones, *sālagrāma* (round sacred stones symbolizing Viṣṇu), and may contain small figures of gods. A typical *vṛndāvana* is a structure of three superimposed square stone terraces: a base, body or central short shaft, and a top layer or slab that is surmounted by a running leaf design on all the four sides (figure 4.1).[11] It is normally installed on a raised platform; it is divided into three parts, each separated by a horizontal projecting slab. The lower part is normally short, the central part might be more elongated, and the upper part consists of small stones in the form of leaves called "*tene*" (leaf) that runs all around the *vṛndāvana*. This is a simple type and many *vṛndāvanas* follow this iconographic type. An example of this type is that of Raghuvarya *Tīrtha* in *Nava Vṛndāvana* at Anegondi (figure 4.1).

However, one can notice slight variations in the size and form of the icon. There is the *vṛndāvana* of Vidyānidhi *Tīrtha* at Yaragola, which has a rounded top, that appears in the shape of a lotus bud or even a *liṅga* (figure 4.2). The last variation is quite distinct. They appear to have been erected from one large stone, marked by symbolic motifs, such as those of Rāghvendra Swāmi (figure 4.3).

However, Among the twenty *mūla vṛndāvanas* in the Kṛṣṇa *maṭha* at Udipi, there is one which is round in shape (figure 4.4). The *vṛndāvanas* in Puthige *matha* are very simple–in the form of three

Figure 4.2 ***Vṛndāvana*** **of Vidyānidhi** ***Tīrtha*****, Yaragola.**

Figure 4.3 Votive *vṛndāvana* of Rāghvendra Swāmi, Bengaluru.

flat stones placed one above the other (figure 4.5). There is also the architectural type, such as that of Raghottama *Tīrtha* at Tirukoilur that resembles the plinth of a Hindu temple (figure 4.6). Regarding the relief imagery on them, some have figures of gods, which could be their *iṣṭa devatā* (favorite god)[12] or devotees. They may depict figures of Kṛṣṇa with the *gopis* as on that of Raghunanda *Tīrtha* (1492 CE). The *vṛndāvana* of Raghuvarya *Tīrtha* consists of figures that allude to his biography (figure 4.1). Some may even contain an image of a tortoise on its base such as those of Satya Abhinava *Tīrtha* at Nachiargudi near Kumbakonam. The *vṛndāvana* of Yogindra *Tīrtha* in Śrirangam (1671 CE) has images of *avatāras* of Viṣṇu on its upper part, on each of the leaves (figure 4.8). The *vṛndāvanas* of Rāghvendra Swāmi are particularly interesting and consist are elaborately carved normally with arches and lotus designs.[13] Above the *vṛndāvana* is placed a small

Figure 4.4 *Mūla vṛndāvanas* in *Kṛṣṇa maṭha/temple*, Udipi.

Figure 4.5 *Vṛndāvanas* in Puthige *maṭha*.

Figure 4.6 *Mūla vṛndāvana* of Raghottama *Tīrtha*, Tirukoilur.

Figure 4.7 *Mūla vṛndāvana* of Śripādarāja *Tīrtha*, Mulbagal.

Figure 4.8 ***Mūla vṛndāvana*** **of Yogindra** ***Tīrtha,*** **Srirangam.**

metal image of Kṛṣṇa (figure 4.9), and sometimes of Vāyu, the Wind God, which might also be located in a small shrine in the *maṭha* (figures 4.9 and 4.10).

Worship of a *vṛndāvana* is quite similar to that of a God in a Hindu temple, which includes the chanting of Vedic *mantras*, offerings of flowers, lights, and incense (figures 4.3 and 4.9). *Vṛndāvanas* are normally erected on the banks of rivers and temples, but the growth of built environment in these areas has led to their incorporation into either *maṭha* or temple architecture. Due to the importance accorded to the worship of *vṛndāvanas*, these objects have become a part of *maṭha* architecture and are thus enclosed within a permanent structure.

Figure 4.9 ***Vṛndāvanas*** **in Uttaradi** ***maṭha*****, Hospet.**

ORIGINS OF THE *VṚNDĀVANA*

The practice of erecting *vṛndāvanas* began in the late medieval period, around the fourteenth century CE, and has continued till today.[14] However, its origins have been a conundrum. The multidisciplinary method of inquiry begins with an examination of its form, as the most prominent feature of the *vṛndāvana* is its non-anthropomorphical or aniconic form. I then turn to the history of relic enshrinement which might have affected its formation. Archaeological evidences of memorials cannot be ruled out in the region as well as the influence of Buddhist *stūpas*.

The earliest *vṛndāvana* is in Anegondi, the early capital of the kingdom of Vijayanagara kingdom[15] near Hampi Vijayanagara. The site is known as *nava vṛndāvana* and is on an island in the river Tungabhadra in Northern Karnataka. The earliest *vṛndāvana* is that of Guru Padmanābha *Tīrtha* (1317–1324), near which are eight other later *vṛndāvanas*, the most important being that of Śri Vyāsarāya *Tīrtha* (1447–1539). These include the *vṛndāvanas* of Śri Jaya *Tīrtha* (1365–1388), Raghuvarya *Tīrtha* (of

Figure 4.10 Lord Vāyu.

Uttaradi *maṭha*, 1502–37), Kavindra *Tīrtha* (1392–98), Vageesa *Tīrtha* (1398–1406), Śrinivasa *Tīrtha* (1539–1584), Rāma *Tīrtha* of Vyāsarāya *maṭha* (1564–84), Sudheendra *Tīrtha* of Rāghvendra Swāmi *maṭha* (1614–23), and of Govinda (1534), who did not hold any office but was a devoted disciple of Vyāsarāya *maṭha*[16] (figure 4.13).

Padmanābha Tirtha was the direct disciple of Madhvācārya (founder of Dvaita philosophy). His *vṛndāvana* was installed by the succeeding pontiff, Narahari Tirtha in *nava vṛndāvana*, in 1324 CE at Anegondi. Later, all Dvaita *maṭhas* began to commemorate their deceased Gurus and house their *vṛndāvanas*. Thus they can be found in or near all Desastha *maṭhas*, Uttarādi *maṭha*, Śripādarāja *maṭha*, Vyāsarāya *maṭha*, Sosale Vyāsarāya *maṭha*, Kundapura Vyāsarāya *maṭha*, Rāghvendra Swāmi *maṭha*, Mulabagilu *maṭha*, Majjigehalli *maṭha*, Kudli *maṭha*, and Balegaru *maṭha*.[17] They are housed as well in the Ashta-*maṭhas* in Udipi, in the Kṛṣṇa, Palimaru, Adamaru, Puttige, Siruru, Sode, Kaniyuru, and Pejawar as well as in further denominational *maṭhas*.

BURIAL PRACTICES AND MORTUARY RITUALS

The Hindu burial practice for *sanyāsins* and yogis in almost all parts of India consisted of a few simple practices. There is no cremation as the body does not have to be purified by fire.[18] They were understood to have performed their own cremation during initiation, and hence there was no postmortem cremation; instead they were buried or immersed in rivers.[19] All formal burial feasts and *srāddha* ceremonies were normally avoided, as they were performed when an individual decided to become a *sanyāsin*.[20] Traditionally, the bodies of ascetics would be floated down the river (in a sitting position) or buried inside the ground, with a *maṇḍapa* or canopy above the ground to mark the area. In Dvaita *maṭhas*, the funerary practice for the pontiff consists of a simple but distinct ritual performed by the members of the *maṭha*: embalming of the body and its transfer into the *vṛndāvana*.

After the death of a Guru, his body is washed, and clothed with a saffron cloth. His legs are crossed and are placed in a sitting posture, facing east or north east and sand and salt are piled over it.[21] Coconuts are broken to crack the skull which affords the imprisoned soul to be "liberated" from the body.[22] It is taken in a procession (followed by monks and disciples) and placed in a pit, in a sitting posture (with the arms on a wooden frame) and heaps of salt, mustard, and camphor poured over it.[23] Above the body are placed *sālagrāmas* (figure 4.11), precious stones, beads, and gold objects and even small images of deities.[24] A stone slab is placed over it. After about a month, a stone memorial (*vṛndāvana*) is constructed with slabs of dressed stone above the pit.[25] This is filled with precious stones, gold, and *sālagrāmas* as well.[26] After the ritual deposition of the embalmed body, the sacralizing ritual of *pratishthāpana* (or establishing the image) is conducted which consists of recitation of Vedic chants, offering lights, flowers, an orange robe, and *vaiṣṇava* sacred marks, such as the *śankha* and *cakra*. Blessed food is distributed and it is now known as a *vṛndāvana*.[27] The object is now considered sacred and can be worshipped.[28]

It is interesting to note that the relics in a *vṛndāvana* can be "divided" to install a new *vṛndāvana* and hence a new branch Dvaita *maṭha*. However, since it is a whole-body relic, it cannot be divided in the strict sense of the term. But a particle of soil (*mritige*) or deposit from the original (*mūla*) *vṛndāvana* can be reinstalled to create secondary *vṛndāvanas* (*mritige vṛndāvanas*).[29] A Dvaita *maṭha* that has a *mūla vṛndāvana* (with the deceased body) is known as a *mūla maṭha*. Furthermore, each original monastery (*mūla maṭha)* can have various branches in different geographical areas, called *shakha maṭha* or branch monasteries (*mritige maṭhas*). For instance, the *mūla maṭha* of the Pejawara *maṭha* is in Udipi, while its branches are scattered. The *mūla vṛndāvana* of Rāghvendra Swāmi is in Mantralaya, while his *mritige* or votive *vṛndāvanas* are in various places and number about a hundred in South India alone. Moreover, the deceased bodies of the succeeding heads of a *mūla matha* have also been entombed (and still continue to be enshrined) in the *maṭha* at Mantralaya, near the *vṛndāvana* of the founder Guru, Rāghvendra Swāmi. The division or reinstallation of the relics (rather a symbolic division through the soil) led to the proliferation of the *maṭhas* along with their secondary *vṛndāvanas*. With the growth of sectarian Dvaita (Madhva) *maṭhas*, *vṛndāvanas* in the sanctum, came to play a seminal role in popularizing the relic cult.[30]

In one of the branch or *shākha maṭhas* or *mritige maṭha* (with a votive *vṛndāvana*), as in the Vyāsarāya *maṭha*, the objects that have been kept in the *mritige vṛndāvana* of Rāghvendra Swāmi (which is 9 ft by 3 ft) in Bengaluru, have been listed. Within the *maṭha* on a board the objects are listed in Kannada (figure 4.3). "On February eleventh, 1937, on *mahā Śivarātri*, Lakshmi Hayagriva, Tikācārya of the Kundapura Vyāsarāya *maṭha* (contemporary of Yati Lakshmi Manoja *Tīrtha*) in the morning at 9.00 am, the *mahotsava* (great celebration) *prāṇa pratishthāpana* (installation) of the *vṛndāvana* took place. Worship in the form of *kumbhābhiṣekha, pancāmṛta abhisekha, alankāra, naividya, mahāmangalārti* were performed. *Tīrtha prasāda* (blessed food) and *phala mantrākshate* were distributed to 6,000 devotees. Three images were kept above the *vṛndāvana* and precious objects placed in it include – *guru rāyara mritige samputa* (part of soil of the Guru); fifteen *sālagrāmas* from sacred sites; idols of Rāma, Kṛṣṇa, Vyāsarāya (on a lion); a conch that is turned toward the south side; two *sālagrāmas* encased in *ratna*; a garland of *navaratnas* (nine precious stones); a coin embossed with the figure of Rāma. These seven items are sacred for the continuous lineage of Gurus.[31]

The practice of embalming and deposition of ascetics affiliated to the Dvaita order, still continues till today. On July 18, 2018, *Prajavani*, the Kannada paper, published details about the mortuary ritual conducted for the head of the Sirur *maṭha* in Udipi, Lakshmivara *Tīrtha* Swāmi, who died on July 15, 2018, from food poisoning. Normally the deceased body of the ascetic would be dipped in the sacred tank before the Udipi *maṭha* but since the body had gone through post mortem, certain rituals were omitted. A 5 ft by 5ft hole (1.5 by 1.5 meters) was dug in the ground. Coconuts were broken on his head till it cracked. The body was wrappped in about 20 kg of cotton cloth, 100 kg of salt, 100 kg of pepper, 100 kg of mustard, 100 kg of green camphor, and covered with soil. A Tulsi plant was planted above it. The symbols of *śankha*, *cakra*, *gada*, *kamandalu* were placed; a spoon of *tirtha* or blessed water was "dropped" in the mouth, and the ascetic staff kept in front. The body was removed from the pit, taken in a procession, given a *darśan* of the icon of Kṛṣṇa in the temple (although this was only through the *kanakana kindi*, the small window), and placed within the stone container. On the twelfth day a *vṛndāvana* was constructed with dressed stone slabs. It appears that the process of mummification was an ancient practice. The *Satapatha Brahmana* contains rules for funeral rites that included removing the intestines; cleaning the internal cavity; placings chips over the eyes, nostrils, mounth; and anointing the body, before cremation.[32] This is an example of the lived reality for a large number of deceased Dvaita saints in present times.

Relic to Icon

Vṛndāvanas are normally erected on the banks of rivers and temples, but the growth of built environment in these areas has led to the incorporation of *vṛndāvanas* into either *maṭha* or temple architecture. The practice of erecting *vṛndāvanas* began in the late medieval period, around the fourteenth century CE, and has continued till today.[33] Due to the importance accorded to the worship of *vṛndāvanas*, these objects have become a part of *maṭha* architecture and are thus enclosed within a permanent structure. It was not merely the placement of the *vṛndāvana* in an architectural setting that established the object as an icon, as *vṛndāvanas* in open air were also worshipped daily with Vedic rites and function as icons. It was the ritual of *pratishthāpana* that transformed the relic into an icon.

As the division of Dvaita *maṭha* into separate branches increased in different regional areas in Karnataka, each with its own lineage of Gurus, the number of *vṛndāvanas* increased proportionately. Thus there are innumerable *vṛndāvanas* in many sacred (*matha-vṛndāvana*) sites in Karnataka. Among the major sites are Udipi, which consists of twenty *vṛndāvanas* in the Kṛṣṇa *maṭha*, Mulbagal with five, Malkhed with seven, Sode with twelve, Gokarna with eight, and Kolar with four. Among the many

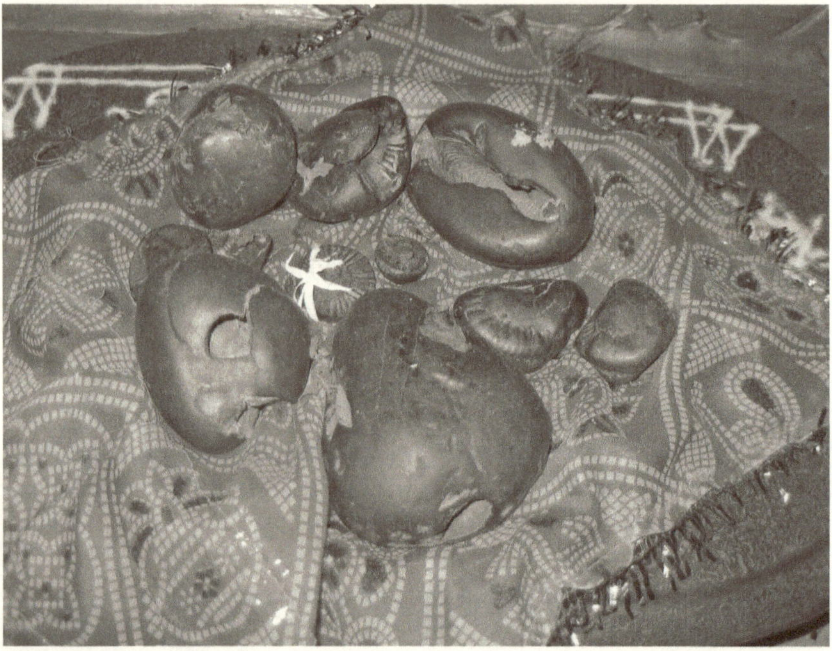

Figure 4.11 *Sālagrāmas.*

vṛndāvanas the most famous *vṛndāvana* pilgrimage site is Mantralaya, where the *vṛndāvana* of Rāghvendra Swāmi is housed apart from twelve *vṛndāvanas* of later Gurus all belonging to Raghavedra Swāmi *maṭha.*

The mritige or secondary *vṛndāvanas* are housed in the central part of a *maṭha* which are spread out. However, these *vṛndāvanas* are inside a *maṭha* which need not be constructed near a river bank. Secondary *vṛndāvanas* are normally installed and housed in the central part of a *maṭha.* In the secondary or branch *matha*, they are on a raised platform and not in a closed space as is the *garbhagriha* of a temple. However these sacred platforms function as the sanctum sanctorium and cannot be entered by anyone except the *matha* Gurus and other 'approved' *ācāryas.* But the *mūla vṛndāvanas* are normally near a river or a sacred site in the open and there was no structure around it. Later, perhaps in the nineteenth century, a built form grew around it due to its importance as a place of pilgrimage. Thus structural expansion of a *mūla maṭha* architecture has taken place in phases depending on its requirements or financial stability, such as the *maṭha* in Udipi, Mantralaya, Sode, and Malkhed. The architectural setting does not raise the sanctity of the *vṛndāvana*. While architecture merely serves as a form of shelter to the *vṛndāvana* (as well as to residents and pilgrims), ritual adds sanctity and status. The main reason it is considered as an icon is the ritual worship that is accorded daily apart from the *pratishthapana* and to a lesser degree, the structure around it.

RELIC WORSHIP IN BUDDHISM AND HINDUISM

The anomaly of whole-body mummification and enshrinment within Hinduism is a paradox and invites an investigation of its influence on the creation of the *vṛndāvana*. Relic veneration has been an important form of religious practice, particularly in Buddhism.[34] Relics have followed Buddhism wherever it spread but have been considered as polluting and even nonexistent in Hinduism.[35] The remains of a Hindu are usually cremated and the ashes immersed in the river, prefarably in river Ganges.

A relic is defined in Latin as something left over or remaining behind.[36] According to Vincent Smith, they comprise of the bodies of saints, or portions of them, such objects as the saints made use of during their lives or as were used at their martyrdom, that can be applied to non-Christian Asiatic usage.[37] Buddhalogists have classified relics into three categories: *śāririka* (the bodily remains of the Buddha or of other Buddhist saints), *paribhogikā* (objects that came into contact with the saint), *uddesika* (commemorative, such as a *stūpa*) or *dharma* relics (those that are related to the doctrine).[38] Other terms used for relics are *dhātu garbha*, the receptacle for ashes; *dagoba*; and *kumbha*, relic urn.[39] The Sanskrit word for relic is *dhātu*, meaning "a constituent element or essential ingredient of the body."[40] While Buddhists prefer the terms *dhātu* and *śārira*, in the Vedic tradition the terms *asthi*[41] (bone) and *bhasma* (ash) refer to funerary relics.[42] The ceremony of collecting the bones after burning a corpse was known as *asthi samcayana* while its immersion in the Ganges was called *asthi samarpaṇa*. If the body was cremated, then the bones and ashes are evident. However, in the case of the *vṛndāvana*, which contains the entire deceased mummified body, I have used the term "whole-body relic" that denotes an expanded meaning and also due to the lack of a proper equivalent term in Sanskrit or Kannada.[43] In this context it would be useful to draw attention to the fact that the whole-body relics were housed in *vṛndāvanas* for ascetics (*sanyāsins*) belonging only to the Vaisnavite Dualist order, and not for pontiffs of other Vedānta monasteries.

Normally, a death of a Hindu makes the family impure for ten days. During these unclean days, no religious ceremonies are performed. It is forbidden for food to be cooked in the house, or sweets to be enjoyed, as well as reading of religious scriptures. It is important to perform the post-cremation death rituals and relics are considered sacred at that time.[44] The normal Hindu funerary practice is cremation, and the relics, namely bones and ashes, are submerged in rivers.[45] After the death of the individual, the body is taken to the cremation ground. Three days after cremation, the son or chief mourner sifts through the remains to extract the unburnt bones and ashes which are collected in a clay urn.[46] These relics are sacred as they are considered to have originated from the sweat of Brahma and hence cannot be trampled by men or animals. Relics go through a temporary post-funerary ritual journey[47] of ten days, called *pinda pradhāna* (feeding and honoring).[48] On the tenth day, is the bone-gathering day. During the bone-gathering ceremony, or *asthi sancayana srāddha*, the unburnt bones are placed in an earthen pot.[49] The ritual process includes offerings of water, food (*pinda*), clothing, shelter in the form of umbrella, flowers, and lights.[50] Some of the bones from the urn are now collected and each wrapped in a wet clay and worshipped with water, milk, yogurt, honey, and clothing. The ashes and bones are now given back to the chief mourner (normally the son) who goes to the river for immersion (preferably river Ganges). Thus for a temporary period, relics are considered sacred. On the eleventh day the chief mourner sets the soul free and on the twelfth day is the *sapinda śrāddha* or ball uniting ceremony, when three round balls of boiled rice are made, to represent the great-grandfather, the grandfather, and the father of the dead; and a long obloing ball represents the dead. Hymns are recited; the long ball is cut in three and each of the three parts is mixed into one of the three round balls as a sign that the dead has been incorporated with his ancestors. From now on, only three ancestral 'heads' come to be recognized and the chief mourner has to remember only three names of his deceased fathers (father, if he has expired, grand father and great grandfather). On the thirteenth day, the chief mourner comes home and worships Ganapati. On the fourteenth day, sweet food is cooked and enjoyed by all. During the first year after a death, in every month on the new moon day and on the lunar day on which the death took place, a memorial ceremony or *śrāddha* is held. After the first year, the death anniversary is performed annually.

Vṛndāvana and *Stūpa*

At first sight the *vṛndāvana* appears to be unmistakably Buddhist in character. However, a brief survey of the history of erection of memorials and relic worship points to a different direction. Memorials and commemorative structures containing relics of bones and ashes have been known to exist as *stūpas* and *cetiyas/caityas* or *aidukas/eidukas* and *liṅgas* in Buddhism and pre-Buddhist traditions. But the form of the *vṛndāvana* recalls the parallel aniconic form of the Buddhist *stūpa*. A comparison between the two can provide valuable insights into the origins and meaning. *Vṛndāvanas* are empowered with the relics of the Guru, just as the *stūpa* is with those of the Buddha. The similarities beween the memorials, in form, and method of proliferation necessitates a close examination of the influence of the *stūpa/caitya* on the *vṛndāvana.*

The *vṛndāvana* associated with the death of a Guru is strikingly similar to the association of the *stūpa* with the *parinirvāṇa*—extinction of the Buddha who was also an ascetic. Both are commemorative monuments, housed in the monastery, containing relics. Both have parallels in the worship of the relic, which was perhaps extended to mean the *śārira* (entire body) of the guru. Along with the relics, *sālagrāmas* are placed in the *vṛndāvana* which may be analogous to the beads, gold flowers, leaves, and pearls in the Buddhist *stūpa* of local monks, as in the Buddhist site at Bhattiprolu, Bavikonda, Gantasala, Gummadidurru, Amaravati, and Nagarajunakonda. In addition, a relic from the original *vṛndāvana* (in which the original embalmed body is deposited) can be divided to be reinstated to form new "commemorative" (secondary) *vṛndāvanas*. This is similar to the practice of creating new *stūpas* by a division of relics, such as the *stūpa* of tooth relic in Kandy, Śri Lanka. The "duplication" and multiplication of *vṛndāvanas* recalls the Buddhist practice of transportation of relics to found new *stūpas* as well as the practice of erecting *stūpas* for local monks as we find in Bodh Gaya, Takht I Bahri, Kanheri and Amravati, Sanchi, Taxila, and Nagarjunakonda.[51]

The *stūpa* and *vṛndāvana* follow a canon, such as division into three parts. In fact, one of the *vṛndāvanas* in Udipi can be compared to the votive *stūpa* in Bodh Gaya.[52] The stupa of Kiangsu Pao Hua resembles a *vṛndāvana*, type 2, with lotus design and a rounded top. Some symbolic articulations on the *vṛndāvana* recounts those on the *stūpa* such as the ladder, the *cakra* (wheel), lotus, and footprints.[53] Other parallels between

Buddhist and Hindu monastic objects may be found in the worship of the bowl and waterpot. The gifting of objects in Hindu funerary ceremonies such as the robe, furniture, umbrella, bowl, and waterpot, which belonged to Buddhist and Hindu ascetics, are similar.

Finally, *stūpas* are empowered with the relics of the Buddha, just as the *vṛndāvana* with those of the Guru; both are considered to have powers of bringing about miracles. The efficacy of relics and miraculous properties of relics of Buddhist and Dvaita Gurus are similar. While a *vṛndāvana* is a square shrine surmounted by leaves or *tene*, the Indian Buddhist *stūpa* is round with a square base, with a triple umbrella. The *vṛndāvana* is a whole-body relic, in other words, a human mummified icon. Both the *vṛndāvana* and the *stūpa* formed the focus of a pilgrimage, and the (*mūla*) *vṛndāvana* and *mūla maṭha* have become important centers of Hindu pilgrimage. It raises the question as to how far the *vṛndāvana* was a symbolic appropriation from Buddhism or continuations of pre-Buddhist forms and practices or whether there was a common denominator.

Hindu and Buddhist Memorials

The similarities in aniconism and method of proliferation in Hinduism and Buddhism, however, do not necessarily determine that the *vṛndāvana* was influenced by the Buddhist *stūpa*. It is pertinent to enquire whether there existed the practice of raising memorials prior to Budhdist period and thus a continuation of Vedic practice or whether it was appropriated and reworked upon a Buddhist practice. Although the *vṛndāvana* is a relic, commemorative memorial, and a tomb, it is necessary to investigate whether the tradition of commemoration of dead was broader than what we know from the Buddhist tradition. In particular, can the origins of the *vṛndāvana* be traced from a pre-Buddhist or Hindu tradition of erection of *caitya/stūpa*?

Commemorative structures containing relics of bones and ashes have been known to exist as *stūpas* and *cetiyas/caityas*. They contained three types of relics of the Buddha as narrated elaborately in the *Mahaparinibbana Sutta* (fourth century BCE).[54] Buddha is said to have suggested to his diciples, the erection of a *stūpa* for him after his *nirvāṇa*. This was in accordance with the prevailing practice with regard to distinguished persons particularly for a *kshatriya* (warrior class). Scholars have different interpretations of the two terms. Although architecturally, the *caitya* and *stūpa* connote different types of religious buildings, the terms were used interchangeably.[55] This was particularly the case in Western India. At Nagarajunakonda the earlier *stūpas* were called *mahācaityas*.[56] It appears that the function and concept of the *stūpa* and *caitya* were quite similar. *Caitya* is derived from the word *citi*, a funeral pyre[57] or a mound over bones or ashes of a departed saint, or a commemorative structure. In the *Mahaparinibbana Sutta* Buddha enjoined to build a *dhātu caitya*.[58]

Stūpa is derived from the Pali word *thupa* meaning a conical heap or mound containing relics as hair, nails, or bones.[59] It was of three different types, namely *śārīraka* (bodily relics), *pāribhogika* (over robes and things used), and *uddeśik* (commemorative of Buddha's life including place of birth, previous births, and votive ones.[60] Thus a *caitya* and *stūpa* have conceptual and functional similairites. According to Subrahmanyam, "All edifices containing sacred objects are *caityas* but not all *caityas* have edificses."[61] In Hindu texts, as well, a *caitya* was a religious edifice, built to commemorate an event, and connected with *yajnasthana*, a relic casket, a burial ground, a memorial built out of stone,[62] houses of gods[63] and on full and new moon days, it would be propitiated at the altar by an umbrella, a small flag and goat's flesh.[64] They were sacred and popular—either as death markers, associated with trees,[65] a tree shrine, or as a memorial shrine.

Furthermore, *stūpas* were built even over the relics of kings, along with precious objects of god and silver, copper, and semiprecious stones and animals.[66] Even householders, belonging to Vaiṣṇava demonition, had memorials built over the bones, and a Tulsi planted on it. These were known as *rudra bhūmis*. They were known to Buddhists and pre-Buddhists. Smith writes, "Such a burial tradition was in vogue in pre-Buddhist times, particularly in the sub Himalayan region."[67] Thus, a renewed consideration of available evidence points out that the construction of memorials is more ancient than Buddhism. Equally if not more important are Jain *stūpas* particularly in the early phase, as evidenced from the *stūpa* relics from Kankali Tila in Mathura. Flugel points out that Jains distinguished between *smarak* and *samādhi mandir* (erected by Terapanth Sventambara Jains). However there are no existent Jain *stūpas* in Karnataka[68] although Jainism has been popular here from early times. There is no indication of relic worship in early Jainism.[69] Although *nisiddhis* or memorial stones in the form of pillars have been erected for (particularly war) heroes, these did not contain relics.

However, a pertinent issue is whether the practice evolved from the erection of *aidukas* as memorials. *Eduka*, *aiduka*, *eluka* was a relic (bone) chamber, also called *dagoba* or *dhātugarbha*,[70] which had a funerary significance. It was non-anthropomorphic in form, with a quadrangular platform upon which other similar tiers were raised, frequently three in number, resulting in a stepped shape, and ultimately topped by a circular member. Elements of the *aiduka* have been described in *Viṣṇudharmottara Purāṇa* (third century CE). It consisted of three superimposed *bhadrapīṭhas*, a long staff or *yasti*, *bhūmikas*, *amalasaraka*, as well as symbols of the sun and moon.[71] In addition, the *aiduka*, which was a memorial in a *smaśāna* (burial ground), was also four-cornered (like the *vṛndāvana*). The square ones were used by the gods, while the round ones were said to be used by *asuras*.[72] *Aidukas* were also surmounted by *liṅga*, which resemble some *vṛndāvanas*, which confirms that *aidukas* were Hindu memorials while *stūpas* were Buddhist and Jain.[73] Granoff and Shah contend that the *aiduka* was basically a Saiva structure.[74] If the *liṅga* is said to have evolved from the *aiduka*, it is appropriate to question whether the *aiduka* was a Śaiva death marker as stated in the *Viṣṇudharmottara Purāṇa*. It is likely that the *liṇga* type stones unearthed in the Indus Valley site of Dholavira and at Śringeri[75] were probably death markers.[76] The latter are considered to be burial stones of Advaita ascetic pontiffs, the *jagadgurus*.[77] *Liṅgas*[78] have been used as death markers for ascetics of the Viraśaiva order and one can find burial grounds called *rudra bhumis* where *liṅgas* are installed even for ordinary mortals who wish to be commemorated in this way.[79] Similarly, *liṅgas* were erected to mark the graves of teachers[80] and on burial sites of Pāśupata teachers. The *liṅgas* are described as the *gurvvaatana* or dwelling place of the gurus and were memorilas to Kapilesvara and Upamitesvara.[81]

The relevance of *aidukas* or relic chambers as an influencing factor for the erection of a *vṛndāvana* cannot be dismissed. The overwhelming literary and epigraphical evidence of *liṅgas*, as memorials being at the site of the residence of ascetic teacher, throw ample light on the *vṛndāvana* in *maṭhas* which were (and still are) residential sites of ascetics. In addition, the *aiduka* provides an ingenious explanation for the form of the *vṛndāvana*: it was square, with a rounded top, resembling type 2 (figure 4.2). It is possible that each faith, Buddhist, Śaiva, or Vaiṣṇava elaborated upon the basic structure and added its own symbolic meaning to memorial/marker.

That the *liṅga* has been a death marker for Śaivite ascetics is a valid trajectory. Medieval inscriptions in South India inform us about edifices over royal personages of Hindu faith. An inscription of the Cola king, Rajaditya (ninth century CE) from Sokapuram in North Arcot District, mentions the erection of a Siva temple on the spot where his father was buried, and the practice continued till medieval times.[82] Furthermore, the pyramids built by Śaivites employed techniques similar to the construction of layered *stūpas* (layers built up with boxes of earth, stones, and rubble).[83] In 1990, Glen Yocum noticed ten *sannidhānams* in the form of shrines that resembled small temples that one could enter. These marked the graves, and were oriented toward the east; they contained either a *liṅga* or a platform (*pīṭha*) with footprints. According to Yocum, "The mutt may in many ways be like a temple, but temples are not located on gravesites and do not have festivals set by death anniversaries.. . . A mutt is also like a grave."[84] It is likely that the bodies might have been buried below the shrines.[85] Thus Śivaliṅgas and *caityas* were both erected in memory of the dead.[86] Evidently, there are parallels in Buddhist and Saiva practices regarding relics and memorials. Fleming states, "There were shared practices and discourses about bodily remains among communities that lived side by side."[87] According to Marco, Buddhist *stūpas* and Vedic *smasanas* or cremation grounds correspond to one single architectural type.[88]

Self-Immolation

Recent evidences from ancient China have revealed that the tradition of self-immolation and whole-body relic entombment was prevalent as well among Buddhist monks. The mummified body of the deceased monk, Huineng (author of Sixth Platform Sutra, 638–713 CE), the sixth Patriarch of Chan Buddhism, has been found. Known as a mummy of Huineng Xu Hengbin (683–713 CE), it is part of the three mummies and was found in the Nanhua monastery near Shaoguan, Qujiang County, in Guangdong Province.[89] Huineng's body resisted decay and his lacquered body was a life-size portrait, with clear facial features. Nearby is a stone *stūpa* that marked the site of the burial of Xu Yun (1839–1959) who is said to have closed his eyes in meditation posture holding a rosary.

Another mummified body of Zhiyi (538–574 CE), the founder of the eponymous tradition, was found intact in his tomb on the south side of Mount Tiantia.[90] In addition, two bodies were discovered buried in a large earthenware tub sealed at the rim; its remains were later removed and were gilded and enshrined. It is interesting to find that even round stones similar to those of Hindu *sālagramas* that were (and still are) used to cover the whole-body relic in the *vṛndāvana* were found in the tomb of Nanhua, Xiaxing.[91] Matteini mentions that "Huineng's lacquered body, together with that of an earlier Indian master Arya Jnanabhaishgya housed in a neighboring temple, became the object of a local cult that interested the local ruling clan of the Liu."[92] Once a year, the "true body" of Huineng would be taken across the counties and inside the royal palace in lavish processions that ensured good harvest and abundant rain.[93]

The above East Asian tradition is similar to the Jain practice of *sallekhana*, or practice of starvation till death.[94] This practice prevailed in Japan till the nineteenth century. Instances of self-immolation while alive or immolation through meditation (*jeevan samādhi*) have been found in Japan. Kōbō Daishi, who founded the esoteric Shingon school of Buddhism in 806, is said to have performed *samādhi maraṇa*. In the eleventh century a hagiography of Kūkai appeared claiming that, upon his death in 835, the monk did not die at all but crawled into his tomb and entered *nyūjō*, a state of meditation so profound that it induces suspended animation.[95] It is said to be an example of *sokushinbutsu*—a Buddhist ritual of self-mummification that was practiced by ascetic monks from the eleventh to twentieth centuries in Japan, Russia, Tibet,[96] Mongolia, and Thailand.[97] According to Kosugi Kazuo there were three stages where the relics were enshrined: natural mummified corpses, which were venerated and found in mountain caves (fifth and seventh century CE), whole-body relics that were enshrined in locations and could accommodate worshippers more easily, and, from seventh century CE onward, whole-body relics which were gilded and placed on a dais or into a *stūpa*.[98]

The existence of whole-body relics in China opens a new perspective in the quest for the origins of the *vṛndāvana*.[99] All the Buddhist, Jain, and Hindu practices encompass a multiplicity of religio-social meanings, and have a common cultural fabric. There was a religious conviction of the efficacy of self-immolation both by the performer and the viewer.[100]

It does not concern us here whether East Asian Buddhist practices were influenced by the Indian tradition,[101] but the issue is whether the tradition of whole-body relic was influenced by the Chinese practice. The influence of Chinese Buddhists in South India cannot be dismissed easily.[102] A Buddhist temple was constructed exclusively for the Chinese monks during the rule of Pallava king Narasimha Varman II (695–722 CE).[103]

In addition, the Kalyani inscription of 1476 CE of Dhammocheti, king of Pegu, refers to the visit of the monks to Padarikarama monastery and worship of Buddha under the instructions of the Chinese rule.[104] A Buddhist establishment was referred by Walter Elliot in 1846. He prepared the plan and details of a brick-built Buddhist *pagoda* (twelfth century CE) of Chinse origin that existed at Nagapattinam till 1867.[105] The thirty meters tall, mulitstoreyed *pagoda* is a good example for non-Indian Buddhist architecture, at Nagapattinam for the benefit of Chinse monks, during the period of the Chinse ruler Xian-Chun (1267 CE).[106] Furthermore, Chinese ceramics have been found in the excavations at Hampi, proving that trade existed between the two states during the Vijayanagara period (fourteenth to sixteenth century).[107] One cannot rule out the Chinese influence, but it is important to examine the Hindu tradition.

It is said that there is a big gap in historical evidences between the decline of Buddhist *stūpas* by ninth century CE in South India and the erection of *vṛndāvanas* in the fourteenth century. Having established that there existed an ancient practice of erection of memorials, it is relevant to examine the evidences of Buddhist and Hindu memorials in South India that might have influenced the *vṛndāvana*. However epigraphical and literary evidences need a careful examination. Buddhism flourished in parats of Tamil Nadu at Kanchipuram and Nagapattinum, Andhra Pradesh, and Karnataka till the twelfth century CE. Inscriptions and archaeological evidences support the practice of building memorials in South India. Buddhist settlements from pre-Asokan times, fourth to third century BCE to the Viṣṇukundins in sixth century CE have been found in the valleys of Vamsadhara, Goshthani, Tandava, Godavari, Kṛṣṇa, and Bahuda rivers.[108] The Kalyani inscription at Zaingganaing (Burma) of Dhammacheti (1472–92 CE) mentions Ananda Thera, a native of Kanchipuram, who was well versed in the Tripitakas, visited Pugama (Pagan) in Burma.[109] Buddhist deities were worshipped in *viharas* till twelfth century CE and at Kadarika in South Kanara till tenth century. A bronze icon of Lokeśvara was installed by King of Alupa in a *vihara*.[110] Inscriptions in Balligame, Dambal and Loliwad dating to eleventh to twelfth centuries CE mention construction of *viharas* and installation of icons of Tara Bhagavati for worship. The Shikarpur inscription of 1065 CE refers to the establishment of Jayanti Prabudha *vihāra* at Balligame[111] and Gummadidurru, Andhra Pradesh where Buddhism survived uptill fouteenth–fifteenth century CE.[112] It is likely that the Buddhist (or non-Buddhist) practice of constructing memorials was prevalent till the rise of the *vṛndāvana*.

Sallekhana

Many of the Chinese practices of mummification of the whole body and enshrinement, particularly between the eighth and twelfth centuries CE, and their veneration recalls the Jain practice of *sallekhana*,[113] and *samādhi maraṇa, sanyāsa maraṇa* (death through renunciation). The art of mortifying the body, was a common practice in Jainism.[114] Jainism gave porminecnce to *sallekhana* or death by ritual starvation (under conditions such as old age, incurable disease, or intolerable personal problems). Fasting unto death (or death by starvation) was common and mentioned in the *Mahābhārata* and *Rāmānyana*.[115]

Those who invited death, without violating the code of conduct, became models for the Jain *sangha* and their memory was preserved by erecting commemorative monuments. At Sravanabelagola, Settar has recorded about one hundred and fifty men and women as having invited death within a span of 1500 years. In the Digambara tradition,[116] pillars were constructed in Sravanabelagola for those who went through ritual death. Here there are about 570 inscriptional evidences between the sixth and tenth centuries.[117] In fact, Chandragiri was known as the *Samadhi-betta* (mountain of meditation unto death) where the history of such deaths on the mountain goes back to third century BCE. But after the tenth century, the practice of self-immolation declined which was taken over by the tradition of erection of memorials or *nisiddhis*. Interestingly, even householders or *sravakas* practiced *sallekhana* or ritual death.

Jeeva(n) samādhi by Hindu Saints

There is a long history of self-immolation or *jeevan samādhi* by Hindu saints. The funerary practices of Dvaita Gurus recall the entombment, rites, and rituals of Nath *yogis*. A revealing evidence comes from the more popular Nath Siddha Yoga traditions in Maharashtra.[118] Jnaneswar (1275–1290 CE) is said to have performed meditation till death or *sanjivani samadhi* (eternal enlivening meditational state) at Alandi on the thirteenth day of the dark half of the Kartik month, in October 1296, in his twenty-second year, and his *samādhi* (memorial) was built at the site.[119] Normally, the body of a Nath *yogi* is washed, covered with a saffron cloth, called Kavi Shathi, rubbed with ashes, and a *rudraksha* palced around the neck. His legs are crossed and placed in a basket and placed in a pit dug near a river. The pit could be 5 or 6 ft, and round in shape. It would then be covered with salt till the head. Coconuts are broken on the head till the skull opens. The whole body and head is immersed in salt. Over the grave a small structure is erected on which a *liṅga* is placed. Worship is offered by *brāhmins* with flowers, lights, incense, and blessed food such as coconut, sugar, and rice. Worship is accompanied with music and prostrations, particularly by barren women. Unlike the cremation ritual for an ordinary Hindu, the ceremony is not polluting and the relative of the ascetic do not have to take a bath, but the *brāhmiṇs* bathe three times a day. For ten days, the *samādhi* is worshipped. There is also an annual death ceremony/celebration that is held and the sacred site is transformed into a pilgrimage place.[120]

There is yet another recorded *jeevan samādhi* (self-immolation) of Hindu ascetics in South India from Tamil Nadu. Thiruvalluvar was a Jain saint who practiced *jeevan samādhi* which was referred to as *vadakirutthal* (facing north).[121] In the *adheenam* of a Śaiva Siddhānta *maṭha* in Thirvavaduthurai, the founder Namachivayamurthi performed *jeevan samādhi*, but there is no memorial with whole-body relic like the *vṛndāvana*; instead there is a stone portrait of the Guru seated in a teaching pose.[122] Saddhananda Swāmigal in Patanjali Temple, at Kulashekharapuram, is said to have performed *jeevan samādhi* and a *liṅga* was placed at the site. Other such sites include Tirnelveli, Chennai, and Kanchipuram. In Andhra Pradesh, Veerabramhendra Swamy performed *jeevan samādhi* in 1693 CE at Kandimallayapalle (also known as Brahmagiri *maṭham*) in Cuddapah, where the square underground hole can still be seen. Other saints who followed the practice have memorials at Kandimallayapalle, Cuddapah (where Eswaramma performed *jeevan samādhi*), Sadu Siddaiah Swamy at Mudumala (Cuddapah), and Yadati Govinda Swamy at Palugurallapalle.[123]

In the light of strong evidences within Hinduism, that by the Chinese Buddhists practice of self-immolation cannot offer sufficient support for the origins of the *vṛndāvana*. But its practice by Hindu saints was perceived with awe and reverence, and might have played an important role in the installation of the whole-body relic below a stone memorial.[124] The early Dvaita *sanyāsins* did not immolate themselves, and the early *vṛndāvanas* were not constructed for ascetics who immolated themselves. There were only two Dvaita ascetics, namely, Vādirāja (fifteenth to sixteenth century CE) and Rāghvendra Swāmi (seventeenth century

CE) who performed meditation unto death and their whole-body relics have been enshrined in the *vṛndāvana*.

A compelling argument can be made from the fact that the whole-body relic of Rāmānujācārya, the founder of Śri Vaiṣṇava *maṭhas*, has been preserved in the temple of Śrirangam in Tamil Nadu. This tradition can also be traced to twelfth century CE, in the visual evidence of the relic of Rāmānujācārya, founder of Śri Vaiṣṇava *maṭha*, who is said to have performed *jeevan samādhi* and his body still remains in the fifth circumambulatory path of the temple of Ranganatha Swāmi temple in Śrirangam. It is more likely that the practice of self immolation in Cuddappah (where pits have been found) might have played a role in the creation of the *vṛndāvana* near Hampi, as the site of Cuddappah is not far from Anegondi. There appears to be a constant change in the burial traditions depending on the region, religious traditons, and historical circusmtances. An examination of medieval archaeological remains can add to our investigation.

ARCHAEOLOGICAL EVIDENCES

The practice of entombment and construction of *vṛndāvana* in Anegondi began in the fourteenth century CE. A close examination of the local area and other regions provides some evidences of memorials as well. There are strong evidences for the existence of construction of commemorative monuments (with and without relics) till about eleventh century CE. Practices between the eleventh and the fourteenth centuries can only be speculative. But *vṛndāvana* type of memorials can be seen at various sites. Commemorative structures have been known to exist in Western India (state of Maharashtra) and these are known as *samādhis, candas*, and *thades*.[125] Prominent kings such as Peshwa Bajirao I and Ranoji Sinde had such (stone) *samādhis* built and these were superimposed by a *chatri* (a royal umbrella) above. *Candas* are square or rectangle stone objects with a *liṅga* above, erected for ascetics, and royalty (figure 4.12).[126] More importantly, the archaeological evidences from Poona district of stone markers for the dead have also been called *vṛndāvanas*. These are square in structure, about three to four feet in height, surmounted by the Tulsi plant. This recalls the *vṛndāvana* (of the pontiff of a Dualist monastery) at many sites, particularly in Anegondi. The former were installed for *satis*, saints, and kings and resemble the Guru *vṛndāvanas*.[127] There are *vṛndāvana*-type memorials dedicated to Sahaji, his son Sivaji, and Sivaji's son Sambhaji, although none of them died at the site or are cremated there. It may be added that there was abundance of cultural exchange between Maharashtra and Karnataka, and the entire region was under the hegemony of dynasties, such as Chalukyas, Rashtrakutas, Hoysalas, and Yadavas, which was conducive for religious and social exchange. One can never overlook the fact that such memorials also extended futher into Maharashtra (figures 4.12 and 4.13).

However, these practices do not provide an answer to the enshrinement of the whole body of the ascetic, although the deceased body of the ascetics were considered pure as mentioned in the sacred texts. There is yet another line of argument that might provide a clue to the origins of the *vṛndāvana*. The practioners of rigorous asceticism were known as *yatis*. The practice has been mentioned in earlier texts, such as the *Baudhayana Pitru Medha Sutra*.[128] Dvaita Guru-philosophers placed emphasis on a *yati*, more than a *muni* or *sanyāsi*. *Yatis* were a seprate class of ascetics with more rigorous principles of asceticism.[129] He is enjoined to live by the side of water on the sand banks of a river or before the gate of a temple or to sit on the bare earth. Kane mentions that the practice of burying the deceased body of a *yati sanyāsin* is still practiced.[130]

The site of Anegondi, offers interesting archaeological evidences as well.[131] Behind the Kodandarama temple on the southern bank of the

Figure 4.12 Memorials stones, Sasvad, Poona District, Maharashtra.

Figure 4.13 ***Nava Vṛndāvana*****, Anegondi.**

Tungabhadra was found an ash mound, which, according to oral tradition is said to have contained the cremated remains of Vali, referred to in the epic, *Rāmāyaṇa*.[132] Historically speaking, Anegondi, during the Vijayangara period, grew to be a place for the burial of kings.[133] Hariharadevaraya Tirumaladevaraya's youngest son, was cremated in the fields next to the Chintamani temple complex. A more recent royal site reserved for those of direct descent of kings of Anegonid is on Magota Hill. In addition, northeast of Anegondi is the Awduth *maṭha*, a building that marks the site of cremations and burials for Hindus. Natalie has studied the settlement patterns in Anegondi and she refers to the burial graves of kings and of Banajigas which she calls as remembrance altars.[134] Beside the *maṭha* are a series of *vṛndāvanas* or remembrance altars associated with the Banajigas.[135] To the rear are the Liṅgāyat graves and beyond them, the graves and tombstones of other castes.[136] One can notice numerous stones that have a *vṛndāvana*-like shape carved from single blocks of stone with a *tulsi* plant on them. In addition, here are some *vṛndāvanas* that do not belong to Madhva Dvaita Vaiṣṇava sect, thereby asserting that the erection of *vṛndāvanas* as memorials was quite widespread in the local region.[137]

In addition, with the rise in the status of the living Guru during the Vijayanagara period, the entombment of the past Guru appeared logical. The capital and its surroundings were considered sacred by the early Vijayanagara kings, the Sangama rulers (1346–1486) who occupied the area around Anegondi, and later south of the Tungabhadra river (in the sacred center) around the Virupaksha temple at Hampi.[138] The kings extended the status of a holy local town to a cosmic city with its rational plan, such as seven walls, radial roads, and zoning which authenticated and expressed imperial power.[139] More importantly, the kings of Vijayanagara considered themselves as followers of Vaidik (Vedic) *dharma* and patronized all denominations of Hinduism, particularly those that were essential for royal legitimacy and status. Thus it is not surprising that the earliest *vṛndāvana*, is in Anegondi, the early residence of the Vijayanagara emperors.

Conclusion

It is possible that the *vṛndāvana* of a Madhva Guru was contiguous to the practice of erecting *samadhis* for kings, saints in Maharashtra and Karnataka. It is very likely that the practice might have spread to other parts. There is no solid basis for Buddhist Chinese evidences and they fail to support the credence of its traditions in South India. It might have been influenced by the practices of Tamil saints or Rāmānujācārya. In addition, there was a strong tradition of erecting portraits of Ālvar saints within shrines at the capital city of Vijayanagara, Hampi, which was an influencing factor as well. A more convincing argument for the influence of the practice whole-body relic entombment of Dvaita ascetics comes from the tradition of Nath yogis, particularly in the similarity of funerary rites. It is likely that the tradition of *jeevan samādhi*, might have filtered through Maharashtra along with the form of the *vṛndāvana* and the burial rituals from Nath yogis. It is well known that there were numerous cultural exchanges between Malkhed and Anegondi, Belgaum, and Bijapur. The southern regions of Maharashtra and the northern regions of Karnataka were contiguous and had open boundaries. The fact that the mercantile community, Śaivites, Liṅgāyats as well as those belonging to Rāmānujācārya and the Nath traditions in Maharashtra (like the Buddhists) had a tradition of erecting death markers and memorials indicates that building such structures was probably a common practice.[140] Each had their own distinctive markers and commemorative structures. Thus it is not surprising to find the *vṛndāvana* of Dvaita pontiffs were close to popular *samadhi* sites.

Although there is no archaeological record about *samādhis* before the eleventh/twelfth century CE, it does not mean that the practice did not continue as oral tradition. Considering the variety of stone death markers for ascetics in the region, and the popularity of marking it with trees or plants, it is not surprising to find Dvaita Gurus adopted the form and practice to symbolize the lineage of past Gurus. There might have been a common practice of erecting *vṛndāvana* with whole-body relics too. The practice of embalming within Dualist school of *mathas* appears to be a revival of a tradition, although the archaeological evidences of the continuity of tradition might have been lost.[141] Innumerable *vṛndāvanas* continued to be installed and the tradition still continues today.

There is another relevant aspect about the *vṛndāvana*, namely its meaning arising from etymological, mythological, and ontological connotations. The meaning behind institutionalization of the deceased Guru in the *vṛndāvana* was connected to a certain philosophical principle of life and death. It was a relation between the human and divine. The layers of meaning attributed to the Guru *vṛndāvana*, namely, God and Guru, asceticism and devotion, aniconic and iconic, will be examined in the next chapter.

NOTES

1. Śaṅkarācārya established four Advaita *maṭhas* at Puri, Dvaraka, Śringeri, Badari and revitalized the ten orders of Saiva ascetics along monastic lines. Cenkner, *A Tradition of Teachers, Śankara and the Jagadgurus Today*. Columbia, Mo.: South Asia Books, 1983, p. 109.

2. Śringeri and Kanchipuram are centers of Advaita, Melkote, and Śrirangam of Visishtadvaita, Udipi, Sode, Malkhed, Anegondi of Dvaita *maṭha*.

3. These are living institutions and have a large number of disciples.

4. The whole-body relic of the ascetic head pontiff (who has been called Guru, with a capital G) of each denomination of Dvaita *maṭha* was consecrated beneath the stone "box" *vṛndāvana*. In an earlier article of mine: Rao, Nalini. Relics, Icons, and Portraits in Hindu Institutions: An Examination of the Worship of the Teacher. In *Across the South of Asia: A Volume in Honor of Professor Robert L. Brown*. Delhi: DKPW (2020), I had mentioned that the whole-body relic was placed inside the "box". But on further research I found that it is placed beneath the "box".

5. For lack of any particular word in the local Kannada language, the term used by Michele Matteini "whole-body relic" appears to be a good description of the relic in the *vṛndāvana*. Matteini, Michele. On the "True Body" of Huineng. *RES* (Spring/Autumn 2009): 41–60.

6. Vaiṣṇavas hold that Viṣṇu is the greatest god. The image of Lord, Kṛṣṇa was installed in the "temple" Udipi in 1250 CE by Madhvācārya (see chapter 5).

7. Simoons, J.Frederick, *Plants of Life, Plants of Death*. Madison, WI: University of Wisconsin Press, 1998, pp. 7–40.

8. Sarma, Deepak. *An Introduction to Madhva Vedanta*. Aldershot: Ashgate, 2003.

Sharma, B.N.K. *Philosophy of Śri Madhvacarya*. Delhi: Motilal Banarsidass, 1986. Reprints, 1992, 2002, 2008.

Rao, Hayavadana. *Poornaprajna Vijaya: Life and Teachings of Śri Madhwācārya*. Trans Dhadra Kṛṣṇamoorthy. Chennai: Śri Kṛṣṇa Śri Raghavendra Trust, 2010.

Govindacarya, Bannanje. *Acharya Madhwa: Life and Works*. Upadhyaya. Udipi: U.P. Isavasya Pratishanam, 2011.

9. Schopen, Gregory. Relic. In *Critical Terms for Religious Studies*. Ed. Taylor, C. Mark. Chicago: The University of Chicago Press, 1998; Strong, John S. *Relics of the Buddha*. Motilal Banarasidass. 1997; Germano, David and Kevin Trainor. *Embodying the Dharma: Buddhist Relic Veneration in Asia*. NY: State University of New York Press. 2004; Scharf, Robert H. On the Allure of Buddhist. *Representations* No. 66 (Spring 1999): 75; Settar, S. *Inviting Death: Indian Attitude Towards the Ritual Death*. Leiden; New York: Brill, 1989. Settar, S. *Pursuing Death. Philosophy and Practice of Voluntary Termination of Life*. Dharwad: Karnatak University, Institute of Indian Art History, 1990.

10. Settar, S. and Sontheimer, G.D., Ed. *Memorial Stones: A Study of their Origin, Significance and Variety*. New Delhi: South Asia Institute, Germany: University of Heidelberg, 1982.

11. The *vṛndāvana* is a built sculpture made up of dressed stone slabs of different sizes and as the uppermost layer appears like a slab, and is smaller in size than the other two parts, I have called it a slab. On July 19, 2019, the *vṛndāvana* of Vyāsarāya *Tīrtha* was vandalized and later re-built.

12. Examples are the *vṛndāvanas* of Vyāsarāya, Narahari, and Madhavendra *Tīrtha*.

13. The arches might have been influenced by the shape of Buddhist *caityas* or *liṅga*, and the ladders by the balustrade seen on Buddhist *stūpas*, denoiting the ascent and descent of Buddha. A book stand is a common motif for saints who used this object to keep their scriptures and often found before Jain Tīrthankaras in sculpture and paintings.

14. *Prajavani*, the Kannada newspaper, published a news about the rituals that were performed for the pontiff of the Uttaradi *maṭha*.

15. Hampi (Vijayanagara) was the later capital of the kings of Vijayanagara kingdom. See Rao, Nalini. *Royal Imagery and Networks of Power at Vijayanagara: A Study of Kingship in South India*. Delhi: Originals, 2010, p. 15.

16. Pandurangi, K.T. *Dvaita Vedānta*. Bangalore: Studies and Research Foundation, 1923, pp. 60–62.

It is not necessary for the pontiffs to belong to the same sub-*maṭha* or branch *maṭha* order to be entombed in one place, as they all belonged to the *Dvaita maṭha*.

The dates correspond to the years the head occupied the pīṭha of their monastic denomination.

17. Apart from these there are two branches of Aksobhya *Tīrtha maṭha*, one in Kudli and the other in Balegaru. Other *maṭhas* in Tulu region are the Subrahmanya *maṭha*, Bhandarkeri maṭha, Bhimana Katte *maṭha*, Citrapura *maṭha*.

18. Oman, John Campbell. *The Mystics, Ascetics, and Saints of India; A Study of Sadhuism, with an Account of the Yogis, Sanyasis, Bairagis, and Other Strange Hindu Sectarians*. London: T.F. Unwin, 1903, pp. 158–161.

19. Marco, Giuseppe De. The Stupa as a Funerary Monument: New Iconographical Evidence. *East and West* 37.1 (1987): 224.

20. Pandey, Raj Bali, *Hindu Samskaras: Socio-Religious Study of the Hindu Sacraments*. Delhi: Motilal Banarsidas, 1969, pp. 271–273.

21. In other parts of India, when a *sanyāsin* dies, his body is buried in a grave like a pit, in which the body is made to sit up facing east or north east with its arms supported on a wooden rest.

22. Oman. *The Mystics, Ascetics, and Saints of India*.158–161.

The coconuts that are broken on the head is said to have miraculous powers of begetting children to women who have problems conceiving. Discussion with principal of Pejawar *maṭha* school.

23. His body rests on a T-shaped wooden structure.

24. *Sālagrāmas* are round black stones, the aniconic symbol of Viṣṇu. The *sālagrāmas* are formed out of fossils. According to personal communication to the author by the head of a *maṭha,* in other parts of India, when a *sanyāsi* dies, his body is buried in a grave like a pit, in which the body is made to sit up facing east or northeast with its arms supported on a wooden frame or support.

25. The term "relic" has been used to denote the embalmed body of the *ācarya*.

26. See page 102 which refers to the list of things placed inside the *vṛndāvana* in Vyāsarāya *maṭha*.

27. In Kannada, the death of a saint is referred to as *vṛndāvanastha aadaru*, probably referring to final *moksha* or liberation. In the Sri Vaisnavite tradition, blessed food, *payasa* (sweet dish made of milk) is distributed to women who would like to conceive but are unable to do so. In the Dvaita tradition, the coconuts that are broken on the head of the deceased ascetic are distributed to 'barren' women.

It is believed that the *vṛndāvana* is sealed. It is believed that an *ācārya* removed the stone covering of the *vṛndāvana* of Sri Vādirāja *Tīrtha* in his meditation and was overjoyed, but before he could see it, the cover reverted back to its original position. Acharya, U. R. *Udupi: An Introduction.* Sri Krishna Matha, 1989, p. 50.

28. The term *vṛndāvana* is also used, meaning death, while in Śringeri, the center of Advaita *maṭha* of Ādi Śaṅkarācārya, the whole site is called a *vṛndāvana.*

29. Flugel, Peter. The Jaina Cult of Relic Stupas. *Numen* 57.3 (2010): 391.

The antecedents for the distinction between the original and secondary *vṛndāvana* can be found in the terms *samādhi* (a relic shrine) and *smāraka* (a commemorative shrine), the former constructed for *pūjā* and the latter for *darśan* and meditation.

30. *Vṛndāvanas* for Śri Vaiṣṇava Gurus appear to have been influenced by those of Dvaita Gurus.

31. The listing of the objects on a big board hung in the *maṭha* is exceptional. It is also a recent phenomenon.

A similar process takes place in Tibetan Buddhism. Bentor, Yael. *Consecration of Images and Stūpas in Indo-Tibetan Tantric Buddhism.* Leiden: E.J. Brill, 1996, p. 35.

32. It appears that there were various ways of mummification of the deceased body of the Guru.

33. *Prajavani*, the Kannada newspaper, August 2, 2018 published a news about the rituals that were performed for the Uttaradi *maṭha* pontiff.

34. Trainor, Kevin. *Relics, Ritual and Representation in Buddhism: Rematerializing the Śri Lankan Theravada Tradition.* Cambridge: Cambridge University Press, 1997, p. 26.

35. Smith states that the veneration of relics seems to be practically unknown to brahamanical Hindus, one reason being that their ill-defined religion has no recognized founder like Jesus Christ, Buddha, or Muhammad. Smith, Vincent. Relics (Eastern). *Encyclopedia of Religion and Ethics* 10 (1918): 658–662.

36. Relic cult in Buddhism has been discussed by the following scholars:

Schopen, Gregory. *Bones, Stones, and Buddhist Monks: Collected Papers on the Archaeology, Epigraphy, and Texts of Monastic Buddhism in India.* Honolulu: University of Hawai'i Press, 1997.

Schopen, Gregory. On the Buddha and His Bones: The Conception of a Relic in the Inscriptions of Nāgarjunakoṇḍa. *Journal of the American Oriental Society* 108.4 (Oct.–Dec., 1988): 527–537.

Collins, Steven. The Body in Theravada Buddhist Monasticism. In *Religion and the Body*. Ed. Coakley, Sarah. Cambridge: Cambridge University Press, 1997, pp. 185–204.

Eckel, Malcolm David. *To See the Buddha.* San Francisco: Harper, 1992; Eckel, Malcolm David. *The Power of the Buddha's Absence*: On the Foundations of Mahayana Buddhist Ritual. *Journal of Ritual Studies* 4.2 (1990): 61–95.

Strong, John S. *Relics of the Buddha*. Delhi: Motilal Banarasidass, 2007.

37. Smith, Vincent "Relics (Eastern)". *Encyclopedia of Religion and Ethics* Vol 10 (1918): 658–659.

38. Buddhist relics include bodily remains, such as bones, ash, beads, gold, and precious objects; objects that were kept along with the bodily relics, such as bowls and urns; and relics of *dharma* or scriptures. Acording to Schopen, relics are the products or essence of the body, rather than its remainders. Schopen, Gregory. "On the Buddha and His Bones: The Conception of a Relic in the Inscriptions of Nagarjunikonda." *Journal of the American Oriental Society* 108, no. 4 (December 1988): 527–537.

Trainor, Kevin. *Relics, Ritual and Representation in Buddhism: Rematerializing the Sri Lankan Theravada Tradition*. Cambridge: Cambridge University Press, 1997.

John S. Strong views relics as expressions and extensions of Buddha's biographical process. Strong, *Relics of the Buddha*, 229.

39. In Jainism, there are no relics in *stūpas* of ascetics, although remains of Jain teachers have been discovered. Today we hear evidences of relic worship in the form of *samādhi*. Flügel. The Jaina Cult of Relic Stupas, 389–504.

40. Williams, Sir Monier, *Sanskrit-English Dictionary*. New Delhi: Motilal Banarsidass, 1899, p. 513.

41. *Asthi* is a bone in AV, the kernel of a fruit. *Asthi kunda* is a hole filled with bones. Williams. *Sanskrit-English Dictionary*, 122.

42. Another significant word that is mentioned along with Buddhist relic is *cetiya* or *caitya*, a shrine, and a *śāriracetiya*, a shrine memorial. The Buddhist Kalingabodhi Jataka does not refer to *dhātu* but to various types of *cetiya*, shrines, or memorials. The Pali commentary on the *Vibhanga* explicitly states that a *śāriracetiya* or the shrine containing a part of the body was more important than a shrine commemoration, a *paribhogacetiya*. Strong. *Relics of the Buddha*, 20.

43. In the local language, Kannada, the dead body is called *śarīra* and only after the body has been transferred inside the container is it termed the *vṛndāvana*. The term whole-body relic has been used by Johnston. Johnston, F. Reginald. *Buddhist China*. London: John Murray. London: John Murray, 1913; 1976, p. 231.

44. It is important to note that there are slight variants in the rituals depending on the region and group in addition to the accretion of funerary rites from decades.

45. If a child (under 13) belonging to the Virsaitive group dies he/she is buried.

46. Funerary cremation of bodies does not leave bones intact today and does not leave much pristine relicts but a messy jumble of ashes and pieces of charred bones.

47. Oldenberg, Hermann. *Buddha; His Life, His Doctrine, His Order*. London: Williams and Norgate, 1882, pp. 245–246.

48. Oldenberg, Hermann. *The Grhya-Sutras: Rules of Vedic Domestic Cermonies*. Delhi. Motilal Banarsidass, 1886, 1981, pp. 245–246.

It is believed that the spirit that remains goes through a journey, entering seven worlds before it attains *moksha*.

49. The collection of relics is not a public event.

Mitra, Babu Rajendralala. Funeral Ceremonies of the Anicient Hindus. *Journal of the Asiatic Society of Bengal* 39.4 (1870): 24–264, 253–255.

50. If the soul is not a good one, even crows will not eat it or it takes three hours for them to do so; but if the person is good, then they are eaten quickly. The theory is the type of death one has depends on the type of life one has lived.

51. Bentor, Yael. Tibetan Relic Classification. *Tibetan Studies (Proceedings of the Sixth Seminar of the International Association for Tibetan Studies)*, 1994, p. 30. Old images were also ground to dust and mixed with the material to make new images. The dust may be used for making *tsah tshas—stūpas* which were then deposited in new images.

52. The Udipi *maṭha* contains about twenty *vṛndāvanas* of Gurus of Ashta *mathas*. Beneath them are the whole deceased bodies of Gurus except those of Vadiraja Tirtha.

53. The leaf-like design, according to some, might be a continuation of inverted Bodhi leaves which are the *asvattha* leaves that were sacred in pre-Buddhist times.

54. Dikshitar, V.R. Ramchandra, "Origin and Early History of Chaityas," *The Indian Historical Quarterly* 14.14 (1938): 450.

55. In Nagarjunakond, Bavikonda the structure which houses a statue of the Buddha is known as Buddha *caitya*, whereas the one which enshrines the *stūpa* is known as *stūpa* caitya. Both the forms can be found in Western India as well.

56. Dikshitar, V.R. Ramchandra, "Origin and Early History of Chaityas," p. 440–443

57. Apte, V.S. Sanskrit-English Dictionary. Delhi: Motilal Banarsidass, 1965.

58. *Mahaparinibbanasutta*, Chap III, secs 36–47. Law, B.C. *History of Pali Literature*. Varanasi: Indica Books, 1933, p.100. Strong, *Relics of the Buddha*, 39.

59. B.C. *Law Historyof Pali Literature*, 100.

60. Barua, B.M. *Barhut: Aspects of Life and Art.* Bk III. Calcutta: Indian Research Institute Publications. 1937, p. 133.

61. There were other types of *stūpas*, namely *Angara thupa* (over burning coal) and *Kumbha thupa* or *stūpa* over the vessel. Subrahmanyam, B. *Buddhist Relic Caskets in South India*. Delhi: Bharatiya Kala Prakashan, 1998, p. 34.

62. *Yajnavalkya*, II, 151, (as *pasanadi bandhyah*) built of stone.

63. In the *Ramayana*, it is stated that the whole region was spotted with hundreds of *caityas*. Ramayana (V.12.14 and V. 43.3).

64. *Arthasastra*, Bk. 1, 20; Bk. XII.5, Bk. IV, ch. 3, Bk. V. ch. 2.

65. The *Śabdakalpadruma*, refers to *caityas* as a Asvattha tree. In the law books of Manu and Yajnavalkya, *caityas* were trees generally in the burial ground which marked the boundary limits of the village. The *Rāmāyaṇa* alludes to *caitya-vṛkṣas*, trees in the burial ground. Valmiki refers to Ravana as looking like a *smaśāna-caitya*, meaning the *caitya* or tree growing in the burial ground, (*Ramayana* II. 6. 11) References are also found in the Mrccha-katika (Act X 12.). Dikshitar. Origin and Early History of Chaityas, p. 443. Referred by Subrahmanyam, B. *Buddhist Relic Caskets in South India*, P. 37.

66. According to Satyanarayanachar, Principal of Pejawar *matha*, Bengaluru.

In the *Satapatha Brahmana* are mentioned round burial mounds or smasanas SB 13. 8.1–2.

67. Smith. Relics (Eastern), 658–662.

68. Flugel, Peter. The Jaina Cult of Relic Stupas. *Numen* 57.3 (2010): 389–504. Jaini, Padmanabha. *The Jain Path of Purification.* New Delhi: Motilal Banarsidass, 1979, p. 193.

69. Bruhn, K. "Jaina Rituals of Death." In *The Study of Jaina Art. Jain Studies in Honour of Jozef Deleu*, eds. Smet, Rudy and Watanabe, Kenji. Tokyo: Hon-no-Tomosha, 1993, pp. 53–66, 54.

70. *Viṣṇudharmottara Purāṇa*. Ch.84 of *khanda* 3.

Shah, Priyabala. Aiduka. *Journal of the Oriental Institute* 1 (1951–2): 271–278; Aiduka. *Journal of the Oriental Institute, M.S.* (1952): 278–285.

71. Pal has argued that the *aiduka* was a Buddhist *stūpa*. Pal, Pratapaditya. The Aiduka of the Viṣṇudharmottarapurana and Certain Apects of Stūpa Symbolism. *Journal of the Indian Society of Oriental Art* No. 4 (1971–72): 49–62.

72. Shah, P. Aiduka,1952, p. 279.

73. Shah, P. Aiduka,1952, p. 284.

74. Granoff, Phyllis. Relics, Rubies and Ritual: Some Comments on the Distinctiveness of the Buddhist Relic Cult. *Rivista degli studi orientali, nuova Serie* 81, Fasc.1.4 (2008): 59–72.

A clear description of the *aiduka* occurs in the *Viṣṇudharmottara Purana* as a place for memorializing the dead and preserving their ashes and bones. Shah, Priyabala. *Viṣṇudharmottara Purana. Introduction. Vol 2.* Gaekwad Oriental Series. Bombay: Oriental Institute, 1961, pp. 168–175. Strong. *Relics of the Buddha*, p. 15.

75. These are near the Vidyaranya temple and are part of the monastery.

76. Such stones have been found in Indus Valley sites and interpreted as death markers. Bisht, R.S. How Harappans Honoured Death at Dholavira in *Sindhu–Sarasvati Civilization-New Perspectives. A Volume in Memory of Dr. Shikaripur Rnnganath Rao. Proceedings of the International Conference on the Sindhu-Sarasvati Valley Civilizations: A Reappraisa*l. Edited by Nalini Rao. Los Angeles; New Delhi: Nalanda Intrnational and DK Printworld, 2014, pp. 265–318.

77. In fact, in Śringeri, the term *vṛndāvana* is referred to the site in Śringeri, on the banks of a river where memorial stones have been installed. Śri Ādi

Śankarācārya is said to have disappeared in the Himalayas and his body was never found. Other sites with Śivaliṅga on riverbeds are Somnath, Hampi, and Kolar.

78. *Liṅga* has been known as the aniconic form of the greatest God, Śiva, and is worshipped in this non-figural form in Hindu temples.

79. However Liṅgāyats always bury their dead. They do not make an exception. The grave is dug. It is about 9 by 5 feet and entered by three steps.

From a recent discussion with the head of the Pejawar *matha*, I gathered that construction of memorials (for the Hindu commoner) was practiced, for those who desired memorials. They might be in the form of a square stone with a conical top. The shape was not of particular importance.

80. Shah, Umakant Premanand. *Studies in Jaina Art*. Banaras: Jaina Cultural Research Society. Parsvanath Vidyapeeth, 1955, pp. 43–64.

81. Panigrahi notes that in Mathura and in Bhubanesvara, *liṅgas* were erected for each generation of teachers. Panigraphi, K.C. *Archaeological Remins at Bhubaneswar*. Bombay, 1961, pp. 225–227.

82. ARASI, 1907–08, 1909, pp. 1–3.

83. Bakker, Hans. Monuments to the Dead in Ancient North India. *Indo-Iranina Journal* 50 (2007): 27.

84. Yocum, Glenn E. "A Non-Brahman Tamil Shaiva Mutt: A Field Study of the Thiruvavduthurai Adheenam." In *Monastic Life in the Christian and Hindu Traditions, A Comparative Study*. Leweiston: NY: Edsin Mellen Press, 1990, p. 265.

85. Similarly, bodies of saints were buried under ground with a *maṇḍapa* above, near the Sun temple at Modhera, Gujarat.

86. In Nepalese art are paintings of cremation grounds with a *liṅga*.

Buhnemann, Gudrun. Sivalingas and Caityas in Representations of the Eight Cremation Grounds from Nepal. *Pramanakirtih: Papers Dedicated to Ernst Steinkellner on the Occasion of His 70th Birthday*. Wiener Studien zur Tibetologie und Buddhismuskunde; Heft 70. Wien, 2007, p. 24.

87. Fleming, Benjamin J. Relics, Lingas, and Other Auspicious Material Remains in South Asian Religions. *Material Religion* 10.4 (2014): 464.

88. Marco, De Giuseppe. The Stupa as a Funerary monument: New Iconographical Evidence. *East and West* 37 (1) 4: (1987), p. 241.

89. Matteini, Michele. "On the 'True Body' of Huineng," RES (Spring/Autumn 2009), pp. 41–60.

Law states that there is a long hist of self-immolation dating back to fifth century CE in medieval China. Law, Eastern: The Study of Buddhist Self-Immolation Beyond Religious Tradition and Plitical Context: The Necessity of Protogetical Analysis. *The International Journal of religion and Spirituality in Society* 7.3 (2017): 25.

90. Yetss, Perceval, Notes on the Disposal of Buddhist Monks Died in China. *Journal of the Royal Asiatic Society*, (1911) pp. 699–725.

91. http:// rufodao.qq.com/a/20171225/001196.htm

92. Matteini. On the "True Body" of Huineng, p. 44.

93. Matteini. On the "True Body" of Huineng. This is mentioned by Zanning (919–1001), author of Biographies of Song Monks and former ambassador of the Song state to Guangdong.

94. Johnston, F. Reginald. *Buddhist China.* London: John Murray. *First Edition.* 1913, p. 231.

95. Kukai is believed to emerge in approximately 5.67 million years to usher a predetermined number of souls into *nirvāṇa.* This is similar to what has been said of Rāghvendra Swāmi as well. https://www.atlasobscura.com/articles/so kushinbutsu

96. In Tibet the whole-body relics are on public display for a certain time and then enclosed in a *stūpa* which was out of view.

97. https://strangeremains.com/2015/01/30/read-about-self-mummificati on-an-extreme-way-of-saving-money-on-embal

98. Bruijn, Eric et al., "Die Mumie in Inneren–eine übermodellierte Mumie eines buddhistichen Mőnchs," In *Mumien: Der Traum vom ewigen Leben*, ed. Alfried Wiexzorek and Wilfried Rosendahl. Manheim: Reiss-Engelhorn-Museen, 2015, pp. 337–42.

99. Croissant, Doris. "Der unsterbliche Leib. Ahneneffigies und Reliquienportrat in der Portratplastik Chinas und Japans," in *Das Bildnis in der Kunst des Orients,* ed. M. Kraatz, J. Meyer zu Capellan, D. Seckel. Stuttgart: Franz Steiner Verlag. 1990, pp 235–268.

100. According to Yun Hua Jan, monks self-immolated as acts of devotion, imitating *bodhisattavs* who sacrifed themselves. Yun Hua Jan. Buddhist Self-Immolation in Medieval China. *History of Religions* 4.2 (1965): 249.

According to Law, it had religio-cultural as well as socio-political dimensions. Law, Eastern: The Study of Buddhist Self-Immolation, p. 25.

101. Doris Croissant denies that the mummy portrait is an extension of the Indian relic cult. See note 99 above

102. Buddhism survived in pockets in South India till the fourteenth to fifteenth century Subrahmanyam, B. *Buddhist Relic Caskets*, 20.

103. Ramachandran, T.N. The Nagapattinam and other Buddhist Bronzes in Madras Museum. *Bulletin of the Madras Museum*, New Series General Section VII.1 (1954): 14.

104. *IA*. Vol. XXII, 1893, p. 29.

105. Subramanyam. *Buddhist Relic Caskets in South India.*

106. *IA*. Vol VII, 1878, p. 224.

107. Sinopoli, C. Earthenware Pottery of Vijyanagara: Some Observations. In *Vijayanagara: Progress of Research 1997–1983*, ed. M.S. Nagraja Rao. Mysore: Directorate of Archaeology and Museums, 1983, pp. 68–74.

108. Subrahmanyam. *Buddhist Relic Caskets in South India*, pp. 4–5.

109. *IA*. XXII, 1893, p. 29.

110. Mitra, Debala. *Buddhist Monuments.* Calcutta: Sahitya Samsad, 1971, p. 190.

111. *EC* Vol. VII, 5 K. / SK, 170.

112. Subrahmanyam. *Buddhist Relic Caskets in South India.*

113. Sallekhana is death by fasting and the criteria was old age, incuarabel disease or acute problesm. Other types of deaths, included *ārādhana maraṇa* (death through worship), *pancapāda maraṇa* (death through prayer), *paṇḍita maraṇa* (death through knowledge or wisdom), and *samādhi maraṇa* (death through meditation). *Paṇḍita maraṇa* was considered the wisest of deaths releases from all bondages. Settar, S. *Inviting Death: Indian Attitude towards the Ritual Death.* Leiden; New York: Brill, 1989, p. xxxv.

114. Jainism believes in the docirnes of *ahimsa,* (non violience) *asteya* (not stealing), *satya* (truth), *brahmacharya* (chastity for laypeople and celibacy for Jain monks and nuns) and *aparigraha* (non-possessiveness). Its three jewels comprises of right knowledge, faith and action Long, Jeffery D. *Jainism: An Introduction.* London. I.B. Tauris, 1988, pp. 154–165.

115. Hopkins, W. On the Hindu Custom of Dying to Redress a Grievance. *Journal of American Oriental Society* (1900): 151–153.

116. Settar, *Inviting Death*, xxvi; *EC* Vol. II, 81.

117. Chandragiri in Sravanana Belagola, Karnataka was known as Samadhi Betta meditation unto death (third century BCE). Settar, *Inviting Death*, x, 136–40.

118. Bronkhorst, Johannes. *Greater Magadha. Studies in the Culture of Early India.* Leiden; Boston: Brill. Handbook of Oriental Studies, Section 2 South Asia, 19, 2007, p. 4. For details, see Bronkhorst, Johannes. Les reliques dans les religions de l'Inde. *Indische Kultur im Kontext.* Rituale, Texte und Ideen aus Indien und der Welt. Festschrift für Klaus Mylius. Hrsg, 2005, p. 55.

119. He drew up all the *prāṇa* and gave up the physical body. He was initiated into the Nath Yogi tradition (founded by Gorakshanath) which emphasized *hatha* yoga. He was influenced by the Mahanubhava sect that belived in the worship of Kṛṣṇa as Vitthala.

120. Dubois, J. A. *Hindu Manners, Customs and Ceremonies*. Oxford: Clarendon Press, 1908, 538 ff.

121. Somasundaram, Ollilingam, Tejus Murthy, A.G., and Vijaya Raghavan, D. Jainism Its Relevance to Psychiatric Practice; with Special Reference to the Practice of Sallekhana. *Indian Journal of Psychiatry. Wolters Kluwer-Medknow* 58 (2016): 471–474.

122. Yocum, Glenn E.A Non–Brahman Tamil Shaiva Mutt: A Field study of the Thiruvavduthurai Adheenam.In *Monastic Life in the Christian and Hindu traditions*, ed. Austin Creel and Vasudha Narayanan (in book), 1990, p. 250.

Hopkins. On the Hindu Custom of Dying to Redress a Grievance, Journal of American Oriental Society, 21. Second Half. (1900) 151–153.

123. Many ascetics committed self-immolation in Tamil Nadu and Andhra Pradesh.

124. It was known as *jeevan samādhi* when a living saint immolates himself to death and is said to have been imbued with eternal life force. In this spiritual

practice, life is not allowed to go out of the body. The seed cells in the body never get damaged. Such a person stops the functions of the body after completion of his or her mission by his or her own will. Rāghvendra Swāmi performed *jeeva samādhi* (In Karnataka, known as *jeeva samādhi*) and his whole-body relic is in Mantralaya, in Northern Karnataka.

125. A *thade* may have been erected in memory of a woman who performed *sati*, or a man who had died a heroic death. As they do not have any inscriptions or decorations, it is difficult to date them. Khare, D.C. "Memorial Stones in Maharashtra." In *Memorial Stones in South India a Study of Their Origin, Significance and Variety*. Edited by Gunther D. Sontheimer and S. Settar. Dharwad: Institute of Indian Art History, Karnataka University; New Delhi: South Asia Institute, Germany: University of Heidelberg, 1982, pp. 251–254.

126. Images of kings were kept in small houses. Bhasa in his drama, *Pratima Nataka* makes a reference to *pratima grihas* that housed the images of Dilipa, Raghu, and Dasaratha and was located in the outskirts of the city of Ayodhya.

127. The 'memorial' *vṛndāvanas* can be found in Theur, Raigad, Simhagad, Brahmanaa, and Vadgaon in Maharashtra. These were erected to perpetuate the memory of persons at places where they were not cremated and the one from Sikhara Singhanapur (Satara District) resembles the *vṛndāvana* in the Madhva Deo, S.B. A Sati Memorial from Markandi. In *Memorial Stones in South India a Study of Their Origin, Significance and Variety.* Edited by Gunther D. Sontheimer and S Settar Settar, S., and Sontheimer, G. D., Dharwad: Institute of Indian Art History, Karnataka University; New Delhi: South Asia Institute, Germany: University of Heidelberg, 1982, pp. 255–259.

128. It is probable that *yatis* in Greater Magadha practiced rigorous asceticism. Bronkhorst, Johannes: *Greater Magadha: Studies in the Culture of Early India*. Leiden – Boston: Brill. Handbook of Oriental Studies, Section 2 South Asia, 19.2007, p. 85.

129. The term *yati* is derived from the root *yam* meaning to control. *Yati* is also the name of an ancient clan which is connected with the Bhrgus in two passages of the *RV* VIII. 3.9 and 6.18. Reference provided by Chakraborti, *Asceticism in Ancient India*, 10.

130. Kane, Pandurang Vama. *History of Dharmasastra (Ancient and Medieval, Religious and Civil Law*). 5 Vols. Government Oriental Series, Class B, No.6. Poona: Bhandarkar Oriental Research Institute, 1930–53. Vol. IV, p. 229.

Olivelle, Patrick. *Rules and Regulations of Brahmanical Asceticism. Yatidharmasamuccaya of Yådava Prakasa*. Edited and translated. Albany: State University of New York Press, 1995, p. 176 ff.

Briggs, George Weston. *Gorakhnåth and the Kanphata Yogis*. 1938. Reprint Delhi: Motilal Banarsidass, 1982, p. 39 ff.

131. Evidences of such memorials have been found in Nepal. Bouillier, Veronique. Naitre Renoncant, Une Caste De Sannyasi Villageois Au Nepal Central. Nanterre: Laboratoire d'Ethnologie. 1979, pp. 139, 175.

132. Anegondi and the surrounding areas were associated with the mythology of Vali and Sugriva in the *Rāmāyana*. The entire area is associated with events and personalities in the epic; Hanuman, Sita, Anjaneya, Vali, and Sugriva. Rao, N. *Royal Artistic Imagery and Networks of power at Vijayanagara*. Originals. 2010, p. 15.

133. Sewell, Robert A. *Forgotten Empire (Vijayanagar) A Contribution to the History of India*. London: Swan Sonnenschein & Co., 1900. Reprint, New Asian Educational Services New Delhi, 1983, 1991, p. 295.

134. Tobert, Natalie. *Anegondi: Architectural Ethnography of a Royal Village. Manohar, Amerrican Institute of Indian Studies*. New Delhi: Manohar, American Institute of Indian Studies, 2000, pp. 6–10, figures 10, 11; plates 15, 16.

135. *Banjiga* stands for the original words, *banija, vanijya* meaning merchant or trader. The Salu Mule Banajigas who were merchant guilds played an important role in the expansion of the economy and built environment, especially in textile production. Sinopoli, Carla M. and Morrison, Kathleen. The Vijayangara Metropolitan Survey: The 1988 Season. In *Vijayanagara: Progress of Research 1987–1988*. Eds. Devaraj, D.V. and Patil, C.S. Mysore: Directorate of Archaeology and Museums, 1991, pp. 55–80.

136. Finally, in the central part of the town of Anegondi, is a house where in their backyard, is a garden with a *vṛndāvana*. Tobert. *Anegondi*, 148, fig. 17, house no. 41.

137. Hariharadevaraya, Tirumaladevaraya's youngest son, was cremated in the fields next to the Chintamani temple complex. Venkatadevaraya was cremated near the entrance gate to Gangavati. A more recent royal site reserved for those of direct descent of kings of Anegondi is on Magota Hill.

138. Anegundi in Gagavati taluk, meaning, "elephant pit" is said to have been the place where the elephants were kept. It is situatied on the left bank of river Tungabhadra, opposite the ruined capital of the Vijayanagara Empire, now called Hampi. After, the battle of Talikota (also called Rakkasagi-Tangadi) in 1565, both Hampi and Anegundi were destroyed by the conferacy of Muslim kings.

139. Smith, Bardwell and Reynolds, Holly Baker. *The City as a Sacred Center: Essay on Six Asian Contexts*. Leiden: E. J. Brill, 1987.

Historical evidences show that with the rise of Mahayana Buddhism, a gradual infiltration of Hindu ideas and religious concepts influenced Buddhism (and vice versa) which narrowed the division between the followers of Buddha and orthodox Hindu groups.

140. In addition was the power of the Banajiga community during the period. Rao, N. *Royal Artistic Imagery*, 20.

141. Paul Demieville, the French sinologist who has discussed Buddhism mummification in various cultures remarks on the absence of mummification in India, while reporting several Buddhist mummies in Central Asia Demieville, Paul. Momies d'Extreme-Orient, *Jounal des Savants*, 1.1. (1965): 144–170.

Chapter 5

Multivalent Symbolism of the *Vṛndāvana*

In the last chapter, the quest for the origins of the *vṛndāvana* was undertaken through an analysis of historical and archaeological evidences. The reinvention of its visual iconography was influenced by two ancient and pervasive traditions, non-figural "abstract" form, and sacredness of relics. However, the material sources do not throw ample light on its symbolic meaning. The reasons for its sacred status can be found in the mythological, metaphysical, and ontological meanings. The rationale for the transformation of meaning from a relic to an icon is embedded in traditional intangible concepts. Some related queries that I aim to answer: Why was the icon/relic "decorated" in the form of a portrait? Why did the deceased body of the Guru matter so much? What was the original meaning or intent behind "naming or renaming" the icon as *vṛndāvana*? How does the Guru's *vṛndāvana* relate to Vṛndāvana, the garden of Kṛṣṇa? We now enter a dark and "quasi-historical" realm, but a conceptual analysis can help us bridge the gap between God and Guru, as well as the meaningful transformations through time.

Etymological Meaning

The term *vṛndāvana* is a multilevel concept and has varied meanings and interpretations. Etymologically, it means a group of knowledge, a multitude, or an assembly[1]. In medieval Vaisnavite literature, the term appears as *yativṛnda* meaning, a group of *yatis* (or a veneration of *yatis*). A *yati is a sanyāsi*, but his status is much higher. He is a self-realized intellectual and can impart multileveled teaching.[2] He has a multifaceted personality and as the head of a *maṭha* represents the institution. The term *vṛndāvana* can also be translated as *vṛnda* (collection)-*avana* (protection), thereby meaning protection of collective knowledge or protection of a collection of knowledge, standing for the Guru himself. In fact, the Guru was considered to be a repository of philosophical and spiritual knowledge. Having ascertained the formation of the word *vṛndāvana* as related to *vṛnda*, one might suppose a connection with *vṛndāraka* (chief), *vṛndiṣṭha* (best), and the formation in groups. The terms *vṛndāvṛndāiha* and *vṛnda* also mean a multitude, an assembly, and thus its association *yativṛnda*—assembly of ascetics[3]—might also be another aspect that might have led to the adoption of the term by the pontiffs of the Dualist school.

Mythological Story of Vṛndā

Mythologically, the term *vṛndāvana* has its origins in the *Śaiva* and Vaiṣṇava versions of the mythological tale of Vṛndā described in the *Padma Purāṇa*.[4] In the story of *samudra manthana*, or Churning of the Ocean, Jalandhara, the demon, could not be defeated by either Śiva or Viṣṇu due to the devotion of his wife, Vṛndā toward him. But Jalandhara finds it difficult to overcome his enemy, Śiva. Hence, he decides to seduce Śiva's wife, Pārvatī. Disguised as Māyaśiva or pseudo, wounded Śiva, he approaches Pārvatī. Struck by the sight of Mayaśiva, and seeing him carrying the "skulls" of her two sons, Gaṇapati and Subrahmaṇya, she begins to weep. Mayaśiva requests Pārvatī to console him by embracing him. Pārvatī resents this plea and educates him by explaining that sexual enjoyment is forbidden in times of misery, fear, meditation, vomiting, fever, during a journey, royal visits, marriage festivities, during offerings, and in the presence of elders and teachers. She questions him, as to how could he make this request to her who was mourning the death of her sons. Pretending to be grief-stricken Mayaśiva replies that she who does not give sexual pleasure to a man in distress would go to hell. Hearing this Pārvatī goes near him. At that moment, Viṣṇu's "vehicle" Garuḍa (eagle) appears in the sky.

In the Vaiṣṇava version of the story, Viṣṇu had been requested by the demigods to defeat Jalandhara. He sends Garuḍa to find out how the battle between the *devas* (gods) and *asuras* (demons) was progressing. Garuḍa flies to Mt. Kailas and finds Mayaśiva with Pārvatī. He reports that to Viṣṇu who recognizes that she had been deceived by Jalandhara. In order to avenge the act, he cheats on Jalandhara's wife, Vṛndā. Avoiding his own wife, Lakṣmī, accompanied by Ananta, and masking himself, with a yellow scarf, he visits Durgakanana, the abode of Vṛndā. There he constructs an *āśrama* (hermitage) and lives with the animals who take a human form and become his disciples.

It was then Viṣṇu's turn to "excite" *kāma* (sexual love) in Vṛndā's heart in order to attract her to his hermitage. She imagines her husband, Jalandhara lying with wounds on his body. Due to the miraculous powers of Viṣṇu, she finds living inside the palace unbearable. She boards a chariot and enters her garden where she is overjoyed to see the beautiful flowers and celestial maidens which reminds her of Jalandhara. Accompanied by her maids, she goes in search of him from one *vana* (forest) to another till she witnesses a ghastly sight. Here she sees huge trees interspersed with black rocks and hears the roar of lions and tigers. She requests the charioteer to hasten back home. But the charioteer loses his way. Fortunately, Vṛndā's maid carefully steers the chariot toward another forest which is far more frightful than the last one. Here there was neither any wind nor sound, except for *yoginī*s (female yogis).

Vṛndā moans and frets that there was no peace of mind for her anywhere in this world. Meanwhile, the charioteer, Samaraduti, sees a huge black mountain and attempts to steer the chariot, but the horses refuse to move. Placing her hands on the pearl necklace on her breast Vṛndā stands up and jumps out of the chariot. A fierce yellow colored demon with five hands, seven eyes, three legs, tiger-like shoulders, and a chin resembling that of a lion, approaches her. Seeing this horrible sight, she closes her eyes and trembles in fear. The ugly demon whirls the chariot into the air and devours all the horses and grasping the queen threatens to kill her unless she concedes to make him her husband. He adds that Vṛndā's husband had been killed by Śiva in the battle and that she should drink the sweet liquor made with flesh. Upon hearing these words, Vṛndā faints.

Meanwhile, Viṣṇu in the guise of an ascetic (Mahāviṣṇu) with a matted hair, wearing barks of trees, appears before her. He sneers at the demon who disappears in an instant. Vṛndā takes refuge with the ascetic who fabricates the myth that he was Devaśarma, son of Bhāradvāja Muni. He had renounced all worldly pleasures and had come to this forest to perform penance, and that, if it pleased her, she could come and stay in the *āśrama* and perform penance as well. Both travel to another forest far way and reach the *āśrama*. There Mahāviṣṇu appears before her in the form of Jalandhara and they embrace each other.

Days later, at the end of a sexual act, Vṛndā discovers that, instead of Jalandahra, it was an ascetic who was embracing her. She is shocked and the ascetic admits that he was Mahāviṣṇu, husband of Lakṣmī, while Jalandhara had gone to conquer Śiva and get Pārvatī for himself. He says, "We appear separate, your husband Jalandhara has been killed in the battle, hence embrace me." Vṛndā is furious and curses Viṣṇu saying that his wife would be cheated by a "false" ascetic as well. Viṣṇu disappears and Vṛndā resumes her penance and immolates herself. The nymphs shower flowers upon her; the deceased body of Vṛndā is cremated by Smaraduti who jumps into the funeral pyre of Vṛndā. At the end of the story, the nymphs are said to create an image of Vṛndā from the ashes in the funeral pyre, and float it down the river Ganges. Later she is transformed into a Goddess, known as Vṛndā Devi and a devotee is supposed to visit her temple before entering the site of Vṛndāvana (in Mathura).[5]

A few points may be observed in relation to this legend. It demonstrated the power of chastity and *pativratā dharma* (loyalty to one's husband) of a woman. Vṛndā's act of self-immolation transformed her into a heroine. It drew the admiration of ascetics, who linked her with their desire for God. It may be added that Vṛndā's self-immolation in the forest (*vana*), or forest of material pleasures, is similar to that of ascetics who immolate themselves spiritually (and physically) as they comprehend the deceptive nature and temporality of the material world. It may not be incorrect to add that the icon was known as the forest of Vṛndā, although there are many unanswered questions.

Tulsi Vṛndāvana

A more conspicuous connection may be found in the story of Tulsi Vṛndāvana.[6] Tulsi (holy basil) is a plant that is considered sacred. It is worshipped by women in almost every Hindu household (figure 5.1). In the story of Vṛndā, mentioned above, before Vṛndā immolates herself in her husband's funeral pyre, Viṣṇu ensures her that she would be reincarnated in the form of a Tulsi plant on earth. In the *Bhāgavata Purāṇa*, Vṛndā is transformed into Tulsi, the goddess, and she is also the wife of Kṛṣṇa.[7] The *vana* (garden, forest, or orchard) is denoted by the sacred pot with the tulsi plant that is worshipped by women in almost every Hindu household. However, in popular memory, Tulsi Vṛndāvana has been a symbol of ideal wifehood, and a goddess, while the story of Vṛndā's *vana* (narrated in the *Padma Purāṇa*) has been forgotten.

Figure 5.1 Tulsi Vṛndāvana.

Tulsi is also considered a medicinal plant that is planted over memorials of saints and in burial sites. Pre-Buddhist *caityas* were marked by trees and plants, and were also related to cremation grounds and burial places.[8] Hence above many *vṛndāvanas*, such as in Anegondi, one can find a Tulsi plant. The importation of Tulsi Vṛndāvana as a death monument may also be traced to an incident in the life of Ādi Śaṅkarācārya. He is said to have built a Tulsi Vṛndāvana on the site of his mother's death at Kaladi in Kerala. It is possible that the present *vṛndāvana* grew out of what Śankara built over the site of his mother's death. Tulsi (basil), with its many medicinal properties, may be said to have appropriated the spirit of the ascetic as did Vṛndā in the *Padma Purāṇa*.[9] More importantly, the pot, in which the Tulsi plant is grown, is in the form of a cuboid stone/brick structure, which resembles the shape of the Guru's *vṛndāvana* (figures 5.1 and 4.1).

VṚNDĀVANA AND THE GARDEN OF KṚṢṆA

Tulsi is also the wife of Kṛṣṇa and the leaves of the plant are sacred for the worship of the latter. During the festival of Tulsi *lagna* (marriage of Tulsi), an image of Kṛṣṇa is placed near the plant and the ritual marriage is celebrated. Having established the link between Tulsi and Kṛṣṇa, we now move on to another link, the relation between Kṛṣṇa and Guru *vṛndāvana*. Above every stone sepulchral *vṛndāvana* of the Guru in a Dvaita *maṭha* (within the sanctum sanctorum) can be found a small metal image of a Vaiṣṇavite god, such as Kṛṣṇa or Rāma or Narasimha (figure 4.9). The image of Lord Kṛṣṇa had been installed in the "temple-*maṭha*" in Udipi in 1250 CE by Madhvācārya,[10] who had found the image in a ship that was sailing southward.

The story of Kṛṣṇa is popular all over India. He was the mischievous child, wondrous boy, endearing lover, cowherd, strategist, friend of Arjuna, and the philosopher in the *Bhagavad Gītā*. A description of the life of Kṛṣṇa involves legends, myths, images, and narratives, both textual and contextual. In terms of the historical period regarding the evolution of his personality, concept, and deification, it can be placed between 11th and 1st centuries BCE. He has been viewed by scholars as a transformation from the Vedic God, Viṣṇu to Vāsudeva-Kṛṣṇa as well as that of the folk hero into an *avatāra* of Viṣṇu.[11]

As mentioned above, the *Bhāgavata Purāṇa* also connects Tulsi and Kṛṣṇa to Tulsi and Rādhā (Kṛṣṇa's beloved). Vṛndā Devi (Goddess Vṛndā) is said to have donated her enchanting forest as a gift to Rādhā. In fact, it is not possible for the aspiring devotee to enter the site of Vṛndāvana without first getting the blessings of Vṛndā Devi. She is exalted and considered to be one of the principle deities of Vṛndāvana. The feelings of affection that Rādhā has for Vṛndā Devi are worthy of praise.[12] Numerous events are documented to have occurred here: this is where Kṛṣṇa performed the divine dance (*rāsalīla*) with Gopis and spread the message of divine love with his lover Rādhā, stole the clothes of the bathing (*gopīs*) maidens, who prayed for attaining him, and here he destroyed an entire succession of demons.[13] Today the (garden/town) stands within the original forest of Vṛndāvana on the banks of the river Yamuna. Consequently, it is a major pilgrimage destination for Hindus, and contains innumerable temples. Thus, the constructs of the term Vṛndāvana undergoes transformation from the forest of Vṛndā, a goddess, a sacred site, and a theological concept.

VṚNDĀVANA IN *THE PURĀṆAS*

There is an immense corpus of Vaiṣṇava literature of different genres: mythological, metaphysical, devotional, and commentarial on Kṛṣṇa's

Vṛndāvana. Kṛṣṇa is said to have spent his youthful days dancing with Rādhā and the *gopīs* in the (blissful) garden of Vṛndāvana. Marcuo Corcoran has analyzed the term as it appears in the *Purāṇas* (quasi-historical texts), particularly the *Viṣṇu Purāṇa*, *Bhāgavata Purāṇa*, and *Harivaṃśa*.[14] Vṛndāvana as an ethereal place of Kṛṣṇa is alluded to in all the three *Purāṇas* although there are slight variations in meaning. In the *Bhāgavata Purāṇa* (sixth to ninth centuries CE) Vṛndavana has metaphysical implications and the text insists on the unity of Kṛṣṇa, the immanent, and Viṣṇu, the transcendent, through the theory of *līla* (play) and *avatāra* (incarnation). In the *Harivaṃś*a, Vṛndāvana is a terrestrial and extraterrestrial site although there is some ambiguity between the two. In the *Viṣṇu Purāṇa* (300–100 BCE), Vṛndāvana is a terrestrial place as well as a celestial one. In the epic, *Mahābhārata*, both the transcendent and immanent forms of Kṛṣṇa have been described, but it treats Kṛṣṇa as a hero and historical events take place in time and space while retaining Viṣṇu as a transcendent deity. Vṛndāvana as a place of beauty and enchantment, love and bliss, is described in the *Bhāgavata Purāṇa*. Here, *gopis* (girlfriends of Kṛṣṇa) are said to gather (in the *vana*, garden) attracted by the music of Kṛṣṇa's flute. It is described as a beautiful orchard (or forest) blossoming with flowers, lit by moon beams, adorned with trees rustling in the breeze from the Yamuna river.

Historicity of Kṛṣṇa

It is important to include a brief note about the historicity of Kṛṣṇa and how it affects historical interpretation of Kṛṣṇa's Vṛndāvana. The principal difficulty in the study of ancient history of India lies in the identification of material evidences to comprehend the existence of leaders, who played a seminal role in ancient Indian history. The discovery of the underwater city of Kṛṣṇa's Dvaraka has shaped the trajectory of study of the historicity of Mahabharata, which can be effectively employed in a collaborative investigation that utilizes literary evidences along with materially grounded phenomena of built environment and significant antiquities. The recent underwater excavations at Dvaraka (in Western India) attest the historicity of Lord Kṛṣṇa of the Mahabharata period.[15] It has now added a new dimension to our understanding of mythical Kṛṣṇa and proved that he was a historical personality who lived around 1400 BCE in the post-Harappan period in Gujarat, Western India. This discovery was possible due to the evidences in the *Mahābhārata* which treats Kṛṣṇa as a hero and describes his city quite accurately. The textual link between a historical folk hero with the mythology of Viṣṇu implied a process of deification which seems to have occurred between 4th and 7th centuries CE.[16] His human aspect had bearing on his deification, relation with Viṣṇu as an *avatāra*, the theological concepts, and the relation with the garden/forest of Vṛndāvana, where he danced with Rādhā. It is possible to corroborate the description of the site of Vṛndāvana in the *Purāṇas*[17] as well as its existence as an actual geographical site with the form and meaning of the *vṛndāvana*.

Historical evidences support the view that the Vṛndāvana was an actual geographical site related to Kṛṣṇa and that saints and kings were cognizant about it. The connection between Kṛṣṇa and Mathura existed even as early as 1307 CE. In the Jain *Vividhatīrthakalpa* in Prakṛta (1307–1332 CE) assigned to 150 years before the rediscovery of the Vṛndāvana (as described by the Vallabha or the Gauḍīya Gosvāmīs), it was stated that it is in Mathura and is said to be the birthplace of Kṛṣṇa Vāsudeva.[18]

Description of Vṛndāvana

Vṛndāvana is a popular site of pilgrimage as well as in the memory of devotees as the place where Kṛṣṇa[19] danced with Rādhā and performed his *līla* or divine sport. From a perusal of Puranic literature, the earliest description of Vṛndāvana appears in the *Harivaṃśa* and the *Viṣṇu Purāṇa*. In the *Harivaṃśa* it is described as *vraja*, and surrounded by trees.[20] As an earthly place, in the *Viṣṇu Purāṇa* (100–300 BCE) it is a terrestrial and celestial place with four enclosures and lotus leaves. It is described as one with the Bhandira tree, water (river Yamuna), and mountain (Govardhana) with connotations of cosmos, creation and potential form, thus transforming it from a holy site (for gaining merit) to total immersion of mind and body and partake in the divine play.[21] In both the *Purāṇas*, we find both a spatial and metaphysical description of the term. One can find a clear description of Vṛndāvana explained in the form of a symmetrical, ordered site in the *Brahma Saṁhitā* that has a Vaiṣṇava interpretation. It is said to be a hexagon surrounded by a quadrangle called *śvetadvīpa*, the four corners of which form the fourfold abode of the four forms of Vāsudeva, Sankarṣṇa, Pradyumna and Aniruddha.[22]

If we examine the description in the *Padma Purāṇa*, it is stated that there are twelve woods[23] and has eight petals within a sixteen-petaled lotus. Apart from the narrative and metaphysical element, the integration of the geographical and symbolic ideas, one can discern the twelve *vanas* as situated on the various petals of these lotuses.[24] Thus the Vṛndāvana appears as a *mandala*, with four doorkeepers, eight petaled lotus, four Vyūha forms of Viṣṇu (Vāsudeva, Sankarṣṇa, Pradyumna, and Anirudh) with a *yogapīṭha* (yogic throne).[25] Furthermore, the Vṛndāvana is on a higher level than the rest of the Mathura-*mandala*:[26] it is the pericarp of the thousand-petaled lotus and is also its center, where Kṛṣṇa lives.[27] In addition, there are four doorkeepers, who are followed by the cowherd boys and the cows. On the outside of the *yogapīṭha*, on each of its four sides, lies a golden *pīṭha* in which one of the four *vyūhas* are enthroned. Finally, the outermost doorkeepers are the four Viṣṇus:[28] white, golden, red, and black—each having four arms.[29]

Vṛndāvana, Kṛṣṇa, and Guru

A close reading of the texts that describe the site reveals a close link between the shape and description of the sacred site to the form of the sacred icon of the deceased Dvaita pontiff. The elaborate descriptions of Vṛndāvana as a sacred symmetrical site consisting of numbers and symbols can be corroborated by visual form of the Guru *vṛndāvana*.[30] The description can be compared to the Guru *vṛndāvana* built for Padmanabha Tīrtha (figure 4.1), which is square in shape. It stands for the four *vyūha* forms of Viṣṇu: Vāsudeva, Sankarṣṇa , Pradyumna and Aniruddha.[31] The four sides symbolize the *bhāgavata rūpa*, God's form; *ananta rūpa*, (eternal form), *sveta rūpa* (pure form) and *vaikuṇtha rūpa* (heavenly form).[32] In addition, each of the four sides have three lotus petals, a total of twelve petals or leaves. On some other *vṛndāvanas*, one can find lotus leaves near the pedestal. The *vṛndāvana* leaves or "*tene*" as they are called can be related to the twelve lotus petals, which can also be corroborated to the twelve woods in the *Padma Purāṇa*.[33] In addition, the dimensions of the site are twelve *yojanas* long and nine *yojanas* wide. The basic pattern of twelve *vanas* is preserved even in the *Varaha Purāṇa*,[34] which can be corroborated with the number of leaves upon the Guru's *vṛndāvana*. From a description of lotus petals in the metaphysical space of Kṛṣṇa in the *Purāṇas*, it appears that the Guru's *vrndavana* connoted both leaves or "*tene*" of the Tulsi and the lotus flower and its petals. Figure 4.2 clearly reveals the lotus form and petals; so do many other *vṛndāvanas*, particularly at the base of the icon.

Furthermore, the concept of *vyuhas*—forms of Viṣṇu, Sankarṣṇa, Vāsudeva, Pradyumna, and Aniruddha—form an important aspect of Madhvācārya's Dualist philosophy and religion. In fact, it is the worship of Viṣṇu (rather than Kṛṣṇa) that was accorded greater significance by the Dvaita Gurus. Hence it was natural to incorporate the concept of four Vyūha forms of Viṣṇu into its four sides.[35] Yet, another reason why it might have been a term appropriated by Dvaita saints in the fourteenth century, and named the relic/icon of the Guru as such, is that the word meant the garden of Kṛṣṇa and Kṛṣṇa was the main deity of Vaiṣṇavites. More importantly, Madhvācārya had come across the image of Kṛṣṇa (which is said to have been in a ship sailing from Dvaraka) and had installed the image in the temple at Udipi.[36]

The Dvaita Gurus were aware of the location of the site of Vṛndāvana; the location of the site of Vṛndāvana was known as a sacred geographical and pilgrimage site associated with the (mythical) sport of Rādhā and Kṛṣṇa, near Mathura. This can be confirmed by the evidence in Bilhana's *Vikramankadevacarita* (written in the eleventh century). In the Jain *Vividhatīrthakalpa* in Prakṛta (1307–1332 CE) is mentioned the site as located near Mathura.[37] They knew about the twelve woods and Vṛndāvana as one of twelve woods situated in Mathura area.[38] In addition, Nimbarka (seventh century CE), who hailed from the South, is said to have lived in Vṛndāvana near Mathura. In fact, F. S. Growse identifies the site of Mathrua in 1071 CE when it was seen by Mahmud of Ghazni.[39] In addition, both Madhvācārya and Narahari *Tīrtha* (who built the first Guru *vṛndāvana*) had visited Vṛndāvana near Mathura. Thus it can be said that the Dvaita Gurus were aware that Vṛndāvana was a sacred geographical site near Mathura and the very first one that was installed by Narahari Tirtha, must have come to be known as such. It does not appear as though the Guru *vṛndāvana* was known as a burial ground (*samādhi*) and later renamed as *vṛndāvana*. Narahari Tirtha creatively appropriated the sacred geographical and symbolic space. Such an ethereal place had immense significance and meaning that was attributed to the *vṛndāvana* of the Guru, who had attained, liberation, and eternity.[40]

Vṛndāvana as *Ānanda*

The meaning of *vṛndāvana* stemming from ontological and metaphysical perspectives is enormous, particularly related to the concept of Vṛndāvana and Kṛṣṇa's *līla*. In the *Bhāgavata Purāṇa* (sixth to tenth century CE), Vṛndavana has metaphysical implications and it relates the term with the theory of *avatāra*. The *Virahamanjari* of Nandadasa alludes to the place as an eternal one. In the *Bhramara Gīta* it is the place of unmanifest *līla* (divine play), it can be detected in the verse where Kṛṣṇa revealed himself to be one with the *gopīs* and then cast again the net of illusion and hid his form of sport (*bihara*). In the *Braj Bhasa* texts and poetry of *Biharinadasa*, it is "nonmaterial" and can be compared to the concept of "eternal" as it occurs in the *Laghubhagavatāmṛta*. Kṛṣṇa's Vṛndāvana (like *Vaikuṇṭha* of Viṣṇu) is untouched by creation; it is not a material creation but is in time and space, in a symbolic sense.[41] The concept of *ānanda* (bliss), where Kṛṣṇa danced with the *gopīs*, is echoed in the *Bhāgavad Purāṇa* (vi.4.48). A similar idea is expressed in the *Bhāgavata*. To quote B.N.K.Sharma, "In me whose attributes are infinite both individually and collectively and constitute my essence." What is blissful is the infinite and as expressed in the *Chāndogya Upaniṣad* (vii.23) "what is infinite is blissful. There is no lasting bliss in what is limited."[42] The *ānanda* or bliss in Dualist philosophy arises from a constant dependence of the *jeeva* on *brahman* and *ānanda* of *jeeva* is different from *ānanda* of *brahman*.[43]

RELIC TO PORTRAIT

In the eternal state of *ānanda*, the body of the Guru is eternal as well. However, there is yet another aspect that can be questioned. If the Guru lived in the *vṛndāvana*, where was the need for "decorating" the nonfigural *vṛndāvana* with facial features and anointing it with sacred materials. Ritual worship of a *vṛndāvana* is similar to the honors paid to a God in a Hindu temple with incense, flowers, and lights, *namaskāras* or ritualized reverence, *japa*, music, and Vedic chants. The bathing consists of *paṇcāmṛta* (mixture of water, milk, honey, fruits, and butter) that is distributed as blessed food or *prasāda*; while on festive occasions, processions of the portable image of God Kṛṣṇa is taken around the premises of the *maṭha*. During ritual worship, the *vṛndāvana* is decorated with Vaiṣṇavite symbols: *śaṅkha* (conch), *cakra* (wheel), *gadā* (club), *padma* (lotus),[44] and *nama* (vertical line on the forehead).[45] It is articulated with eyes and often (particularly Thursdays—the day of the guru) a silver plate engraved with bodily features of the Guru is physically affixed to the stone *vṛndāvana*. A saffron cloth, similar to that worn by a *sanyāsi*, is draped over it, and it appears like a generic portrait of the Guru.

Portraiture has largely been defined as a close resemblance of the physical characteristics of an individual to those of his or her image; although in Indian art, resemblance to outward form was rare, and not consciously cultivated, and the aim of portraiture is to capture an inner essence of the person. As long as the image could be recognized as representing an individual it served the purpose for which it was created; there was no need to create a resemblance to outward appearance and it may be termed as a generic portrait.[46]

Regarding portraits of ascetics and Gurus, those of Nammalvars in temple shrines existed in South India, such as those in Mẹlkote in 1350 CE. Rāmānujācarya was deified in the Varadarajaswamy temple within fifty-five years of his death, which is attested by a record of Kulottunga II, 1191 CE. There is also a shrine dedicated to Rāmānujācārya at Govindarajaperumal temple in Tirūpati.[47] It is said that he caused his own image in the form of an idol and consecrated it in the Yadugiri Yatiraja *matha* in Melkote.[48] His body is in the fifth *prākāra* (circumambulatory path) of the temple of Ranganāthaswāmī temple in Śrirangam. His body is said to be still there and is coated every year with camphor and *kumkum*, as well as herbs. Thus the portrait traditions were constantly recreated in the face of changing society.

The transformation of the non-figural *vṛndāvana* into a portrait made the image more impressive, and it was considered as alive. However, the *vṛndāvana* comes to life not merely by way of outward "decorations" or worship but through ritual of *prāṇa pratishthāpana* (suffusion of the life giving breath into the *vṛndāvana*). After the body is placed within the pit, and a memorial installed, the ritual takes place (see p. 101). There is yet another belief about life after death. In Dvaita philosophy, there is no absolute death for the individual soul or *jeeva*, particularly for the ascetic. The deceased body is said to possess an element of *jeeva* (*amsa of jeeva*). The *jeeva* is symbolized by Vāyu, whose metal image is placed above the *vṛndāvana*. Vāyu is the lord of Breath/Wind and is also called Prāṇa Devaru, God of life-breath (figure 4.10).

Prāṇa is life energy (life force) and is both a physical and psychological force. In the *Taittiriya Upaniṣad* (11. 1–6), it is that which circulates. It is believed that there are five *prāṇas*, which characterize the wind channels of the body. These are *prāṇa* that travels along the channel from the top of the head till the navel; *apāna* that travels from base of spine to the navel;

samāna is where the two breaths meet; and it is distributed by *vyāna* which is conveyed by *udāna* as *tejas* (energy) throughout the body. The way this should relate to one's life as it does for an ascetic is described as follows: an ascetic aims at freedom from subjection to physical forces, including control over *prāṇas*, celibacy for attainment of a higher power or *prāṇa-śakti*, a radiance and endurance.[49] According to Banerjea, *prāṇa* is a psychological force; it is a provider of enthusiasm, and courage. The force has to be purified by the reconciliation of dichotomies (as likes and dislikes, *rāga*, *dvesha*).[50] Through purification and identification of one's *anthakarana* (inner instrument) and detachment, one can elevate *prāṇa* so that one can go beyond likes and dislikes. In Dvaita philosophy, *prana* is a conscious force, a discipline of the mind, equanimity, and even awakened consciousness.[51]

In Hindu mythology, *prāṇa* is linked to the Vedic God, Vāyu. It is said that God Nārāyana in *tretayuga* appeared as Vāyu, devotee of Rāma (also called Hanuman in North India and Hanumantha in Karnataka); in *dvāparayuga* Nārāyana manifested himself as Bhimasena and became the recipient of Kṛṣṇa's grace and in *kaliyuga* took the *avatara* of Madhvācārya who became a great scholar like Vedavyāsa.[52] In addition, Vāyu is also a personification of *tattvajñāna* (true knowledge).

VṚNDĀVANA AND THE BHAKTI MOVEMENT

There is another meaning of *vṛndāvana* that can be related to the concept and religious movement of *bhakti*. Was it a substantiation of an attitude/belief/devotion toward the Guru, particularly during a period when the *bhakti* movement (devotional movement) was popular in medieval India? *Bhakti* has been defined in a variety of ways: it is love toward God, religious devotion, surrender, *brahmānubhava*, experiencing communion with God, without finding any fault in him by the *śiṣya* (disciple). This may include *sakhya* or friendliness or, *dāsya* or service type of love, *madhurya* or sweet. The *bhakti* movement percolated from North to South India to the doctrines of the Śaiva Nayanmars and Vaiṣṇava Ālvār saints of eighth century CE.[53]

The *bhakti*-infused popular Hinduism was incorporated by the Vedānta Gurus, and particularly by the schools of Vaiṣṇava *bhakti* by Rāmānujācārya, and Madhvācārya who reinterpreted the Vedic concepts and praised epic heroes such as Rāma and Kṛṣṇa. They incorporated the devotional contents thereby achieving a new doctrinal synthesis that included devotion. But the *bhakti* movement in the South, also hardened the tenets and principles, and became more conservative. There developed a sharper distinction between the philosophical doctrines of Ādi Śankarācārya, Rāmānujācārya (as well as Madhvācārya). Śaṅkarācārya gave more importance to *jñāna* and *śraddhās* (knowledge and sincerity), which precedes *bhakti*. According to him *bhakti* is concerned with *saguṇa brahman* and is directed toward a personal object, and a personal attachment to Gods. The Vaiṣṇava philosophers accused him of having cut at the root of *bhaktivāda*, the doctrine of love and faith, arguing that if there is only one universal spirit, there is no scope for love or devotion which postulates two separate entities—the lover and the beloved.

Rāmānujācārya placed *bhakti* on a firm philosophical basis by his doctrine of Viśiṣṭādvaita *vāda* and united various communities through ritual, and *tirtha yātrā* (pilgrimage). His followers were divided into Vadagalai and Tengalai subtraditions, with their respective affinities with Sanskritic *Vedas* and Tamil *Prabandhas*, advocating surrender or *prapatti* thereby broadening the theories of *bhakti* to include *mokṣa*. But the Gurus of Dvaita order, particularly Vyāsarāya, elaborated the concept of *bhakti*. Apart from defining it as a personal, subjective, and emotional devotion and surrender (and *tirtha yātrā* or pilgrimage), he included action, and from yoga, the perfection of tasks. He incorporated the idea of constant meditation, as well as *japa*, *vrata*, *upavāsa* during *ekādasi*, *sravana* or listening to attributes of God, and *smarana* (remembering God). Such a synthesis of various shades of *bhakti* and its interpretations, with its broad understanding, appealed to the *haridāsas* (servants of God). The *haridāsa* movement in the Deccan, particularly Karnataka, propagated devotion through the *kīrtanas* (songs) of the poets and saints of the Dvaita *ācāryas* and Gurus that indirectly led to the popularization of the cult of Gurus.

One of the early Gurus who inaugurated the *haridāsa* movement in Karnataka was Narahari *Tīrtha* in the fourteenth century CE. Later ascetic Gurus such as Pādarāja *Tīrtha* (disciple of Vyāsarāya) and his two disciples Purandara Dāsa Kanaka Dāsa popularized the *bhakti* movement. Other Gurus followed them, including Vādirāja *Tīrtha*, Rāghvendra Swāmi, Vijaya Dāsa, Gopal Dāsa, Jagannatha Dāsa, Pranesh Dāsa, and Mohan Dāsa. The movement can be distinguished into two—the Vyāsa Kuta and the Dāsa Kuta—on the basis of musical compositions and content. The Vyāsa Kuta musical compositions were devoted to Vyāsarāya and it emphasized Vedic knowledge, the *Upaniṣads*, *Darśanas*, metaphysics, and use of Sanskrit, while the Dāsa Kuta saints propagated through the message of Dvaita philosophy in Kannada. In the songs composed by Narahari *Tīrtha*, *bhakti* is directed toward Viṣṇu which can be seen in the small metal image of the God above the *vṛndāvana*.

Regarding the relation between the *vṛndāvana* (and Dvaita *maṭha*) to the *bhakti* movement, it may be mentioned that it was Narahari *Tīrtha* in 1324 CE who constructed the first *vṛndāvana* of his Guru, Padmanabha *Tīrtha*, 1317–1324 CE at Anegondi. He was also the earliest saint who began the Dāsa Kuta *bhakti* musical tradition in Karnataka. Does this mean that the *vṛndāvana* was a substantiation of *bhakti*? Another question arises, whether the *vṛndāvana* reinvented the meaning of Guru *bhakti*. Guru *bhakti*, which can also be called Guru *bhava* (feeling), meant an unshakable faith in the words and teachings of the Guru: The Guru *śiṣya* (*devotee/student*) relationship, particularly the idea that the "*sisya* belives that the Guru knows what kind of change is required and that he can bring it about," while the Guru believes "that the disciple can be transformed."[54] The presence of the Guru and the link between the material and immaterial was ennobled in the chants on the Gurus, such as the Dvādasa *stotra*, Śri Rāghvendra Swāmi *stotra*, and others. These Guru *stotras* describe the powers of both the Guru and the *vṛndāvana* as one which can provide all material and spiritual benefits, attain liberation, and shower divine grace upon the devotee.[55] It may be added that the interaction between *bhakti* and the Dvaita Guru (past and present) led to an altered and expanded meaning that was inclusive of all layers of society.

The redefined concept of Guru *bhakti* was also partly due to the narrative biography and miracle stories that the Guru is said to have performed. Madhvācārya is said to have performed impossible feats, such as moving the gigantic boulder (Bhiman Kallu), and affected the sprouting of seeds, all of which is narrated in the *Madhvavijaya*. Vādirāja *Tīrtha* is said to have cured a leper, made the chariot of the God move by the power of his spiritual music and transformed Jain images into Vaiṣṇava images.[56] Rāghavendra Swāmi is said to have healed the sick, brought a child back to life, restored the vision to the blind, turned nonvegetarian food to fruits, revived a boy from snake bite, revived a boy who had drowned, and even made dead wood sprout. Even Thomas Munroe, a British Collector from Bellary, who visited Mantralaya to check about the land grant and introduction of the concept of "acre" is said to have a vision of the Swāmi and talked to him in person, although the latter had already committed *jeevan samādhi*.[57]

Stories about their perceptions of sacred immanence and the icon being "attentive and responsive" have been narrated about Mantralaya and other pilgrimage sites of the Gurus. There were implications of the icon of the Guru both in Dvaita *maṭhas*, Vaisnavism as well as in the religious life of the people. The *vṛndāvana* had transformed devotional practices within Vaisnavism which intensified *bhakti* toward the Guru within the institution/relic or icon. This was also possible due to the architectural space provided by the *matha* around the icon that led to a transformed sacred space for the community to gather to chant *bhakti* music. It reinforced the idea of constant faith on God, the living Guru and the philosophy of the founder Guru. It was no more a mere stone "box," an aberration, but the eternal form of Viṣṇu.

The non-figural form can be related to the nature of interchangeableness between the *nijarūpa* (true form) and *nityarūpa* (eternal form). The figural form (of the Guru, while living) is true form as in reality. It is a manifestation of eternal form (beyond form), which is non-figural (the *vṛndāvana* as well as the *sālagrāma*).[58] Concepts that were linked to Śiva and Viṣṇu were attached to that of the Guru. It can be perceived as the *vṛndāvana* being the *nityarūpa* and after worship, the portrait as the *nijarūpa*, and there does not appear to be any dynamic tension between the two as the theory of *avatāra* had solved the conflict even for the Guru. The *vrndavana* as a symbol was more powerful than (figural) portrait.

The scene of this duality is seen as divine play of *prakata* (manifest) and *aprakata* (unmanifest). In the texts, Krishna eternally performs his *lila* through *prakatas* (appearances) and sometimes through one appearance such as his birth in this life, similar to that of the Guru: Kṛṣṇa's *līla*, a play of life and death, of concealment and appearance. Just as the transcendent entity of Kṛṣṇa's *vṛndāvana* becomes a sacred, blissful, mystical space, the *vṛndāvana* of the Guru is symbolic of divine *ānanda* of the Guru.

NOTES

1. Williams, Monier. *Sanskrit-English Dictionary*. New Delhi: Munshiram Manoharlal, 2002, p. 1011.
2. See ch. 4, p. 117, endnotes 128, 129.

3. Olivelle, Patrick. *Vasudevsrama Yatidharmaprakasa: A Treatise on World Renunciation*. Publications of the de Nobili Research Library. Vienna: Gerold & Co. in Komm: Delhi: Motilal Banarsidass, 1976–77.

4. The mythological story in the *Padma Purāṇa* is part of the narrative of Mayasiva. *Padma Purāṇa*. Ed. Vishvanath Narayan Mandalika. Poona: Anandashram,1894.

5. Mathura is a sacred pilgrimage site near Delhi in North India.

6. The term *vṛndāvana* is spelt with a small "v" and italicized with diacritical marks denoting the tomb/memorial of the Guru, But words that denote the geographical and metaphysical site is in capital letters, but not italicized -Vṛndāvana; wife of Jalandhara is spelt Vṛndā, as a plant it is Tulsi Vṛndāvana, in order to distinguish the multiple usage of the term.

7. Vṛndā is said to have cursed Viṣṇu who was turned into a *sālagrama*, the aniconic form of Viṣṇu, found in the rivers, Narmada and Gandaki.

8. While the memorials of Saivite Gurus are planted with the plant of a *bilva*, those of Vaisnavite Gurus have a Tulsi plant.

9. It is also believed that Tulsi leaves have an antifertility and ascetic property.

10. The Dvaita monastery was a Vaisnavite one that considered Viṣṇu to be the highest God and Kṛṣṇa was the most important *avatāra* of Viṣṇu. Madhvācārya had found the image of Kṛṣṇa in the ship sailing in the sea. See pp. 66, 151.

11. Recent excavations have proved that Kṛṣṇa was a historical personality and that his deification process occurred gradually. Rao, S.R. *The Lost City of Dvaraka*. Delhi: Aditya Prakashan, 1999.

12. Rādhārani once arranged for Kṛṣṇa and Vṛndā to sit together on the same throne during their pastimes in the forest. At that time Rādhārani arranged for the performance of the wedding ceremony of Kṛṣṇa and Vṛnda.

13. In the *Surasagara* as well, the *vana* is also the scene of the meeting of Rādhā and Kṛṣṇa. Another text, *Vṛndāvana Sata Līla* by Dhruvadāsa (1629), consists 116 verses in praise of Vṛndāvana where the eternal sport of Rādhā and Kṛṣṇa took place. Dhruvadasa. Vrndavana Sata Lila in *Bayalisa Lila*. Vrndavana. 1971. V. 115. (publisher not known).

14. Corcoran, Maura. *Vrndavana in Vaisnava Literature: History, Mythology, Symbolism. New Reconstructing Indian History and Culture*. No. 6. Delhi: DKPW, 1995, p. 92.

15. Using literary evidences, oral traditions, and narratives with the materially grounded phenomena of built environment, archaeology and antiquities, S.R. Rao proves the existence of Kṛṣṇa as a human being. Rao, S.R. *The Lost City of Dvaraka*. Delhi: Aditya Prakashan. 1999.

16. Rao. *The Lost City of Dvaraka*, p. 17.

17. I use Marcuo's analysis of Vṛndāvan as mythological, symbolic and geographical site although they overlap textually, and I attempt to find out whether they provide an understanding for the interpretation of Guru *vṛndāvana*.

18. Corcoran, *Vrndavana in Vaisnava Literature*, p. 114.

19. Bryant, Edwin F. *Krishna: A Sourcebook*. Oxford University Press: Oxford, 2007, pp. 123–40.

20. *Harivamsa*. Edited by Parashuram Lakshman Vaidya, Poona: Bhardarkar Oriental Research Institute. 1969–71, 53.30.

21. *Visnu Purana*. Edited by Jivananda Vidyasagara. Calcutta: Saraswati Press. 1882. The *Viṣṇu Purāṇa* describes the Vṛndāvana with cattle (V. 6.29-30), grass (V.6.30) but gives importance to the divinity of Kṛṣṇa more than the *Harivamsa* (11.8.23). Corcoran, *Vrndavana in Vaisnava Literature*, 25.

22. Corcoran, *Vrndavana in Vaisnava Literature*, p. 108. Also see *Brahma Samhita*. Commentary by Jiva Goswami. Edited by A. Avalon. Calcutta, 1928, pp. v. 6.

23. Corcoran. *Reconstructing Indian History and Culture*. No. 6. Vrndaban: Vrndavan Research Institute, Delhi: DKPW, 1995, pp. 71, 103.

24. The seventh petal of the outer lotus is said to be Bakulavana while the eighth petal is Talavana where the demon Dhenuka was killed by Kṛṣṇa. Corcoran. *Vrndavana in Vaisnava Literature*. Reference in footnote no. 74, 104, 106.

25. Corcoran, *Vrndavana in Vaisnava Literature*, pp. 101-115. Nineteen *vyūhas* are emanations in human personalities. The four *vyūhas* also stand for four concepts, individual consciousness, intellect, mind, and ego.

26. In the Gauḍīya Theology, *Laghubhāgavatāmrta*, it is described as surrounding Mathura and it designates the whole area as Mathura-*mandala*. Here we find an attempt to depict the vṛndāvana symbolically.

27. *Padma Purāṇa* (4.69.70). Corcoran. *Vrndavana in Vaisnava Literature*, 1995, 105. 104.

28. Corcoran. Śridāma at the western door, Vasudāma at the northern, Sudāma at the eastern and Kinkiṇi at the southern. *Vrndavana in Vaisnava Literature*, p.105, reference number 80. Here we find a subordination of Viṣṇu—as doorkeepers—to Kṛṣṇa's Vṛndāvan.

29. One can find a similarity between the *Padma Purāṇa* and later Braja Bhasa text *Brajabhaktavilasa* by Narayana Bhatta, 1951, Such as the seven successive enclosures or *āvaranas,* the third *āvarana* consisting of the four *vyūhas*: Vāsudeva, Sankarṣṇa, Pradyumna and Aniruddha. In addition are the eight rows of sixteen-petaled lotus, twelve *vanas* and scenes of *līlas* with the *vṛndāvana līla* as the highest *līla* due to the presence of Kṛṣṇa. In the Braj Bhasa text, the *Radha Vallabha* text, the *vana* is known as *vṛndāvana yogapīṭha* and it is placed it the same category as *yogapīṭha* of *gadādhara*.

30. The *vṛndāvana* of Vidyānidhi *Tīrtha* (figure 4.2) displays the lotus petals, while that of Yogindra *Tīrtha* depicts images of deities on the lotus petals that run all around the *vṛndāvana* above (figure 4.8).

31. This information was gathered from discussions with Suvedyendra *Tīrtha*, former head of Rāghvendra Swāmi *maṭha*, Mantralaya.

32. Corcoran. *Vrndavana in Vaisnava Literature*, 137.

33. There is no suggestion of a circular shape in the *Padma Purāṇa.* 4.69. 18.

34. *Varāha Purāṇa.* Ed. Hrsikesh Sastri. Calcutta: 1893, 152.7; 153.45.

35. Viṣṇu is symbolic of an expansive, all pervading essence, who can manifest himself in ten incarnations, Kṛṣṇa being one of them.

36. However the *aidkuas* (burial mounds) were also square like the square Vṛndāvana described in the *Purāṇas.* The square *aidukas* were used by *Daivyah Praha* or gods, while the round ones were said to be used by *asuras* or demons. See Shah, Priyabala. "Aiduka." *Journal of the Oriental Institute.* Vol. 1. 1952, p. 279. For the story of Madhvācārya procuring the image of Kṛṣṇa in a miraculous way, see Padmanabhacharya, C.M., *Life and Teachings of Sri Madhvachariar.* Bombay: C.A. Pattabiraman and C.A. P. Vittal. 1983, pp. 76–78.

37. The Jain texts allude to the site near Mathura. This is 150 years before the rediscovery of the Vṛndāvana as described by Vallabha or the Gauḍīya Gosvāmīs. Corcoran, *Vrndavana in Vaisnava Literature*, reference number 133, p. 114.

38. Corcoran. *Vrndavana in Vaisnava Literature*, reference number 13, p. 114.

39. Growse, F.S. *Mathura: A District Memoir.* Roorkee: Thomason Civil Engineering College Press, 1883, p. 9.

40. Whether *vṛndāvana* was the original "name" given to the memorial or whether it was renamed as such after the rediscovery of the site near Mathura, is not known at this juncture.

41. In the *Vṛndāvan Śata Līla* Dhruvadasa. In *Bayalisa Lila.* Vrndavana. 1971. V. 115. (publisher not known) (116 verses), which praises the Vṛndāvan, and the *Brihad Dharma Purāṇa.* Trans. English and Sanskrit. Syama Charan Banerji. Lucknow: Hathi Trust. 1915. Translation of Sanskrit *Vāmana Purāṇa.* 3 Vols. By Venkatacharya, Sankeeghattam, Mysore: Sri Jayacahmrajendra Book Series. Sri Sharada Electric Press. 1946.

The term *vṛndāvana* occurs in the sixteenth century text, *Brihad Vāmana Purāṇa.* See Rao, V.D.N. *Essence of Pradhana Tirthas.* New Delhi: Ministry of Commerce, pp 30-31. The *Purāṇa* is not traceable, in both later sixteenth-century and seventeenth-century texts, the site is described in superlatives. The *Laghu Bhagavatamrta* describes Kṛṣṇa's pastimes as manifest and unmanifest, eternally and simultaneously taking place somewhere in the world. A further interpretation of the concept was by Rupa Goswami who describes Kṛṣṇa's divine form as connotations of continuous state of being and self-manifestation and Kṛṣṇa as greater than Viṣṇu, even as *mahā vaikuṇtha nāyaka. Laghu Bhagavatamrta.* Rupa Goswami. Hindi Translation by B. P. Misra. 1902; Bombay: Venkatesvara Press, 2014.

42. Sharma B.N.Krishnamurti. *Madhva's Teaching in his own Words.* Edited by K. M. Munshi, RR. Diwakar. Bharatiya Vidya Bhavan. Bombay. 1961, p. 137.

43. In *dhyāna* one sees only the reflection of the *brahman* in the *citta* (consciousness). The term used is *Bimba-pratibimba-bhava* or the relation of "original and reflection"—which is the nearest to this experience. Since we have a

false sense of independence (which is rooted in our *jeeva*), we have a bondage to *saṃsāra*. Thus meditation on the *bimba* aspect of the lord's various aspects has been considered by Madhvācārya to be the essential condition for mystic communion (*aparoksha jñāna*). The devotee must turn in and see this as *pratibimba* (reflected image). Sharma. *Madhva's Teaching in His Own Words*, pp. 137–140.

44. Followers of Madhvācārya apply the mark on the forehead (*nama*) composed It is composed of two white perpendicular lines made with *gopīcandana*, a type of earth obtained on the west coast of India, and a dark line in the middle with a spot in the center. The two white lines are joined by a crossline on the bridge of the nose.

45. Such a tradition of worship most probably began only in the seventeenth century after the demise of Guru Rāghavendra Swāmi in Mantralaya.

46. Rao, Nalini. An Analysis of Political Power through Royal Iconography. *Nidan. International Journal for Indian Studies* 4.1 (July 2019): 157–180.

47. Ranganathan, C., Krishnan, S. and Iyengar, Narayana. *Bhagavad Sri Ramauja's Contribution to Four Swayamvyakta Kshetras-Kanchipuram, Srirangam, Tirupati & Melkote*. Bhagavad Academy of Sanskrit Research. Melkote: Academyof Sanskrit Research. 2015, pp. 90–91.

48. Ranganathan, *Bhagavad Sri Ramauja's Contribution*, 90–91.

49. Banerji, Debashish. *Seven Quartets of Becoming: A Transformational Yoga Psychology Based on the Diaries of Sri Aurobindo*. Los Angeles: Nalanda International and New Delhi: DKPW, 2012, pp. 250–255.

50. Banerji, Debashish. *Seven Quartets of Becoming: A Transformational Yoga Psychology*, pp. 59–64.

51. Sharma. *Philosophy of Sri Madhvacarya*.

52. Madhvācārya is believed to be an *avatāra* of Hanuman and Bhimasena, both known for their fearlessness.

53. Narayanan, M. G. S. and Veluthat, Kesavan. Bhakti Movement in South India. In *The Feudal Order: State, Society and Ideology in Early Medieval India*, Ed. Jha, D.N. New Delhi: Manohar Publishers, 2000, pp. 390–392.

54. Raina, M. K. Guru-Shishya Relationship in Indian Culture: The Possibility of a Creative Resilient Framework. *Psychology and Developing Societies*. 14, 1 (2002). Sage Publications. New Delhi, p. 189.

55. The powers of the Gurus, such as those of the Ālvārs, Śankarācārya, Madhvācārya, Vādirāja and others have been praised. The festival of *Guru Purnima* which is celebrated even today speaks eloquently about the sacred status of the guru and his relationship with his devotees.

56. Havanur, Shrinivas, Havanur, N. Anjana. *Shri Vadiraja Tirtha of Sode Matha*. Havanur: Tara Prakashana & Shri Vadiraja Mrttika Vrndavana, 2003, pp. 20–32.

57. According to an account in the "Madras District Gazetteers," Vol. 1, ch 15, p. 213, Sir Thomas Monroe, then a British Collector of Bellary, was sent to the village of Mantralaya to review the grant issued by the Nawab of Adoni and

to undertake the resumption of the village under British government. When he arrived there, the acting Guru was on a tour to Nanjangud.

However, Munroe was told that that Mantralaya was a gift given by Masood Khan to the saint and hence it belonged to him. Eager to visit the Guru, Monroe entered the *vṛndāvana*. Those around him, heard him conversing in English with someone inside but could not see that person. Then the collector is said to have asked of the people, "Is this the saint you have so extolled?" On reaching Bellary, Monroe recommended to the Governor of Madras Presidency that the status quo on the issue of Mantralaya be maintained, as he was convinced that it was the legal property of the Mantralaya *pīṭha*. Monroe was directed to assume charge as Governor as the then Governor left for England due to personal reasons. The first thing that Monroe, did was to endorse his approval on the note made by himself on Mantralaya. His body was buried near Mantralaya. The Superintendent of Madras Printing Press recorded this in the Gazetteer in the year 1861. An account in the "*Madras District Gazetteers*," Vol. 1, ch 15, 1861, p. 213.

58. *Sālagrāmas* have been known to be round black stones as well as shells of fossils. Depending on the form of the shell, they have been classified and named. They symbolize the aniconic form of Lord Viṣṇu and a garland of *sālagrāmas* decorate the image of Viṣṇu in a Hindu temple.

Chapter 6

Conclusion

This chapter has two purposes, first to acknowledge some of the limitations in my historical analysis and second to recapitulate and reorganize the major arguments in the book.

There are limits on what can be accomplished in a book. The topic is long and complex, and my analysis has been selective. Given the scanty yet multiple sources, and a host of varied interpretations, I have confined the scope of the book exclusively to Hindu *maṭhas* (monasteries) and particularly to those in the state of Karnataka in South India. Although references have been made to artifacts and monasteries in North and Central India, Andhra Pradesh, and Tamil Nadu, I find that a detailed survey of *maṭhas* is essential to explain their variations in organization, economic and political circumstances, and other factors.

The study is more in the nature of a historical narrative than theoretical. I have not analyzed the Guru solely from the perspective of power or authority, neither have I concluded that the icon was entirely a product of the institutionalization of the Guru. More research is essential for a more holistic analysis of such a complex religious organization, particularly from a sociological point of view.

I have argued that in South India, the Hindu monastery was an institution of the living Guru while the Dualist monastic order can be considered an institution of the living as well as the past (deceased) Guru(s) in the form of a *vṛndāvana*. The leadership of the Guru was a key element for the development of the monastery; his "constructed" and intangible status was concretized in the icon, and his sacred presence felt through the relic. The "institution, icon, and relic" played a central role in the local, regional community as well as the religious life of the people. The nature and role of the *maṭha* was shaped by both internal and external factors: the charisma of the Guru and the sociohistorical changes. The "sacred" leadership of the Guru, defined by his learning and wisdom was embedded in the *Vedas* and *Upaniṣads*. The Guru was a realized soul; he was an adviser to the king and the layman, as well to scholar and soldier. The importance attributed to the values of asceticism, and teaching by the Guru, led to their widespread practice within the *āśrama* system as well as in Hindu, Buddhist, and Jain monastic systems. It may be added that the *maṭha* provided an institutionalized base for asceticism and teaching.

During the early medieval period the Guru could unite various groups through the force of religion, particularly Saivism. After the decline of Buddhist monasteries, Hindu *maṭhas* in Central India, Tamil Nadu, and Karnataka began to play a role with the purpose of keeping alive religious ideas and practices. They fulfilled the social needs of teaching, lodging, boarding, and worship. The ascetic pontiff was a dynamic interpreter of the monastic and religious traditions. The sources of his legitimacy were embedded within the traditional concept of not only asceticism but also in the lineage of Gurus. Historical changes, such as the rise of militant kings, trade and urbanism, royal patronage, and the expansion of temples were conducive to the rise of the Guru. The Guru was an organizer, fundraiser, an adviser to the king, and caretaker of the temple. Equipped with the power of scriptural knowledge, yoga, and renunciation, his word was final. By the twelfth to thirteenth century CE the role and function of *maṭhas* far exceeded those of contemporary formal education systems with multiple functions. The dynamism of the Guru led the monastic institution to develop from a semi-structured organization to a multifaceted dynamic and cohesive order.

The Saivite and Vaisnavite monasteries witnessed a complementary development comparable to another religious institution—the Hindu temple. While worship of gods was the focus in the temple, the monastery, grew to be a full-fledged independent philosophical institution between twelfth and fifteenth centuries. The Gurus of the three major Vedānta monasteries of Advaita, Viśiṣṭādvaita, and Dvaita, while continuing some of the functions of earlier monasteries, took upon themselves the task of writing commentaries on the *Upaniṣads*. Their ideologies played a key role in the status and authority of the Guru in the community.

During the late medieval period, Vedānta, as well as the Liṅgāyat *maṭhas*, underwent significant institutional changes. The basis for their development was the organizational structure that was initiated by the Guru. In an Advaita *maṭha*, the Guru was known as a 'world Guru' whose edifice was constructed on an ethical foundation, based on norms of *dharma*, celibacy, yoga, and *śāstras* (scriptures). These and other socio-religious regulations within the Vedānta and Liṅgāyat monasteries, and the power of exposition of philosophical concepts, added to the prestige of the Guru and the *maṭha*. A large body of disciples to uphold the honor of the *maṭha* provided integrity within the institution.

The growth of monasteries into full-fledged independent seminal institutions between the twelfth and fifteenth centuries CE was also due to royal patronage. Vedānta and Viraśaiva *maṭhas* held lands, and with a large number of disciples and followers, they began to resemble estates of kings, and developed into a *saṃsthāna* (kingdom with its own governance). The administration consisted of a large personnel, officers, superintendents, managers, chiefs as well as revenue collectors, and accountants. The spread of *maṭhas* was phenomenal, and branches were established in various regions. The heads were influential in royal courts; they were honored by kings that led to a phenomenal increase of royal patronage. Gurus were consulted in socioreligious issues and their judgment was regarded as final. In turn, royal grants and titles led to prestige of kings, while *maṭhas* constituted part of a network system. They became formidable institutions, and functioned as part of a socioreligious network system.

The multiple functions of Vedānta *maṭhas* such as teaching, feeding, and lodging, necessitated a large precinct with separate yet interconnected buildings, with a place for the Guru and God. The *maṭha* did not require trained architects for its buildings, and could be built of brick and mortar unlike a temple. But it had parallels with a Hindu temple as well, such as consisting of an object of worship, a raised altar (in the semblance of a sanctum sanctorum), an entrance, courtyard, and functional precincts within a courtyard and a functional plan. *Maṭha* architecture was flexible and not governed by rules of *Śilpaśāstras* or any system of measurements or proportion. Being an institution of an ascetic, it avoided visual imagery except for some minor symbolic motifs.

The extended sphere of influence of Vedānta and Liṅgāyat *maṭhas* effected religious and social changes. Cohesive groups came to be formed, which was also the result of ritual practices and elements of identity. The differences in body marks, worship of gods, and philosophical theories provided sustenance for traditional communities. It was not a static but a dynamic, flexible, and popular institution. It was the Guru within the *maṭha* sustained the growth of intellectual thought, ascetic, and teaching traditions in South India.

The status and sacredness of the living Guru in medieval South India ultimately crystallized into an anomaly, the veneration of the icon of the Guru with his whole-body relics. The non-anthropomorphic form of the *vṛndāvana* was similar to the Buddhist *stūpa* and the *liṅga*. Both the *stupa* and the *vṛndāvana* have parallels in the worship of the relics, and are commemorative monuments. Both are part of the monastic precinct. The key difference between the *vṛndāvana* and other memorials lies in the burial of the whole mummified body of the ascetic Guru. There was nothing objectionable about the worship of whole-body relics in Hinduism nor about its display, and it did not violate either the letter or the spirit of Hindu teachings. Neither do the followers of Advaita Vedānta openly decry the worship of relics. It cannot be denied that one of the influences was the Buddhist practice and worship of the *stūpa*. Epigraphical and archaeological evidences prove that there was an overall underlying tradition of worshipping memorials and relics in Hinduism and Buddhism.

The practice of embalming and deposition of relics was not new. The construction of memorials for ascetics was an ancient practice. One can definitely discern a useful pattern of similarity in form between the death markers, and whether the influence was from a *stūpa* or *caitya*, *aiduka*, or *liṅga* or that of Nath Yogis; they were all aniconic (non-figural) and it was important that they remained as such. The construction of *aidukas*, *liṅgas*, and *thades* and deposition of the body in pits in Nath yoga tradition reveals the widespread practices of burial traditions that the *vṛndāvana* substantiated. There were shared ideas and practices about burials among groups. A multiplicity of factors suggests a deliberate amalgamation of various traditions into the iconography of the *vṛndāvana*. The main support probably comes from the presence of whole-body relics which suggests multiple forces at work.

GURU AND GOD

A *vṛndāvana* is different from the place where merely remnants of the mortal body are kept and worshipped. It is not like the Buddhist *stūpa* or the *aiduka*. Viraśaivas have a similar system of burial of the dead, but their structure is not considered a *vṛndāvana*. Thus, in this book, the

Figure 6.1 Guru in a *Maṭha*.

problematic nature and symbolism of the *vṛndāvana* has been investigated from an ontological, metaphysical perspective that has led to its being considered sacred. This is indeed related to the Guru and his status of a God.

On every *vṛndāvana*, within the "sanctum" is a small metal image of a Vaiṣṇavite god, such as Kṛṣṇa (or Rāma or Narasiṃha) and worship is similar to the honors paid to a God in a Hindu temple. Attributions of power and life to the relic as presence of the Guru were done in many ways: through *prāṇapratiṣṭhā* or infusion of life force, *mantras*, and significant articulations of facial features. Such a transformation of the *vṛndāvana* into a living presence was made familiar with ritual dressing. It is now transformed into an object of intense desire, efficacy, and sacredness, acting as a renewal of devotion to the cultic personality of the past Guru.

The similarity of ritual worship of a *vṛndāvana* and the God probably meant that the Guru in a *maṭha* was equal in status and sacredness to that of God. Madhvācārya was said to be an *avatāra* of Hanuman and Bhima.

Prominent Dvaita Gurus were linked to the divine lineage of gods. The life of the Guru was a biography of knowledge, renunciation, and miracles (figure 6.1). But the Dvaita *maṭhas* did not adhere to the Advaita philosophy (of Ādi Śaṅkarācārya) of *aham brahmāsmi* (I am *brahman*) and took care to negate that by placing an image of a God above the *vṛndāvana* and making sure that there were no stone sculptures of the Guru in a *maṭha* unlike that of a God. Furthermore, in terms of ritual, there were (and still are) forms of worship that is offered to a *vṛndāvana* and not to a God, such as dressing of the image with a saffron cloth. In addition, since the Guru is an ascetic, the two ingredients of worship, namely turmeric and *kumkum* are avoided. In addition, the annual death anniversary of the past Guru is celebrated, which is not the case for a God. The Guru in a Dvaita *maṭha* is similar to a God but is not equivalent to a God.

The *vṛndāvana* was a reinvention and reinterpretation that could be understood from various perspectives symbolized by the *vṛndāvana*. The Guru was probably conceived as "seen" as he existed in bodily form, as a relic. The non-anthropomorphic form of the icon revealed the ascetic nature of the Guru and it meant that he was merely "invisible." This was consistent with the belief stated in texts, that the body and life of the Guru is eternal. He could be brought back to life through ritual (like the Gods). The rubric of the non-figural form was linked to beyond form, potential form, capable of innumerable forms, and self-manifested form. The Guru was more than a specific Guru but also one in the abstract: a principle, and a source of individual potency. By establishing the icon, the monks of the Dvaita *maṭha* had the power to transform dead organic matter into a sacred object, similar to the *līla* of manifestation and non-manifestation of Kṛṣṇa, eternally and simultaneously taking place somewhere in the world. The *vṛndāvana* reflects this analogy by the deposition of non-figural aniconic symbols of Viṣṇu, the *śālagrāmas* in the icon, which echoes conceptually in the textual description of Kṛṣṇa as the manifest and unmanifest, occupying both terrestrial and celestial space.

Various meanings stemming from those attributed to Gods can be applied to the symbolism of the *vrndavana*. It is the *nityarūpa* (eternal form) of the Guru; after worship, the "portrait" with facial features is the *nijarūpa* (true form) and there does not appear to be any dynamic tension between the two as the theory of *avatāra* had solved the conflict even for the Guru. The scene of this duality is seen as divine play of *prakaṭa* (manifest) and *aprakaṭa* (unmanifest). In the texts, Kṛṣṇa eternally performs his *līla* through *prakaṭas* (appearances) and sometimes through one appearance such as his birth in this life, similar to that of the Guru. The *vṛndāvana* as a symbol was more powerful than (figural) portrait.

In regard to the relation between God and reality, *vṛndāvana* acted as a bridge between the two concepts. *Vṛndāvana* was the site where Rādhā and Kṛṣṇa performed the *rāsalīla*, the dance of joy and bliss, and one can think of them only in the context of *vṛndāvana*. *Līlā* is the divine play of Kṛṣṇa, and this world is said to be a manifestation of Kṛṣṇa's *līla*. The *Harivaṃśa* transforms the *vṛndāvana* from a holy site (for gaining merit) to total immersion of mind and body in one place to take part in the divine play. The *līlas* (play) of manifestation and non-manifestation of Kṛṣṇa is taking place somewhere eternally and simultaneously, just as the transformation of the Guru from life to death and vice versa.

It may be added that the efficacy of the *vṛndāvana* lies not in the connotations of death or the embalmed body or relic but in the life within the Guru as well as in each of the devotees. Here the boundaries between the dead and living, sacred and unholy, aniconic and iconic, relic and icon, were crossed and where the boundaries between the guru and god, were not defined. It reveals the religious exchanges between the dynamic traditions of asceticism and bliss, form and formlessness, the earthly and divine realms with an extraordinary efficacy that can be attributed to the enigma of the multivalent symbol of the *vṛndāvana* and the "relic."

It is probable that the *vṛndāvana* meant different concepts to different groups. To the devotees of Kṛṣṇa, the *vṛndāvana* on this "earth" was a manifestation of the original Gokula Vṛndāvana *dham* (site) of Lord Kṛṣṇa. It is possible that while Kṛṣṇa lived in *vṛndāvana*, by analogy, worship to the *vṛndāvana* meant worship to Lord Kṛṣṇa. To the *paṇḍita* (scholar), it probably meant a group of knowledge; to the *maṭha* staff, the specific Guru himself; to the followers of Dualism, it was the symbol of a Guru who was an *avatāra* of God. Indirectly, the *vṛndāvana* acquired a more powerful symbolism and meaning to the devotee. It established a triangular relationship between the Guru, God, and devotee. The explanation for the sacred status and veneration can be found in the mythological, metaphysical, and ontological meanings. Thus, the rationale for the transformation of meaning from a relic to an icon is embedded in traditional intangible concepts.

The icon/relic could have been installed either near or within the *maṭha*, the institution of the ascetic. It had already developed into a remarkable socioreligious phenomenon that commanded authority in medieval India. The *vṛndāvana* in a *maṭha* was a form of symbolic strategy to mediate de facto sociocultural changes: the power of kings and challenges of *bhakti*. The relic played a central role in the popularization and geographical transportation of the Guru. The growth of relic worship led to the spread of *vṛndāvana*-related pilgrimage sites and substantiated the rise of the Gurus who was exemplified by his life, writings, and philosophy. It was the means for a strong visual spread of religious values and philosophy. The institutionalization of the deceased Guru through enshrinement and public ritual worship led to an intense social and religious activity around the *maṭha* which in turn increased the sacred status of the living Guru. The Guru was indispensable to society and his relics, icons, and institutions fulfilled demands of mass religion.

Hinduism, with its broad umbrella of group affiliations and practices and with no ecclesiastical authority to administer and regulate the boundaries of its tradition, Gurus in monasteries were able to rephrase traditions, interpretation, rituals, iconography, and ideals, and yet maintain a sense of continuity, echoing Vedic and Upanisadic thoughts, across time and space. *Maṭhas* are still popular institutions in South India and their history demonstrates how the ascetic Gurus successfully appropriated and creatively reworked the principles of Vedism within a complex tradition of education, asceticism, and sacredness and connected seemingly disparate genres. The growth of the multifaceted institution from an educational establishment to organized centers of socioreligious power sustained the growth of intellectual thought in South India and provided a structure to Hinduism.

This study is a discourse and I do not profess to have solved the problem of the origin of the *maṭha* or of the *vṛndāvana* or fully comprehended its multiple meanings. I hope the discourse will lead to further research by various scholars.

Appendix

Disciples of Madhvacarya: Gurus of Ashta *Maṭhas*

1. Hrisikesha *Tīrtha*—Palimar *Maṭha*
2. Narasimha *Tīrtha*—Admar *Maṭha*
3. Janardhana *Tīrtha*—Krsnapur *Maṭha*
4. Upendra *Tīrtha*—Puthige *Maṭha*
5. Vaman *Tīrtha*—Shirur *Maṭha*
6. Visnu *Tīrtha*—Sode *Maṭha*
7. Rama *Tīrtha*—Kaniyoor *Maṭha*
8. Adhokshaja *Tīrtha*—Pejawar *Maṭha*

Lineage of Gurus who were heads of Important Dvaita Desastha *Maṭhas* and their Divisions Indicated

Padmanabha *Tīrtha*

Narahari *Tīrtha*

Madhava *Tīrtha*

Aksobhya *Tīrtha*

Jaya *Tīrtha*

Vidyadhiraja *Tīrtha* I

Kavindra *Tīrtha*	Rajendra *Tīrtha*
Vagisha *Tīrtha*	Jayadhwaja *Tīrtha*
Ramacandra *Tīrtha*	Purushottama *Tīrtha*
Brahmanya *Tīrtha*	Vyasa *Tīrtha*

I................................I		I
Vibhudhendra *Tīrtha*	Vyasa *Tīrtha*	Srinivasa *Tīrtha*
Jitamitra *Tīrtha*	Raghunatha *Tīrtha*	Rama *Tīrtha*
Raghunandana *Tīrtha*	Raghuvarya *Tīrtha*	Lakshmikanta *Tīrtha*
Surendra *Tīrtha*	Raghottama *Tīrtha*	Sripati *Tīrtha*
1539 CE	1596 CE	1627 CE
I	I	I
Raghavendra Swami *Maṭha*	Uttaradi *Maṭha*	Vyasaraja *Maṭha*

Succession of Disciples up to Madhvacarya

1. Sri Hamsanamaka Paramatma
2. Sri Chaturmukha Brahma
3. Sri Sanaka *Tīrtha*
4. Sri Sanandana *Tīrtha*
5. Sri Sanatkumara *Tīrtha*
6. Sri Sanatana *Tīrtha*
7. Sri Doorvasa *Tīrtha*
8. Sri Jnananidhi *Tīrtha*
9. Sri Garuda vahana *Tīrtha*
10. Sri Kaivalya *Tīrtha*
11. Sri Jnanesha *Tīrtha*
12. Sri ParaTeertharu
13. Sri Satyaprajna *Tīrtha*
14. Sri Prajna *Tīrtha*.
15. Sri Achyutaprekshacaryaru.
16. Sri Madhvacharyaru

Lineage of Gurus Traced by Raghavendra Swami, *Maṭha* Mantralaya

Sri Madhvacarya

17. Sri Padmanabha *Tīrtha* (1317–1324)
18. Sri Narahari *Tīrtha* (1324–1333)
19. Sri Madhava *Tīrtha* (1333–1350)
20. Sri Akshobhya *Tīrtha* (1350–1365)

21. Sri Jaya *Tīrtha* (1350–1388)
22. Sri Vidyadhiraja *Tīrtha* (1388–1392)
23. Sri Kavindra *Tīrtha* (1392–1398)
24. Sri Vagisha *Tīrtha* (1398–1406)
25. Sri Ramacandra *Tīrtha* (1406–1435)
26. Sri Vibudhendra *Tīrtha* (1435–1490)
27. Sri Jitamitra *Tīrtha* (1490–1492)
28. Sri Raghunandana *Tīrtha* (1492–1504)
29. Sri Surendra *Tīrtha* (1504–1575)
30. Sri Vijayeendra *Tīrtha* (1575–1614)
31. Sri Sudheendra *Tīrtha*
32. Sri Raghavendra *Tīrtha* (1621–1671)
33. Sri Yogeendra *Tīrtha* (1671–1688)
34. Sri Sooreendra *Tīrtha* (1688–1692)
35. Sri Sumateendra *Tīrtha* (1692–1725)
36. Sri Upendra *Tīrtha* (1725–1728)
37. Sri Vadeendra *Tīrtha* (1728–1750)
38. Sri Vasudhendra *Tīrtha* (1750–1761)
39. Sri Varadendra *Tīrtha* (1761–1785)
40. Sri Dheerendra *Tīrtha* (1785)
41. Sri Bhuvanendra *Tīrtha* (1785–1799)
42. Sri Subodhendra *Tīrtha* (1799–1835)
43. Sri Sujanendra *Tīrtha* (1807–1836)
44. Sri Sujnanendra *Tīrtha* (1836–1861)
45. Sri Sudharmendra *Tīrtha* (1861–1872)
46. Sri Sugunendra *Tīrtha* (1872–1884)
47. Sri Suprajnendra *Tīrtha* (1884–1903)
48. Sri Sukruteendra *Tīrtha* (1903–1912)
49. Sri Susheelendra *Tīrtha* (1912–1926)
50. Sri Suvrateendra *Tīrtha* (1926–1933)
51. Sri Suyameendra *Tīrtha* (1933–1967)
52. Sri Sujayeendra *Tīrtha* (1963–1986)
53. Sri Sushameendra *Tīrtha* (1985–2009)
54. Sri Suvidyendra *Tīrtha* (2002)
55. Sri Suyateendra *Tīrtha* (2006–2014)

Glossary

IMPORTANT NON-ENGLISH TERMS USED

Ācārya: Head of a Vedic school, spiritual preceptor.

Advaita: Monism.

Ānanda: Bliss.

Ananta: Infinite, endless

Ārādhana: Worship; Annual celebration of pontiffs.

Ātma(n): Individual self and universal Self (both are possible since in Sanskrit there are no capital letters).

Avatāra: Descent, Divinity incarnate.

Bhāndīra: Indian fig tree.

Bhāva: A Sanskrit word having many meanings, emotion, state of being, inner experience.

Brahma: Creator God.

Brahmacārī: Literally "he who moves in the Brahman"; usually means "celibate student," especially in the religious field (fem. *brahmacārini*).

Brahmacārin: Brahmanical student, belonging to the first stage of life.

Brāhmaṇa: Spiritual power, an attribute of the brāhmin.

Cakra: Wheel or disk.

Caturmāsa: Four months in a year during which pontiffs are supposed to remain in one place; it is now reduced to six to eight weeks.

Citta: Consciousness.

Dharma: Law that has always been there; socio-cosmic order supporting the existence of universe; one's own duty.

Dhyāna: Meditation.

Gaudiya: Relating to Vaiṣṇava sect founded by Chaitanya.

Goloka: Abode of Kṛṣṇa.
Gopīs: Cowherd girls.
Gṛhastha: Householder.
Guru: Spiritual master, traditional teacher.
Iṣṭa devatā: Divinity who has been chosen by a devotee for his personal worship.
Jeevanmukti: Liberation during life time.
Jñāna: Knowledge.
Jñānin: Sage who has realized the Self.
Kaivalya: Literally "isolation"; state of liberation.
Kāma: Desire, sensuality.
Karma: Every action, often the ritual action, performed with the expectation of a given result; secondarily, it means bondage, conditioning due to past actions performed in an interested manner.
Kāvisatti: Saffron cloth worn by ascetics.
Kṛṣṇa: Dark; Incarnation of Viṣṇu, popular god.
Kṣatriya: A member of the second caste.
Līla: Play, especially the divine play.
Mantra: Formula recited during a Vedic sacrifice.
A verse in the Veda or the word of Veda; the name of God that one repeats throughout his life.
Māyā: Fundamental illusion pushing us to believe that the universe is only what we perceive with sense organs.
Illusion.
Mokṣa: Liberation, the fourth and ultimate goal of human life.
Naivedya: Food offering to god or *svāmījīs*.
Nara: Man.
Nārāyaṇa: Another name for Viṣṇu.
Pāda: Feet.
Pāduka: Footwear that is made of wood.
Paramātma: Supreme spirit.
Pīṭha: Pedestal or base.
Prakṛti: Nature.
Prāṇa: Breath, vital energy, in practice a current of sensations that one learns to direct through yoga.
Prāṇāyāma: Regulation of breath.
Prasāda: Divine grace; sacred food or objects (like flowers etc.) received from a temple or a guru.
Purāṇa Traditional texts, especially medieval, collecting all that a Hindu should know about cosmology, myths, rituals, and so on.

Rāja, Rājya: King, kingdom.
Rājadharma: Duties of the king, the royal function.
Rājaśāsana: Royal order, ordinance.
Rāma: One of the most popular incarnate gods of Hinduism along with Kṛṣṇa. He is considered as the model king and hero.
Ṛṣi: "Seer," sage of Vedic times.
Sadguru: True Master.
Sādhaka: Spiritual seeker.
Sādhanā: Spiritual practices.
Sādhu: literally "good man"; religious person, often a wandering one.
Samādhi Experience of absorption, enstasis occurring to a sādhaka.
Saṃsāra: Cycle of births and deaths; the world.
Saṃskāra: Innate tendency, deep conditioning. Rituals equivalent to the sacraments.
Śaṅkarācārya: Famous sage and philosopher of non-duality in the ninth century who spread the teaching of Vedanta.
sanyāsi: Ascetic, renouncer.
Sat-cit-ānanda: Being-consciousness-bliss, one of the names of the Absolute.
Satsaṅga: Meeting with sages (literally "being with Being").
Satva: Purity.
Siddhānta: A principle or teaching.
Siddhi: Parapsychological power.
Śiva: God, both of asceticism and of vitality, of destruction as well as of liberation; he seems to be, among the gods still worshipped nowadays in the world, the one whose cult is the most ancient.
Tīrtha: Sanctified holy water; designation of a religious ascetic.
Upaniṣads: Portion of revealed texts, the last part of the *Vedas*; this teaching has penetrated the whole of Hindu thinking in one way or another.
Upvana: A minor wood of Vṛndāvana.
Vaikuṇṭha: Celestial piece of Viṣṇu.
Vairāgya: Detachment.
Vana: Grove or wood.
Vāsudeva: Name for Viṣṇu or Kṛṣṇa.
Vāyu: God of wind or air.
Vedānta: "The end of the Vedas," the doctrine of non-duality as can be established from the teaching of the Vedas.
Vedas: Sacred texts, whose authority is recognized by all Hindus.
Vijaya: Complete victory.
Vijñāna: Complete knowledge.

Vṛndā: Collection; wife of Jalandhara

Vṛndāvana: Sacred burial site of a *sanyasi* or Guru in the order of Dualism; Vṛndāvana, the sacred garden (orchard) where Krsna danced with the Gopis

Yamuna: River.

Yātrā: Pilgrimage.

Yoga: One of the six Brahmanical philosophical systems, includes theory and especially practice implying body-postures and meditation.

Vyūha: Part of divine.

Bibliography

PRIMARY WORKS

Agni Purana. Edited by Rajendralala Mitra. Calcutta. Translated by T.N. Narasimha. Mysore, Gorakhpur: Bhagavadgita Gita Press, 1985.

Atharva Veda. Edited by Maurice Bloomfield. Strassburg: K.J. Trübner, 1899.

The Bhagavad Gita. Translated by Srimath Swami Chidbhavananda. (Sanskrit and English) Tirupparaitturai, Trichy District: Rai Ramakrishna Tapovanam, 1997.

Brihad Dharma Puraṇa, Translated by Banerji, Syama Charan. English and Sanskrit. Lucknow: Hathi Trust. 1915.

Daksinamurti Sotra with the Varttika Manasollasa of Suresvaracarya. Swami Harshananda. Chennai: Ramakrishna Math, 1992.

Dikshit, T.R.C. *Sannyasa Upanishad*. Madras: Adyar Library, 1929.

The Garuda Purana. Translated by Dutt, Manmatha Nath. Calcutta: Chowkhamba Sanskrit Series Office, 1968.

Garuda Purana. Translated by Vyas, M.P. Banaras: Bombay, 1906.

Harivamsa. Edited by Vaidya, Parashuram Lakshman. Poona: Bhandarkar Oriental Research Institute. 1969–71.

Kryakalpataru, of Bhatta, Lakshmidhara. Edited by KV Rangasvami Aiyangar. *Vol 4. Sraddhakanda*. Baroda: Oriental Institute, 1950.

Laghu Bhagavatamrta, of Rupa Goswami. Hindi Translation by B. P. Misra. 1902; Bombay: Venkatesvara Press, 2014.

Lalita Vistara, Ed. S. Lefmann, 2 Vols. Halle, 1902–08.

Mahaparinibbana Sutta. In Digha Nikaya. Edited by. T. W. Rys Davis et al., 3 Vols. London: Pali Text Society, 1889–1910.

Olivelle, Patrick. *Samnyasa Upanisads: Hindu Scriptures on Asceticism and Renunciation.* Oxford: Oxford University Press, 1992.

Padma Purana. Edited by Mandalika, Vishvanath Narayan. Poona: Anandashram. 1894.

Rgbhasya, of Madhva. Edited by Govindcharya, Bannanje in Sarvamulagranthah, Vol. 4. Udupi: Akhila Bharata Madhwa Mahamandala, 1973.

Sannyasa Upanishad. Dikshit, T.R.C. Madras: Adyar Library, 1929.

Vamana Purana. 3 Vols. Translated by Venkatacharya, Sankeeghattam, Mysore: Sri Jayacahmrajendra Book Series. Sri Sharada Electric Press. 1946.

Varaha Purana. Edited by Hrsikesa Sastri. Calcutta, 1893.

Vairagya Shatakam: Bharthari. Translated by Swami Madhvananada. Calcutta: Advaita Ashram, 1990.

Vayu Purana. Edited by Rajendrala Mitra, Calcutta. 1880–88. Translated by R. P. Tripati.

Vishnudharmottara Purana. Third Kanda. Translated by Priyabala Shah. Baroda: Gaekwad Oriental Institute, 1961.

Visnu Purana. Edited by Vidyasagara, Jivananda. Calcutta: Saraswati Press, 1882.

Vrndavana Sata Lila in *Bayalisa Lila* by Dhruvadasa. Edited by Goswami, Lalitacarana Vrndavana, 1971.

Yajnavalkya Smriti. Edited with the Commentary of Vijnaneśvara, called the Mitakshara, Bombay, 1909. Translated by R. B. Shrishchandra, Allahabad 1918.

EPIGRAPHICAL AND ARCHAEOLOGICAL SOURCES AND ABBREVIATIONS

A Topographical List of the Inscriptions of the Madras Presidency. Edited by V. Rangacharya, 3 Vols. Madras: Superintendent Govt. Press, 1919.

Annual Reports on Indian Epigraphy. New Delhi: Manager of Publications, 1947 onwards.

ARSIE Annual Reports on South Indian Epigraphy. Madras/Calcutta: Govt. Press.

ARASI Annual Reports of Archaeological Survey of India. Calcutta/Delhi: Archaeological Survey of India.

Bhadarkar, D.R. *Index to Epigraphia Indica.* Survey Reports of the Archaeological Survey of India.

CII Corpus Inscriptionum Indicarum, Vol. III by Fleet and Vol. IV by V.V. Mirash.

CII Fleet. *Circle Reports of the Archaeological Survey of India Corpus Inscriptionum Indicarum Vol. III.*

EC Epigraphia Carnatica. Edited by Lewis Rice and others. Madras/ Bangalore/Mysore, 1886–1958.

EI Epigraphia Indica. Archaeological Survey of India. 1882–1977.

IA Indian Archaeology-A Review published by the Archaeological Survey of India. New Delhi.

JBBRAS Journal of the Bombay Branch of the Royal Asiatic Society.

JRAS Journal of the Royal Asiatic Society.

Karnataka State Gazetteer. Bangalore: Shimoga Dist. Publications, Government Press, 1975.

KI Kannada Inscriptions.

Mirash, V.V. *Circle Reports of the Archaeological Survey of India Corpus Inscription Vol. IV.*

QJMS Quarterly Journal of Mythic Society.

SII South Indian Inscriptions, Old and New Series.

The Historical Inscriptions of Southern India (Collected till 1923) and Outlines of Political History. By Robert Sewell. Edited by Aiyangar, S.K. Madras: University of Madras, 1932. Reprint, New Delhi: Asian Educational Services, 1983.

Vijayanagara Inscriptions. Edited by Gopal, B.R. 2 Vols. Mysore: Directorate of Archaeology and Museums, 1985–1986.

KANNADA WORKS

Agnihotri, Gopalcharya. *Sri Uttradi Mathada Guru Prampareya Samkshipta Charitre*. Hubli: Raghavendra Swami Matha, 1972.

Badrinath, S.K. *Shri Raghottama Tirtharu.* Bangalore: Susheela Prakashana (n.d).

Gururajachar, Rajashree. *Kaliyuga Kalpaturu*. Mysore: Sri Parimala Samshodhana Mandir, 2007.

Kolhara, Kulkarni. *Madhva Mathagalu.* Bangalore: Bhagyalakshmi Prakashana, 1996.

Malagi, Jayatirthacharya. Edited by *Shri Suddha Vishesh Sanchike.* Dharwad: Shri Suddha Karyalaya, 1989.

Ruchiracharya, Balagaru. *Pajakakshetra Vaibhava.* Bangalore: Pajaka Seva Trust, 1999.

Satyanatha, Amman. *Navavrindavana Charitre Mahatvagalu.* Translated in Kannada by B.S. Ramachandra and Nagubai Narasappa. Chennai: Arulmigu Amman Pathippagam, 2004.

Vedavyasachar. *Shri Madvadhiraja Guru Sambhavagalu.* Dharwad: P. S. Desai (n.d.).

SECONDARY SOURCES

Acharya, J. H. B. *The Lord of Mantralaya*, Bangalore: Indian Press, 1981.

Acharya, U. R. *Udupi: an Introduction*, Udupi: Sri Krishna Matha, 1989.

Aerthayil, J. "ViraSaivism – A Saivite Revolution in Karnataka." *Journal of Dharma* 15 (1989).

Aiyangar, Sakkotai Krishnaswami. *Evolution of Hindu Administrative Institutions in South India.* University of Madras, 1930.

Aiyangar, SK. "Foundation of Vijayanagar." *Quarterly Journal of the Mythic Society* 2, no. 1 (1920): 13–32.

———. *South India and Her Muhammadan Invaders.* New Delhi: S. Chand & Co., 1971.

Aiyar, C.N.K. and P.S. Tattvabush. *Sri Samkaracharya.* University of Madras, 1902.

Aiyer, Subrahmanya K.V. *Historical Sketches of Ancient Dekhan.* New Delhi: Cosmo Publications, 1980.

Aklujkar, Ashok. Pandita and Pandits in History. In *The Pandit: Traditional Scholarship in India.* Edited by K Parameswara Aithal and Axel Michaels. New Delhi: Manohar, 2001, 17–38.

Allchin, R. "The Attaining of the Void—A Review of Some Recent Contributions in English to the Study of Virasaivism." Religious Studies 7, no. 4 (1971): 339–359.

Altekar, A.S. *Education in Ancient India.* Gyan Publishing House, 1965.

———. *The Coinage of the Gupta Empire and its Imitations.* Corpus of Indian Coins, Vol. 4. Varanasi: Banaras Hindu University, 1957.

Alavi, Rafi Ahmad. *Studies in the History of Medieval Deccan*. Delhi: Idarah-I Adabiyat-I, 1977.

Amur, G.S. and S.H. Ritti. *A Brief Lifesketch of Mrityunjaya Swamiji*. Dharwar: Shri Murughamath, 1968.

Appadorai, A. *Economic Conditions in Southern India*. University of Madras, 1936.

Appadurai, Arjun. "Kings, Sects and Temples in South India, 1350–1700 A.D." *The Indian Economic and Social History Review* 14, no. 1 (1978): 49–73.

———. *Worship and Conflict in South India: the Case of the Sri Partasārati Svami Temple, 1800–1973*, 1976.

Appadurai, Arjun, and Carol Appadurai Breckenridge. "The South Indian Temple: Authority, Honour and Redistribution." *Contributions to Indian Sociology* 10, no. 2 (1980): 187–211.

Apte, Vaman Shivram. *Sanskrit–English Dictionary*. Delhi: Motilal Banarsidass, 1965.

Aravamuthan, T.G. *Portrait Sculpture in South India*. London: The India Society, 1931.

———. *South Indian Portraits, in Stone and Metal*. Luzac and Company, 1930.

Arnold, D. et al. "Caste Associations in South India: A Comparative Analysis." *The-Indian Economic & Social History Review* 13 (1976).

Artal, R.C. "A Short Account of the Reformed Shaiva or Veerashaiva Faith." *Journal of the Anthropological Society of Bombay* 3, no.3 (1909).

Auboyer, Jeanine. *Le Trone et son Symbolisme dans l'Inde Ancienne*. Vol. 55. Presses Universitaires de France, France: 1949.

Ayyar, Jagadisa P.V. *South Indian Festivities*. New Delhi: Asian Educational Services, 1982.

Balasubrahmanyam, S.R. *Early Chola Art*. Part I. New York: Asia Publishing House, 1966.

———. *Early Chola Temples*. Orient Longman, 1971.

———. *Middle Chola Temples*. Faridabad: Thompson Pr., 1975.

Bali, A.P. "Organization of the Vira Saiva Movement: An Analysis in the Sect Church Framework." In *Social Movements in India*, II. Edited by M.S.A. Rao. New Delhi: Manohar, 1979.

Banerjea, Jitendra Nath. "On Indian Images." *Journal of the Indian Society of Oriental Art* 7 (1939): 83–88.

Banerji, Debashish. *Seven Quartets of Becoming: A Transformational Yoga Psychology Based on the Diaries of Sri Aurobindo*. Los Angeles: Nalanda International and New Delhi: DKPW, 2012.

Barrett, T.H. "Stupa, Sutra and Sarira in China, ca. 656–706 C.E." *Buddhist Studies Review* 18 (2001): 1–64.

Barth, A. *Religions of India*. London: Trubner, 1882.

Barua, B.M. *Barhut: Aspects of Life and Art*. Book III. Calcutta: Indian Research Institute Publications,1937.

Beal, Samuel. *The Life of Hiuen-Tsang*. London: Kegan Paul, Trench, Trubner and Co., 1914.

Beane, Wendell Charles. *Myth Cult and Symbols in Sakta Hinduism*. Leiden: E. J. Brill, 1977.

Beavides, G. "Economy." In *Critical Terms for the Study of Buddhism*. Edited by D.S. Lopez Jr. Chicago: University of Chicago Press, 2005, 77–102.

Bedekar, Vijay V., ed., *Education in Ancient India: Shri S.B. Velankar Felicitation Volume: Papers Presented at the Seminar Conducted on Saturday, 29th April 1995 at Thane, Under the Auspices of the Institute of Oriental Study, Thane*. Itihas Patrika Prakashan, 1996.

Beggiora, Stefano. "The Subtle Teacher. Typologies of Shamanic Initiation: Trance and Dream Among the Lanjia Saoras of Orissa." In Rigopoulos, Antonio. Ed. *Guru: The Spiritual Master in Eastern and Western Traditions: Authority and Charisma*. Venice, Italy. Venetian Academy of Indian Studies Series, no. 4. 2004. First Indian Edition, New Delhi: DKPW, 2007, 327–371.

Benard, Elizabeth. "The Living among the Dead: A Comparison of Buddhist and Christian Relics." *The Tibet Journal* 13 (1988): 33–48.

Benn, James A. "Where Text Meets Flesh: During the Body as an Apocryphal Practice in Chinese Buddhism." *History of Religions* 37 (1998): 295–322.

Bentor, Yael. *Consecration of Images and Stupas in Indo-Tibetan Tantric Buddhism*. Leiden: E.J. Brill, 1996.

———. "On the Indian Origins of the Tibetan Practice of Depositing Relics and Dharanis in Stupas and Images." *Journal of the American Oriental Society* 115, no. 2 (1995): 248.

———. "Tibetan Relic Classification." *Tibetan Studies (Proceedings of the Sixth Seminar of the International Association for Tibetan Studies)*. Edited by Kvaerne, per. Oslo: Institute for Comparative Research in Human Culture, 1994, pp. 16–30.

Bhadri, K.M. *A Cultural History of Northern India: Based on Epigraphical Sources form the 3rd Century. B.C. to 700 A.D.* Delhi: Book India Publishing Co, 2006.

Bhagat, M.G. *Ancient Indian Asceticism*. Munshiram Manoharlal Pub Pvt. Ltd, 1976.

Bhagowalia, Urmila. *Vaishnavism and Society in Northern India, 700–1200*. New Delhi: Intellectual Corner, 1980.

Bhandarkar, R.G. *Early History of the Deccan*. Calcutta, 1957, 1931, 1929.

———. "Mathura Pillar Inscription of Chandragupta II." *Epigraphia Indica* 21, no. 1 (1931): 1–9.

———. *Vaisnavism, Saivism and Minor Religious Systems: and Wilson Philological Lectures on Sanskrit and the Derived Languages, Delivered in 1877*. Poona: Bhandarkar Oriental Research Institute, 1929.

Bharati, Swami Agehananda. *The Ochre Robe*. Seattle: University of Washington Press, 1962.

Bharatiya Vidya Bhavan. Voice of the Guru, Jagadgru Sri Candrasekhareandra Sarasvati Svami: The Guru Tradition. Mumbai: Bharatiya Viday Bhavan, 2008 (Anon).

Bhardwaj, Surinder Mohan. *Hindu Places of Pilgrimage in India: A Study in Cultural Geography*. Berkeley: University of California Press, 1973.

Bhatt, Gururaja, P. *Studies in Tuluva History and Culture*. Manipal: Geetha Publishers, 1975.

Bhatt, G.H. *Shri Vallabhacharya and His Doctrines*. Delhi: Butala & Co, 1980.

Bhattacharyya, Ananda. *Introduction in a History of the Dasnami Naga Sannyasis*. Jadunath Sarkar. London: Routledge, 2018, 11–90.

Bhattacharya, Shiva Chandra Vidyarnava. *Principles of Tantra*, 2 Vols. Ed. Sir John Woodroffe. Madras: Ganesh and Co., 1978. First published in 1913.

Bhuler, G. *The Laws of Manu*. Delhi: Motilal Banarsidass, 1886.

Bisht, R.S. "How Harappans Honoured Death at Dholavira." In *Sindhu Sarasvati Civilization-New Perspectives. A Volume in Memory of Dr. Shikaripur Ranganatha Rao. Proceedings of the International Conference on the Sindhu-Sarasvati Valley Civilizations: A Reappraisal.* Edited by Nalini Rao. New Delhi, Los Angeles: Nalanda International and DK Printworld, 2014.

Bloch, Maurice and Jonathan Parry. Eds. *Death and the Regeneration of Life*. Cambridge: Cambridge University Press, 1982.

Boisvert, Mathieu. "Death as Meditation Subject in the Theravada Tradition." *Buddhist Studies Review* 13, no. 1 (1996): 37–54.

Bordern, C. *Contemporary India: Essays on the Uses of Tradition*. Delhi: Oxford University Press, 1989.

Bourdieu, Pierre. *Distinction: A Social Critique of the Judgment of Taste*. London: Routledge and Kegan Paul, 1984.

———. *Outline of a Theory of Practice*. Cambridge: Cambridge University Press, 2005.

Bouillier, Veronique. *Naitre Renoncant, Une Caste De Sannyasi Villageois Au Nepal Central*. Nanterre: Laboratoire d'Ethnologie. 1979.

Boyer, Pascal. *Tradition as Truth and Communication: A Cognitive Description of Traditional Discourse*. Cambridge: Cambridge University Press, 1990.

Breckenridge, James D. *Likeness: A Conceptual History of Portraiture*. Evanston: Northwestern University Press, 1968.

Brian, Ruppert. *Jewel in the Ashes: Buddha Relics and Power in Early Medieval Japan*, 2000.

Briggs, George Weston. *Gorakhnath and the Kanphata Yogis*. Calcutta: Y.M.C.A. Publishing House, 1938. Reprint, Delhi: Motilal Banarsidass, 1973, 1982, 1989.

Brilliant, Richard. "Portraits: The Limitations of Likeness." *Art Journal* Vol. 46, no. 3 (Fall 1987): 171–172.

Bronkhorst, Johannes. *Buddhism in the Shadow of Brahmanism*. Leiden: Brill, 2011.

———. "Greater Magadha." In *Studies in the Culture of Early India*. Leiden-Boston: Brill. (*Handbook of Oriental Studies*, Section 2 South Asia, 19, 2007).

———. "Les reliques dans les religions de l'Inde." In *Indische Kultur im Kontext. Rituale, Texte und Ideen aus Indien und der Welt*. Festschrift für Klaus Mylius. Hrsg., 2005.

Brown, Charles Philip "Account of the Basava Purana: the Principal Book used as a Religious Code by the Jangams." *The Madras Journal of Literature and Science* (1840): 271–292.

———. "Essay on the Creed, Customs, and Literature of the Jangams." *Madras Journal of Literature and Science*, Series I Vol. II, no. 26 (1840).

Brown, Peter. *The Cult of the Saints*. Chicago: University of Chicago Press, 1981.

Brown, Robert L. "Expected Miracles: The Unsurprisingly Miraculous Nature of Buddhist Images and Relics." In *Images, Miracles, and Authority in Asian religious Traditions*. Edited by Richard H. Davis. Boulder: Westview, 1998, 23–35.

Bruhn, K. "Jaina Rituals of Death." In *The Study of Jaina Art. Jain Studies in Honour of Jozef Deleu*. Edited by Rudy Smet & Kenji Watanabe. Tokyo: Hon-no-Tomosha, 1993, 53–66.

Bruijn, Eric et al., "Die Mumie in Inneren–eine übermodellierte Mumie eines buddhistichen Mőnchs," In *Mumien: Der Traum vom ewigen Leben,* ed. Alfried Wiexzorek and Wilfried Rosendahl. Manheim: Reiss-Engelhorn-Museen, 2015, pp. 337–42.

Brunton, Paul. *A Search in Secret India*. New York: Dutton, 1935.

Bryant, Edwin F. *Krishna: A Sourcebook*. Oxford: Oxford University Press, 2007.

Buhler, George. "Further Proofs of the Authenticity of the Jain a Tradition." *Vienna Oriental Journal* 4 (1890): 313–331.

Buhnemann, Gudrn. "Sivalingas and Caityas in Representations of the Eight Cremation Grounds from Nepal." In *Pramanakirtih: Papers Dedicated to Ernst Steinkellner on the Occasion of His 70th Birthday*. Wiener Studien zur Tibetologie und Buddhismuskunde; Heft 70, 2007, 23–35.

Burgess, James. *The Buddhist Stupas of Amaravati and Jaggayyapeta*. New Delhi: Archaeological Survey of India, 1886.

Burghart, Richard. "Renunciation in the Religious Traditions of South Asia." *Man* 4 (1983): 635–668.

Campbell, J. "Basava: A Social Reformer." *Times of India* April 17, 1918.

Campbell, Joseph. *Myths to Live By*. New York: The Viking Press, 1972.

Carus, Paul. "A Buddhist Priest's View of Relics." *The Open Court* 11 (1897): 122–125.

Caycedo, Alfonso. *India of Yogis*. Delhi: National Publishing House, 1940.

Cenkner, William. *A Tradition of Teachers: Sankara and the Jagadgurus Today*. Columbia, MO: South Asia Books, Delhi: Motilal Banarsidass, 1983. Reprint, 1995, 2001.

Chakraborti, Haripada. *Asceticism in Ancient India: in Brahmanical, Buddhist, Jaina and Ajivika Societies from the Earliest Times to the Period of Sankaracharya*. Calcutta: Punthi Pustak, 1973.

Chandrasekharendrea Sarasvati Svami, Sri. *The Guru Tradition*. Mumbai: Bharatiya Vidya Bhavan, 2008.

Channabasavappa, B. *Yediyur Siddhalingeshwara Swamy: Brief Life Sketch.* Bangalore, India: Fifth Centenary Celebration Committee, 1971.

Chatterjee, Mitali. "Education in Ancient India: From Literary Sources of the Gupta Age". *Reconstructing Indian History and Culture*, no. 17. New Delhi: Printworld, 1999.

Chekki, Danesh A. *Religion and Social System of the Virasaiva Community*. Westport, CT: Greenwood Press, 1997.

Chitnis, K.N. "Vira Saiva Mathas in the Keladi Kingdom." *Journal of the Karnatak University (Social Sciences)* 3, (1967).

Clarke, Shayne. *Family Matters in Indian Buddhist Monasticisms*. Honolulu: University of Hawai'i Press, 2014.

Collins, Steven. The Body in Theravada Buddhist Monasticism. *In Religion and the Body*. Edited by Coakley, Sarah. Cambridge: Cambridge University Press. 1997, 185–204.

Coomaraswamy, A.K. *Spritual Authority and Temporal Power in the Indian Theory of Government*. New Haven, CT: American Oriental Society, 1942.

———. "The Traditional Conception of Ideal Portraiture." *Journal of the Indian Society of Oriental Art* (1939): 74–82.

Corcoran, Maura. *Vrndavana in Vaisnava Literature: History, Mythology, Symbolism. New Reconstructing Indian History and Culture*. No. 6. Delhi: DKPW. 1995.

Crane, Robert I. Regions and Regionalism in South Asian Studies. *Program in Comparative Studies on South Asia*, Monograph no. 5.Durham, NC: Duke University, 1967.

Creel, Austin B. and Vasudha Narayanan. *Monastic life in the Christian and Hindu Traditions. A Comparative Study*. Leweiston: NY: Edwin Mellen Press. 1990.

Croissant, Doris."Der unsterbliche Leib. Ahneneffigies und Reliquienportrat in der Portratplastik Chinas und Japans," in *Das Bildnis in der Kunst des Orients*. Edited by M. Kraatz, J. Meyer zu Capellan, D. Seckel. Stuttgart: Franz Steiner Verlag, 1990, 235–268.

Cuevas, B.A. and J.I. Stone, eds. *The Buddhist Dead.Practices Discourses and Representations*. Honolulu. University of Hawaii Press, 2007.

Czerniak-Drozdzowicz, Marzenna. "Rituals of the Tantric Traditions of South India: The Text (Canon, Rule) versus the Practice." *Studio Religiologica* 47, no. 4 (2014): 253–262.

Dallapiccola, A.L. "Gods, Patrons and Images: Stone Sculpture at Vijayanagara." In *Paradigms of Indian Architecture: Space and Time in Representation and Design*. Edited by G.H.R. Tillotson. London: Curzon, 1988 (Collected Papers on South Asia No. 13), 136–158.

Dallapiccola, A.L. and Anila Verghese. *Sculpture at Vijayanagara: Iconography and Style*. New Delhi: Manohar Publications and the American Institute of Indian Studies, 1998.

Dallapiccola, Anna Libera and Stephanie Zingel-AveLallemant, eds. *Vijayanagara – City and Empire: New Currents of Research*. 2 Vols. Stuttgart: Franz Steiner Verlag Wiesbaden GMBH, 1985.

Davidson, M.Ronald. *Indian Esoteric Buddhism: A Social History of the Tantric Movement*. NY: Columbia University Press. 2002.

Dikshitar, V.R. Ramchandra. "Origin and Early History of Chaityas." *The Indian Historical Quarterly* 14, no. 14 (1938): 440–451.

Dehejia, Vidya. "Aniconism and the Multivalence of Emblems." *Ars Orientalis* 21 (1991): 45–66.

Demaitre, Edmond. *The Yogis of India*. London: G. Bles, 1937.

Demieville, Paul. Momies d'Extreme-Orient. *Journal des Savants*, 1, no.1 (1965) 144–170.

Deo, S.B. "A Sati Memorial from Markandi." In *Memorial Stones in S.India a Study of Their Origin, Significance and Variety*. Edited by Gunther D. Sontheimer and S Settar. Dharwad: Institute of Indian Art History, Karnatak University, New Delhi: South Asia Institute, Germany: University of Heidelberg, 1982, 255–259

Derrett, J. Duncan M. "Modes of Sannyāsīs and the Reform of a South Indian Maṭha Carried out in 1584." *Journal of the American Oriental Society* 94, no. 1 (1974): 65–72.

Desai, P.B. *A History of Karnataka*. Dharwar: Kannada Research Institute, Karnatak University, 1970.

Diehl, Carl Gustav. *Instrument and Purpose: Studies on Rites and Rituals in South India*. Lund: C.W.K. Gleerup, 1956.

Dikshit, G.S., ed. "Early Vijayanagara." In *Studies in Its History and Culture (Proceedings of S. Srikantaya Centenary Seminar)*. Bangalore: BMS Memorial Foundation, 1988.

———. "S. Srikantaya on Vidyaranya's Part in the Foundation of Vijayanagara." In *Early Vijayanagara*. Edited by G.S. Dikshit. Bangalore: BMS Memorial Foundation, 1988, 39–45.

Dikshitar, V.R. Ramchandra, "Origin and Early History of Chaityas," *The Indian Historical Quarterly 14*, no.14 (1938): 440–451.

Dimmit, C. and W.J.C. Van Buitenen. *Puranic Myths*. New Delhi: Rupa, 1983.

Dirks, Nicholas B. "Political Authority and Structural Change in Early South Indian History." *The Indian Economic and Social History Review* 13, no. 2 (1979): 115–25.

———. *The Hollow Crown: Ethnohistory of an Indian Kingdom*. Cambridge: Cambridge University Press, 1987.

Doninger, Wendy O'Flaherty. *Asceticism and Eroticism in the Mythology of Shiva*. London: Oxford University Press, 1973.

Drekmeier, Charles. *Kingship and Community in Early India*. Stanford: Stanford University Press, 1962.

Drury, Naama. *The Sacrificial Ritual in the Satapatha Brahmana*. Delhi: Motilal Banarsidass, 1981.

Dubois, J.A. *Hindu Manners, Customs and Ceremonies*. Oxford: Clarendon Press, 1908.

Dumont, L. and D. Pocock. "Pure and Impure." *Contributions to Indian Sociology* no. 3 (1959): 9–39.

———. "The Conception of Kingship in Ancient India." In *Religion, Politics and History in India*. Collected Papers in Indian Sociology. Paris: Mouton Publishers, 1970, 62–88.

———. "World Renunciation Indian Religions." *Contributions to Indian Sociology* 4 (1960): 3–62.

Duncan, Jonathan. "An Account of the Discovery of Two Urns in the Vicinity of Benares." *Asiatic Researches* 5 (1808): 131–32.

Dutt, Nalinaksha. "Notes on the Nagarjunikonda Inscriptions." *Indian Historical Quarterly* 7, no. 3 (1931): 633–53.

Dutt, Sukumar. *Buddhist Monks and Monasteries of India: Their History and Their Contribution to Indian Culture*. London: G. Allen and Unwin, 1962.

———. *Early Buddhist Monasticism: 600 B.C–100 B.C.* Bombay: Routledge, 1960.

Eck, Diana L. *Banaras: City of Light*. London: Routledge and Keegan Paul Ltd., 1984.

Eckel, Malcolm David. *To See the Buddha*. San Francisco: Harper, 1992.

———. "The Power of the Buddha's Absence: On the Foundations of Mahayana Buddhist Ritual." *Journal of Ritual Studies* 4, no. 2 (1990): 61–95.

Falk, Maryla. *Nama-Rupa and Dharma-Rupa: Origin and Aspects of an Ancient Indian Conception*. University of Calcutta, 1943.

———. “Relics, Regalia, and the Dynamics of Secrecy in Japanese Buddhim”. In *Rending the Veil*, ed. Elliot R. Wolfson. New York: Seven Bridges, 1999, 271–87.

Farquhar, J.N. *An Outline of the Religious Literature of India*. Bombay: Oxford University Press, 1920.

Feiss, Hugh. *Monastic Wisdom*. Harper: San Francisco, 1999.

Filliozat, Vasundhara. *Alidula Hampe*. Bangalore: Manasollasa Prakasana, 1982.

———. *Hampe*. Dharwad: Karnataka University, 1976.

———. *Vijayanagara Samrajya Sthapane*. Bengaluru: Kannada Sahitya Parishad, 1980.

Filippi, Gian Guisep. *Concept of Death in Indian Traditions*. New Delhi: D.K. Print World Ltd., 1996.

Fleet, J.F. “The Tradition about the Corporeal Relics of the Buddha”. *Journal of Royal Asiatic Society of Great Britain and Ireland* (Oct., 1906): 881–913; (April, 1907): 341–363.

Fleming, Benjamin J. Relics. “Lingas, and Other Auspicious Material Remains in South Asian Religions.” *Material Religion* 10, no. 4 (2014): 452–471.

——— “Making Land Sacred: Inscriptional Evidence for Buddhist Kings and Brahman Priests in Medieval Bengal.” *Numen* 60, nos. 5–6 (2013): 559–585.

———. “The Form and Formlessness of Siva: The Linga in Indian Art, Mythology and Pilgrimage.” *Religion Compass* 3 (2009).

Flood, Gavin. *The Blackwell Companion to Hinduism*. Oxford: Blackwell Publishing, 2003.

Flügel, Peter. “Jaina Relic Stupas.” Jaina Studies. Newsletter of the Centre of Jaina Studies, SOAS, University of London. Issue 3, March 2008, 18–23.

———. “The Jaina Cult of Relic Stūpas.” *Numen* 57, no. 3 (2010): 389–504.

Fogelin, Lars. “Material Practice and the Metamorphosis of a Sign: Early Buddhist Stupas and the origin of Mahayana Buddhism.” *Asian Perspectives* 51, no. 2 (Fall 2012): 278–310.

Forsthoefel, Thomas A. and Humes Cynthia Ann. *Gurus in America*. State University of New York Press, 2005.

Framarin, Christopher G. “Renunciation, Pleasure, and the Good Life in the Samnyasa Upanisads.” *Philosophy East and West* 67, no. 1 (Jan 2017): 140–159.

Fritz, J.M. "Vijayanagara: Authority and Meaning of a South Indian Imperial Capital." *American Anthropologist* 88, no. 1 (1986): 44–55.

Fritz, J. M., George Michell, and M.S. Nagaraja Rao. *Where Kings and Gods Meet: the Royal Centre at Vijayanagara, India.* Tucson, AZ: The University of Arizona Press, 1984.

Gajrani, S. *Ancient Buddhist Monasteries: India and Nepal.* Delhi: Kalinga Publications, 1998.

Gambhirananda, Swami. *History of the Ramakrishna Math and Mission.* Calcutta: Adviata Ashrama, 1957.

Gangadharan, H. *Glimpses of Suttur Mutt.* Sri Shivarthreswara Granthamala. Mysore, 2001.

Geertz, C. *Myth, Symbol and Culture.* New York: W.W. Norton & Company, 1974.

———. *The Interpretation of Cultures.* New York: Basic Books, 1973.

Germano, David and Kevin Traino, eds. *Embodying the Dharma. Buddhiwst Relic Veneratin in Asia.* New York: SUNY Press, 2004.

Ghosh, A. *Jaina Art and Architecture.* New Delhi: Bharatiya Jnanpith, 1975.

Ghurye, G.S. *Indian Sadhus.* Bombay: Popular Prakasham, 1964.

Gideens, Anthony. *Reflexive Modernization: Politics, Tradition and Aesthetics in the Modern Social Order.* Stanford University Press, 1994.

Glasenappu, Helmuth von. *Madhva's Philosophy of the Vishnu Faith.* Trans. Shridhar B. Shrothriya. Edited by K.T. Pandurangi. Bangalore: Dvaita Vedanta Studies and Research Foundation. (n.d.).

Goetz, Hermann. "Muslims in Vijayanagar, the Record of Monuments." In *Studies in Indian Culture: Dr. Ghulam Yazdani Commemoration Volume.* Edited by H.K. Sherwani. Hyderabad: Maulana Abul Kalam Azad Oriental Research Institute, 1966, 66–70.

Gold, D. *The Lord as Guru.* New Delhi. Oxford University Press, 1987.

Gonda, J. *Ancient Indian Kingship from the Religious Point of View.* Leiden: E. J. Brill, 1966.

———. *Change and Continuity in Indian Religion.* Mouton, 1965.

———. *Visnuism and Sivaism.* Munshirm Manoharlal Pub Pvt Ltd., 1977.

Gopal, B. R. "Political Conditions in Karnataka Before the Establishment of the Vijayanagara Empire." In *Early Vijayanagara.* Edited by G.S. Dikshit. Bangalore: BMS. Memorial Foundation, 1988, 13–18.

———. *Sri Ramanuja in Karnataka: An Epigraphical Study.* Delhi: Sundeep Prakashan, 1983.

Goswami, B.N. "Essence and Appearance: Some Notes on Indian Portraiture." In *Facets of Indian Art*, ed. Robert Skelton. London: Victoria and Albert Museum, 1986, 193–202.

Govindacharya, Bannanje. *Acharya Madhwa: Life and Works.* Translated into English by U.P. Upadhyaya. Udipi: Isavasya Pratishanam, 2011.

———. "Dvaita in Karnataka." In *Avalokana: A Compendium of Karnataka Heritage*, ed. Krishna Swamy. Bangalore: Directorate of Kannada Culture, 1985.

———. *Udupi: Past and Present.* Udupi: Pejavara Matha, 1984.

Graham, William A. *Beyond the Written Word: Oral Aspects of Scripture in the History of Religion.* Cambridge University Press, 1993.

Granoff, Phyllis. "Relics, Rubies and Ritual: Some Comments on the Distinctiveness of the Buddhist Relic Cult." *Rivista degli studi orientali, nuova Serie* 81, Fasc.1.4 (2008): 59–72.

Granoff, Phyllis and Koichi Shinohara. *Monks and Magicians: Religious Biographies in Asia.* Mosaic Press, NY: Motilal Banarsidass, 1994.

———. *Speaking of Monks: Religious Biography in India and China.* Oakville: Mosaic Press, 1992.

Gross, Robert Lewis. *The Sadhus of India: A Study of Hindu Asceticism.* Rawat Publications, 1992.

Growse, F.S. *Mathura: A District Memoir.* NWP and Oudh Gov. Press, 1883.

Guggali, G.H. *The Siddharudha Swami Math in Monasteries in South India*, ed. Swahānanda, 1989, 71–72.

Gunther, D. Sontheimer and S. Settar, eds. *Memorial Stones in S.India a Study of Their Origin, Significance and Variety.* Dharwad: Institute of Indian Art History, Karnatak University, n.d.

Gupta, Mahendranath. *The Gospel of Shri Ramakrishna.* Trans. Swami Nikhilananda. Mylapore, Madras: Sri Ramakrishna Math, 1964.

Gururajachar, S. *Some Aspects of Economic and Social Life in Karnataka (A.D. 1000–1300).* Perasaranga. Mysore: University of Mysore, 1974.

Harper, Katherine Anne and Robert L. Brown, eds. *The Roots of Tantra.* Albany: State University of New York Press, 2002.

Harshananda, *Daksinamurti Stotra with Manasollasa.* Trans. and Annotated by Swami Hashanda. Chennai: Sri Ramakrishna Math, 1992.

Harvey, Peter. "The Symbolism of the Stupa." *Journal of the International Association of Buddhist Studies* 7 (1984): 67–93.

Havanur, Shrinivas, Havanur, N. Anjana. *Shri Vadiraja Tirtha of Sode Matha*. Havanur: Tara Prakashana & Shri Vadiraja Mrttika Vrndavana. 2003.

Heesterman, J.C. *The Inner Conflict of Tradition: Essays in Indian Ritual, Kinship, and Society*. Chicago: University of Chicago Press, 1985.

Heitzman, James. "Temple Urbanism in Medieval South India." *Journal of Asian Studies* 46, no. 4 (Nov. 1987): 791–837.

Hellebradt, Alfred. "Death and Disposal of the Dead (Hindu)." *Encyclopedia of Religion and Ethics,* Vol. 4. Edited by James Hastings. Edingurgh: T and T Clark, 1911, 475–479.

Hileri, George A. *The Monastery: A Study in Freedom, Love and Community*. London: Praeger, 1992.

Hopkins, T.J. "The Social Teaching of the Bhagavata Purana." In *Krishna; Myths, Rites, and Attitudes.* Edited by Milton B Singer. Honolulu: East-West Center Press, 1966.

Hopkins, W. "On the Hindu Custom of Dying to Redress a Grievance." *Journal of the American Oriental Society* (1900): 151–153.

Hunshal, S.M. *The Lingayat Movement: A Social Revolution in Karnatak.* Dharwar, India: Karnatak Sahitya Mandira, 1947.

Huntington, Susan L. "Early Buddhist Art and the Theory of Aniconism." *The Art Journal* 49 (1990): 401–408.

———. *The Art of Ancient India: Buddhist, Hindu, Jain*. New York: Weatehr Hill, 1985.

Ikegame, Aya. "Why Do Backward Castes Need Their Own Gurus? The Social and Political Significance of New Caste-based Monasteries in Karnataka." *Contemporary South Asia* 18, no. 1 (2010): 57–70.

Inden, Ronald. "Ritual Authority and Cyclical Time in Hindu Kingship." In *Kingship and Authority in South Asia*. Edited by J.F. Richards. Madison: University of Wisconsin, 1978, 28–73.

Ishwaran, K. *Speaking of Basava: Lingayat Religion and Culture in South Asia*. Westview Press, Boulder, 1992.

Jacobsen, Knut A., Helene Basu, Angelika Malinar, and Vasudha Narayanan. "Acharya, Diwakar 'Pasupatas.'" In *Encyclopedia of Hinduism*, Vol. 3. Brill: Leiden, 2009–2015.

Jaini, Padmanabha. The Jain Path of Purification. New Delhi: Motilal Banarsidass, 1979.

Jangam, R.T. "Basaveshwara and the Ideal of Social Equality." *Basava Journal* Vol. IIX, no.3 (1985).

Jinhua, Chen. "Sarira and Scepter: Empress Wu's Political Use of Buddhist Relics." *Journal of the Indian Association of Buddhist Studies* 25 (2002): 33–150.

Johnston, F. Reginald. *Buddhist China.* London: John Murray, 1976. First Edition 1913.

Jones, J.J. *The Mahavastu*, Vol. 1–3. London: Pali Text Society, 1949–56.

Joshi, G.B. *Shri Raghavendra-Life and Works*, Vols. 1 and 2. Mantralayam: Sri Gurusarvabhouma Samsodhana Mandiram, Sri Raghavendra Swamy Matha, 2015.

Juergensmeyer, Mark. *Religion as Social Vision.* Berkeley: University of California Press, 1982.

Kane, Pandurang Vama. "Dana (Gifts)." In *The History of Dharmasastra.* Poona Bhandarkar Institute, 1941, Vol. 2, Part 2.

———. *History of Dharmasastra (Ancient and Medieval, Religious and Civil Law).* 5 Vols. Government Oriental Series, Class B, No.6. Poona: Bhandarkar Oriental Research Institute, 1930–53. 2nd edition, Poona: Bhandarkar Oriental Research Institute, 5 Vols., 1968–1977.

Karashima, Noaboru. *South Indian History and Society: Studies from Inscriptions (A.D. 850–1800).* Delhi: Oxford University Press, 1984.

Karashima, N., Y. Subbarayalu, and P. Shanmugam. "Mathas and Medieval Religious Movements in Tamil Nadu: An Epigraphical Study." *Indian Historical Review* 37, no. 2 (2011): 217–234.

Karunaratne, T.B. "The Significance of the Signs and Symbols on the Footprints of the Buddha." *Journal of the Sri Lanka Branch of the Royal Asiatic Society* no. 20 (1976): 47–63.

Katti, Madhav, N. "Some Important Epigraphs of the Sangama Dynasty." In *Early Vijayanagara*, ed.G. S. Dikshit. Bangalore: B. M. S. Memorial Foundation, 1988, 143–152.

Kern, Heinrich. *Manual of Indian Buddhism*, 1896. Reprint used: Varanasi–Delhi: Indological Book House, 1972.

Khare, D.C. "Memorial Stones in Maharashtra." In *Memorial Stones in S. India a Study of Their Origin, Significance and Variety.* Edited by Gunther D. Sontheimer and S Settar. Dharwad. Institute of Indian Art History, Karnatak University, 1982, 251–254.

Kinnard, Jacob N. "The Polyvalent Padas of Vishnu and the Buddha." In *History of Religions* 40, no. 1 (2000): 32–57; and *Buddhist Art and Narrative* (Aug., 2000): 32–57.

Kinsley, D.R. *The Divine Player.* Delhi, 1979.

Krishnamani, M.N. *Shankara: The Revolutionary*. New Delhi: Rajan Publications, 2001.

Krishnaswami, A. *Tamil Country under Vijayanagara*. Annamalai: Annamalai University, 1959.

———. *Topics in South Indian History*. Annamalinagar: Published by the Author, 1975.

Kulke, Hermann. "Royal Temple Policy and the Structure of Medieval Hindu Kingdoms." In *The Cult of Jagannatha and the Regional Tradition in Orissa*. Edited by A. Eschmann. New Delhi: Manohar, 1986, 125–137.

———. Maharajas, Mahants and Historians: Reflections on the Historiography of Early Vijayangara and Sringeri. In *Vijayanagara – City and Empire*: New Currents of Research. 2 Vols. Edited by Dallapiccola, Anna Libera and Lallemant, Stephanie Zingel-Ave. Stuttgart: Franz Steiner Verlag Wiesbaden GMBH, 1985, 120–143.

Kumar, Pintu. *Buddhist Learning in South Asia: Education, Religion, and Culture at the Ancient Sri Nalanda Mahavihara*, Lexington Books, 2018.

Kumara, S and others. eds. *Bhagavad Sri Ramanuja's Contribution to Four Swayamvyakta Kshetras-Kanchipuram, Srirangam, Tirupati and Melkote*. Melkote: Academy of Sanskrit Research, 2015.

Law, B.C. Law, Eastern: "The Study of Buddhist Self-Immolation Beyond Religious Tradition and Political Context: The Necessity of Protogetical Analysis." *The International Journal of Religion and Spirituality in Society* 7, no. 3 (2017): 25–41.

Leclercq, Jean O.S.B. *The Love of Learning and the Desire for God: A Study of Monastic Culture*. Trans. Catharine Misrahi. New York: Fordham University Press, 1961.

Lingat, Robert. *The Classical Law of India*. Translated from the French by J. Duncan M. Derrett. Berkeley: University of California, 1973.

Long, Jeffery D. *Jainism: An Introduction*. London: I.B. Tauris, 1988, 154–165.

Longhurst, A.H. *Hampi Ruins: Described and Illustrated*. Madras: Government Press, 1917.

L'Orange, H.P. *Studies on the Iconography of Cosmic Kingship in the Ancient World*. New York: Caratzas Brothers Publishers New Rochelle, 1982.

Lorenzen, David N. *Religious Movements in South Asia 600–1800*. Oxford University Press, 2006.

———. "Early Evidence for Tantric Religion". In *the Roots of Tantra*. Edited by Katherine Anne Harper and Robert L. Brown. Albany: State University of New York Press, 2002, 25–36.

———. "The Kabir Panth: Heretics to Hindus." In *Religious Change and Cultural Domination*. Edited by David N. Lorenzen. Mexico City: El Colegio de Mexico, 1981.

———. "Warrior Ascetics in Indian History." *Journal of the American Oriental Society* 98, no. 1 (January 01, 1978): 61–75.

———. *The Kapalikas and Kalamukhas: Two Lost Saiva Sects*. Berkeley: University of California Press, 1972.

Madan, T. N., ed. *91 Religion in India*. Oxford: Oxford University Press, 1991.

———. *Non Renunciation: Themes and Interpretations of Hindu Culture*. Delhi: Oxford University Press, I987.

———. "Way of Life: King, Householder, Renouncer." In *Essays in Honour of Louis Dumont*. New Delhi: Viikas, 155–182.

Madugula, I.S. *The Acharya: Sankara of Kaladi, Motilal Banarsidass*. Delhi: 1985, Reprint 2006.

Mahadevan, T.M.P., ed. *A Seminar on Saints*. Madras: Ganesh and Co., 1960.

Mahalingam, T.V. *Adiministration and Social Life under Vijayanagara*. General editor K.A.N. Sastri, 2 Vols. Madras University Historical Series No. 15. Madras: University of Madras, 1940.

Mahipati, Justin E. Abbott, and Narhar R. Godbole. *Stories of Indian Saints: an English Translation of Mahipati's Marathi Bhaktavijaya*. Poona: N.R. Godbole, 1933.

Marco, Giuseppe De. "The Stupa as a Funerary monument: New Iconographical Evidence." *East and West* 37, no. 1 (1987): 191–246.

Mariott, McKim. *Village India: Studies in the Little Community*. Chicago: University of Chicago Press, 1955.

Marriott, McKim and Ronald Inden. "Toward an Ethnosociology of South Asian Caste Systems." In *The New Wind: Changing Identities in South Asia*, ed. Kenneth David. The Hague: Mouton Publishers, 1977, 227–238.

Matteini, Michele. "On the 'True Body' of Huineng." *RES* (Spring/Autumn 2009): 41–60.

Michael, R.B. "Linga as Lord Supreme in the Vacanas of Basava." *Numen* 29 (1982): 2.

Michaels, Axel, ed. *The Pandit: Traditional Scholarship in India.* New Delhi: Manohar, 2001.

Michaels, Axel "The Pandit as a Legal Adviser: rajaguru, rajapurohita and dharmadhikarin." In The Pandit: Traditional Scholarship in India. Edited by Michaels, Axel Michaels. New Delhi: Manohar, 2001.

Miller, David M. and Dorothy C. Wertz. *Hindu Monastic Life the Monks and Monasteries of Bhubaneswar.* London: McGill-Queen's University Press, 1976.

Mills, Martin A. "Ritual as History in Tibetan Divine Kingship: Notes on the Myth of the Khotanese Monks." *History of Religions* 51, no. 3 (2012): 220–238.

Milner, M. Jr. *Status and Sacredness.* New Delhi: Oxford University Press. South Asia Books, 1994.

Mirashi, V.V., ed. *Inscriptions of the Kalachuri–Chedi Era,* Coprus Inscriptionum Indicarum, Vol. V, Parts I–II, Ootacamund, 1955.

Misra, R.N. *Ascetics, Piety and Power. Saiva Siddhanta Monastic Art in the Woodlands of Central India.* New Delhi: Aryan Books International, 2018.

Mitra, Babu Rajendralala. "Funeral Ceremonies of the Ancient Hindus." *Journal of the Asiatic Society of Bengal* 39, no. 4 (1870): 24–264 (sp 253–5).

Mookerji, Satkari. *Buddhist Phisophy of Universal Flux.* Delhi: Motilal Banarsidass, 1935. Orient Book Distributors. Reprint, 1975.

Muck, Terry C. "Relics, Ritual, and Representation in Buddhism: Rematerializing the Sri Lankan Theravada Tradition (Review)." *Buddhist-Christian Studies* 22, no. 1 (2002): 242–243.

Muddachari, B. *Economic History of Karnataka.* Mysore: Udaya Prakashan, 1982.

Mus, Paul, Serge Thion, and Martine Karnoouth-Vertalier. "The Iconography of an Aniconic Art." *Anthropology and Aesthetics,* no. 14 (Autumn 1987): 5–26.

Nagaswamy, R, *Studies in South Indian History and Culture. Professor V.R. Ramacandra Dikshitar Centenary Volume.* Delhi: DKPW, 1997.

Nandi, R.N. "Origin of the Virasaiva Movement." *Indian Historical Review* 2 (1975): 1.

Nandimath, S.C. *A Handbook of Virasaivism.* Delhi: Motilal Banarsidass, 1979.

Narayanan, M.G.S. and Kesavan Veluthat. "Bhakti Movement in South India." In *The Feudal Order: State, Society and Ideology in the Early Medieval India.* Edited by D.N. Jha. New Delhi: Manohar Publishers, 2000.

Oldenberg, Hermann. *Buddha: His Life, His Doctrine, His Work*. London: Willimas and Norgate, 1882.

———. *The Grhya-sutras: Rlues of Vedic Comestic Cermonies*. Delhi: Motilal Banarsidass, 1886, 1981, 245–246.

Olivelle, Patrick. *Renunciation in Hinduism: A Medieval Debate*. Institut für Indologie der Universität Wien, 1986.

———. *Rules and Regulations of Brahmanical Asceticism. Yatidharma-samuccaya of Yådava Prakasa*. Edited and translated. Albany: State University of New York Press, 1995.

———. *Samnyasa Upanisads: Hindu Scriptures on Asceticism and Renunciation*. Oxford University Press, 1992.

———. *The Āśrama System: The History and Hermeneutics of a Religious Institution*. New York: Oxford University Press, 1993.

———. *Vasudevsrama Yatidharmaprakasa: A Treatise on World Renunciation*. Part 2. Translation. Vienna: publications of the de Nobili Research Lib. Gerold &Komm, Delhi: Motilal Banarsidass, 1977.

———. *The Origin and the Early Development of Buddhist Monachism*. Colombo: M.D. Gunasena, 1974, 8–9.

Oman, John Campbell. *The Mystics, Ascetics, and Saints of India; a Study of Sadhuism, with an Account of the Yogis, Sanyasis, Bairagis, and Other Strange Hindu Sectarians*. London: T.F. Unwin, 1903.New Delhi: Cosmo Publications, 1984.

———. *The Mystics, Ascetic and Saints of India: A Study of Sadhuism, with an Account of the Yogis, Sanyasis, Bairagis, and other Strange Hindu Sectarians*. Cosmo Publications, 1984.

Oren, S. "Killing a Myth: A Note on the Lingayat Mutts of Mysore State and their Political Influence." *Journal of Indian History* (1973): (Golden Jubilee volume).

———. "Religion and Social Change: A Study of Tradition and Change in Virasaivism." In *Dimensions of Social Change in India*, ed. M.N. Srinivas et al. Columbia, MO: South Asia Books, 1978.

Orr, W.G. *A Sixteenth-Century Indian Mystic*. London: Lutterworth Press, 1947.

Padmanabhacharya, C.M. *Life and Teachings of Sri Madhvachariar*, 2nd edition, Bombay, 1983.

Pal, Pratapaditya. "The Aiduka of the Visnudharmottarapurana and Certain Aspects of Stupa Symbolism." *Journal of the Indian Society of Oriental Art*, no. 4 (1971–72): 49–62.

Pande, Govind Chandra. *Life and Thought of Sankaracarya.* Delhi: Motilal Banarsidass Publishers, Pvt. Ltd, 1994, Reprint 2004.

Pandey, Rajbali. *Hindu Samskaras: Socio-Religious Study of the Hindu Sacraments.* 2nd rev ed. Deli: Motilal Banarsidas, 1969.

Pandit, M.P. *All Life Is Yoga.* Pondicherry: Dipti Publications, 1975.

Panigraphi, K.C. *Archaeological Remains at Bhubaneswar.* Bombay, 1961.

Pandurangi, K.T. *Dvaita Vedānta.* Bangalore: Studies and Research Foundation, 1923.

Pathak, V.S. *Saiva Cults in Northern India, from Inscriptions, 700 A.D. to 1200 A.D.* Varanasi: Ram Naresh Varma, 1960.

Pellegrini, Gianni. "Figure of Pandita as Guru." In *Guru: The Spiritual Master in Eastern and Western Traditions.* Edited by Rigopoulos, Antonio. Delhi: DKPW, 2007, 305–26.

Pintchman, Tracy. *Guests at God's Wedding: Celebrating Kartik among the Women of Benares.* New York: SUNY, 2005.

Poonacha, K.P. *Excavations at Kanaganahalli (Sannati) Taluk Chitapur, Dist. Gulbarga Karnataka.* New Delhi: Archaeological Survey of India, 2011.

Prasoon, Shrikant. *Indian Saints and Sages: Before Shankaracharya to Vivekananda.* Delhi: Hindoology Books, 2009.

Puranika, K. Hayavadana. *Poornaprajna Vijaya: Life and Teachings of Sri Madhwacharya.* Translated from Kanndada by Bhadra Krishnamoorthy. Chennai: Sri Krishna Sri Raghvendra Trust, 2010.

Raina, M.K. "Guru-Shishya (kp spelling) Relationship in Indian Culture: The Possibility of a Creative Resilient Framework." *Psychology and Developing Societies* 14, no. 1 (2002): 167–198.

Rajagopal, S. *Kaveri: Studies in Epigraphy, Archaeology and History: Prof. Y. Subbarayalu Felicitation Volume.* Chennai: Panpattu Veliyiittakam, 2001.

Rajasekhara, Sindigi. "Inscriptions at Vijayangara." In *Vijayanagara – City and Empire*: New Currents of Research. Vol. 1. Edited by Dallapiccola, Anna Libera and Lallemant, Stephanie Zingel-Ave. Wiesbaden GMBH, Stuttgart: Franz Steiner Verlag, 1985, 101–119.

Raman, K.V. "Political and Social Conditions of Tamil Nadu during the Early Vijayanagara Times." In *Early Vijayanagara.* Edited by G.S. Dikshit, Bangalore: B. M. S. Memorial Foundation, 1988, 27–34.

———. *Sri Varadarajaswami Temple – Kanchi: A Study of its History, Art and Architecture.* New Delhi: Abhinav Publications, 1975, 2003.

Rama Sharma, M.H. *The History of the Vijayanagar Empire*. Ed. M.H. Gopal. Bombay: Popular Prakashan, 1978–80, Vol. 1. *Beginnings and Expansion 1308–1569*, 1978, Vol. 2. *Decline and Disappearance,* 1980.

Ramachandran, T N. "The Nagapattinam and other Buddhist Bronzes in the Madras Museum." *Bulletin of the Madras Museum*. New series general section, 7, no. 1. (1954).

Rangachari, Dewan Bahadur K. *The Sri Vaishnava Brahmans*. Delhi: Gian Publishing House, 1986.

Ranganathan C., Krishnan S. and others. *Bhagavad Academy of Sanskrit Research*, 2015. Melkote.

Rao, B.A. Krishnaswamy. *Outline of the Philosophy of Sri Madhwacharya*. Bangalore: Swetadweepa Publications, 2003.

Rao, Hayavadana. *Poornaprajna Vijaya: Life and teachings of Sri Madhwacharya*. Translated from Kannada by Dhadra Krishnamoorthy, Chennai: Sri Krishna Sri Raghavendra Trust, 2010.

Rao, Krishna. *Udupi: A Great Religious Center*. Manipal: Manipal Rotary Club, 1989.

———. *Outline of the Philosophy of Madwacharya.* Manipal: Manipal Rotary Club, 1989.

Rao, Nagaraja M. S. Ed. *Vijayanagara: Progress of Research 1979–1983*. Mysore: Directorate of Archaeology and Museums, 1983.

Rao, Nalini. "Navaratri in South India: Symbolism and Power in Royal Rituals." *Sagar: A South Asia Research Journal*, 24 (2016): 1–14.

———. *Royal Imagery and Networks of Power at Vijayanagara: A Study of Kingship in South India*. Originals. Delhi, 2010.

———. "Royal Portraits at Vijayangara: Identification and Meaning." In *New Trends in Indian Art and Archaeology: S.R. Rao's 70th Birthday Felicitation,* Vol. 2. Edited by B.U. Nayak and N.C. Ghosh. New Delhi: Aditya Prakashan, 1992, 349–366.

———. "Royal Religious Beneficence in Pre-Modern India: Political and Social Implications." *International Journal of Dharma Studies* 4, Article no. 7 (July 2016): 1–11.

———. "The Heroic Tradition in South Indian Art: Ascetics, Gods, and Kings." In *Ananya: A Portrait of India*. Edited by S.N. Sridhar and Nirmal K. Mattoo. New York: The Association of Indians in America, 1997, 523–543.

Rao, Prabhakar. *Mathas (Mutts) of Madhwa Community*. Singapore, 2009.

Rao, Rama M. *Krishanadeva Raya*. New Delhi: National Book Trust, 1971.

Rao, S.K. Ramachandra. *Sankara and his Adhyasa Bhashya*. Bangalore: Abhijanan, 2002.

Rao, S.R. *The Lost City of Dvaraka*. Delhi: Aditya Prakashan, 1999.

Rao, Vasudeva. *Living Traditions in Contemporary Contexts: The Madhva Matha of Udupi*. New Delhi: Orient Longman, 2002.

Ratnam, Venkata A.V. *Local Government in the Vijayanagara Empire*. Mysore: University of Mysore, 1972.

Read, Herbert. *Icon and Idea: The Function of Art in the Development of Human Consciousness*. New York: Schocken Books, 1965.

Renfrew, C., M. Boyd, and I. Morley, eds. *Death Rituals and Social Order in the Ancient World: Death Shall have No Dominion*. Cambridge: Cambridge University Press, 1962.

Rigopoulos, Antonio. Ed. *Guru: The Spiritual Master in Eastern and Western Traditions: Authority and Charisma*. Venice, Italy: Venetian Academy of Indian Studies Series, no. 4. 2004. First Indian Edition, New Delhi: DKPW 2007.

Ritzinger, J. and M. Bingenheimer. "Whole Body Relics in Chinese Buddhism: Previous Research and Historical View." *Indian International Journal of Buddhist Studies* 7 (2006): 37–94.

Rizvi, Saiyid Atthar Abbas. *A History of Sufism in India*, Vol. 1. Delhi: Munshiram Manoharlal, 1978.

Ruppert, Brian. *Jewel in the Ashes: Buddha Relics and Power in Early Medieval Japan*. Harvard University Asia Center, 2000.

Sacco, A.M. "Serpa Funeral Ceremony." *Tibet Journal* 32, no. 1 (1998): 25–37.

Sadananda, S. "Islamic Influence in Vijayanagara Capital." *Journal of Andhra Historical Research Society* 30 (1964–65): 85–88.

Sadasivaiah, H.M. *A Comparative Study of Two Virasaiva Monasteries: A Study in Sociology of Religion*. Mysore: Prasaranga, Manasa Gangotri, 1967.

Saletore, B.A. "The Raja Guru of the Founders of Vijayanagara and the Pontiffs of Sringeri Matha." *Journal of Andhra Historical Research Society* 9, Part 4 (1935): 33–42.

Sangay, T. "Tibetan Rituals of the Dead." Trans. G. Kilty. *Tibetan Medicene* 7 (1994): 30–40.

Santideva, Siksasamucchaya. *Buddhist Sanskrit Texts, Vol. 11*. Ed. P.L. Vaidya. Darbhanga: The Mithila Institute of Post Graduate Studies and Research in Sanskrit Learning, 1961.

Saraswati, Baidyanath. *Brahmanic Ritual Traditions in the Crucible of Time: Studies in Indian and Asian Civilizations*, Simla: Indian Institute of Advanced Study, 1977.

Sastri, K. Nilakanta. *A Hisory of South India: From Prehistoric Times to the Fall of Vijayanagara*. New Delhi: Oxford University Press, 1958.

Sastry, A.K. *History of Sringeri*. Dharwar: Prasaranga, Karnatak University, 1982.

Sastry, Alladi Mahadeva Trans. *Dakshinamurti Stotra of Sri Sankaracharya and Dakshinamurti Upanishad.* Chennai: Samata Books, 1978. Reprint 2001.

Sathiyanathan, Amman. *Navanidhi Nalgum Navarindavanam Tamil.* Trans. K. Lakshman. The Bountiful Navabrindavana. Chennai: Arulmigu Amman Pathippagam, 2006.

Sawai, Yoshitsugau. *The Faith of Ascetics and Lay Smartas: A Study of the Sankaran Tradition of Srngeri*, Vol. XIX. Publications of the De Nobili Research Library. Edited by Gerhard Oberhammer. Vienna: Institute for Indology, University of Vienna, 1992.

Scharf, Robert H. "Buddhism in China, East Asia and Japan." In *Critical Concepts in Religious Studies*. Edited by P. Willaims, Vol. 8. London: Routledge, 2005.

———. "On the Allure of Buddhist." *Representations*, no. 66 (Spring, 1999): 75.

———. "The Idolization of Enlightenment: The Mummification Chan Masters in Medieval China." *History of Religions* 32, no. 1 (Aug. 1992): 1–31.

Scharfe, Hartmutt. *Education in Ancient India*. Leiden: Brill, 2002.

Schomer, Karine and W.H. McLeod, eds. *The Sants: Studies in a Devotional Tradition of India*. Berkeley Religious Studies Series. Berkeley: Graduate Theological Union, 1986.

Schopen, G. Stupa and Tirtha. "Tibetan Mortuary Practices and an Unrecognized Form of Burial at Sanctos at Buddhist Sites in India." *Buddhist Forum* 3 (1994): 273–293.

Schopen, Gregory. "Relic." In *Critical Terms for Religious Studies*. Edited by Mark C. Taylor. Chicago: The University of Chicago Press, 1998.

———. *Bones, Stones, and Buddhist Monks: Collected Papers on the Archaeology, Epigraphy, and Texts of Monastic Buddhism in India.* Honolulu: University of Hawai'i Press, 1997.

———. "Ritual Rights and Bones of Contention; More on Monastic Funerals and Relics in the Mulasarvastivada – Vinaya." *Journal of Indian Philosophy* 22 (1994): 31–80.

———. "Monks and the relic cult in the Mahåparinibbåna-sutta. An old misunderstanding in regard to Monastic Buddhism." *From Benares to Beijing: Essays on Buddhism and Chinese religion in honor of Prof. Jan Yün-hua*. Edited by Koichi Shinohara & Gregory Schopen. Oakville, Ontario: Mosaic Press, 1991, 187-201.

——— "On the Buddha and His Bones: The Conception of a Relic in the Inscriptions of Nagarjunakonda." *Journal of the American Oriental Society* 108, no. 4 (Oct.–Dec. 1988): 527–537.

Radhakrishnan, K.R. "Thousands Offer Worship to Kapilavastu Relics in Sri Lanka." *The Hindu*. August 20, 2012.

Sears, Tamara I. *Worldly Gurus and Spiritual Kings: Architecture and Asceticism in Medieval India*. New Haven: Yale University Press, 2014.

Sen, Amulyachandra. *Asoka's Edicts*. 1956, 124–125.

Settar, S. *Inviting Death: Indian Attitude towards the Ritual Death*. Leiden; New York: Brill, 1989.

———. *Pursuing Death. Philosophy and Practice of Voluntary Termination of Life*. Dharwad: Karnatak University, Institute of Indian Art History, 1990.

Settar, S. and Sontheimer, G. D., eds. *Memorial Stones: A Study of their Origin, Significance and Variety*. Dharwad: South Asian Studies, Vol. 2, Karnatak University, 1982.

Sewell, Robert. *A Forgotten Empire (Vijayanagar) A Contribution to the History of India*. Swan Sonnenschein & Co., London, 1900. Reprint, New Delhi: New Asian Educational Services, 1983, 1991.

Shah, Chandrakant P. "The Age of Acharyas: Part 2: Jain Temples, Idols and Worship." *Teerthanka Mahaveer's Teerth*, October 1991.

Shah, Priyabala. "Aiduka." *Journal of the Oriental Institute* 1 (1951–2): 271–278. M.S., 1952, 278–285.

———. *Vishnudharmottara Purana: Introduction*, Vol. 2 . Gaekwad Oriental Series. Bombay: Oriental Institute, 1961.

Shah, Umakant Premanand. *Studies in Jaina Art*. Jaina Cultural Research Society. Banaras: Parsvanath Vidyapeeth, 1955. "Lakulisa: Saivite Saint." In *Discourses on Siva: Proceedings of a Symposium on the Nature of Religious Imagery*. Edited by Michael Meister, Philadelphia: University of Pennsylvania Press and Delhi: Oxford University Press, 92–102

Sharf, Robert H. "The Idolization of Enlightenment: On the Mummification of Ch'an Mastgers in Medieval China." *History of Religions* 32, no. 1 (Aug. 1992): 1–31.

Sharma, B.N. Krishnamurti. *History of the Dvaita School of Vedanta and its Literature from the Earliest Beinnings to Our Own Times*. Delhi: Motilal Banarsidass Pub. First ed., 1981. Third rev., 2001. Reprint 2008.

———. *Philosophy of Sri Madhvacarya*. Delhi: Motilal Banarsidass Publishers, 1962. Rev ed., 1986, Reprint, 1992, 2002, 2008.

———. *Madhva's Teaching in His Own Words*. Ed. K.M. Munshi, R.R. Diwalar. Bombay: Bharatiya Vidya Bhavan, 1961.

Sharma, R.K. *The Kalacuri and their Times*. Delhi: Sandeep Prakashan, 1980.

Sharma, R.S. *India's Ancient Past*. New Delhi: Oxford Univ Press, 2005.

Sharma, Sanjay. "Negotiating Identity and Status: Legitimation and Patronage under the Gurjara-Praiharas of Kanauj." *Studies in History* 22, no. 2 (2006): 181–220.

Shastri, A.K. *A History of Sringeri*. Dharwad: Prasaranga Karnatak University, 1982.

———. *Sringeri Dharma Sansthana*. Sringeri: Sringeri Matha, 1983.

Shastri, Venimadhava. "Vidyaranya's Association with the Vijayanagar Empire." In *Early Vijayanagara*. Edited by G.S. Dikshit. Bangalore: B. M. S. Memorial Foundation, 1988, 45–52.

Shastry, A.M. and R.K. Sharma, eds. *Essays on Evolution of Indian Art and culture K.D. Bajpai Felicitation Vol.*, Vol. 1. Vajapeya. Delhi: Agam Kala Prakashan, 1987.

Shaw, Julia. "Archaeologies of Buddhist Propagation in Ancient India: 'ritual' and 'practical' Models of Religious Change." *World Archaeology* 45, no. 1 (2013): 83–108.

———. "Religion, 'Nature and Environmental Ethics in Ancient India: Archaeologies of Human, Non-human Suffering and Well-being in Early Buddhist and Hindu Contexts." *World Archaeology* (2017): 1–27.

Sheridan, Daniel P. "Jayatirtha." In *Great Thinkers of the Eastern World*. Edited by Ian McGready. New York: Harper Collins, 1995.

———. *Texts in Context: Traditional Hermeneutics in South Asia*. Edited by Jeffrey Timm. State University of New York Press, 1991.

Shivarudrappa, G. "Contributions of Veerashaiva Mathas to the Development of Education in Karnatak from 12th to 18th Century A.D." *Journal of the Karnatak University (Social Sciences)* Vol. XI (1975).

Shivarudraswamy, S.N. *Vijayanagara Temples in Karnataka.* Mysore, Directorate of Archaeology and Museums, 1996.

Shukla, A.C. *The Concept of Imitation in Greek and Indian Aesthetics.* Calcutta: Rupa & Co., 1977.

Simoons, Frederick J. *Plants of Life, Plants of Death*, Madison: University of Wisconsin Press, 1998.

Singer, Milton and Bernard S. Cohn, eds. *Structures and Change in Indian Society*. Chicago: Aldine, 1968.

Singer, Milton. *When a Great Tradition Modernizes*. New York: Praeger, 1972.

Singh, Pritam. *Saints and Sages of India*. New Delhi: New Book Society of India, 1948.

Sinopoli, C. "Earthenware Pottery of Vijyanagara: Some observations." In *Vijayanagara: Progress of Research 1997–1983*. Edited by M.S. Nagraja Rao. Mysore: Directorate of Archaeology and Museums, 1983. 68–74.

Sinopoli, Carla M. and Morrison, Kathleen. The Vijayanagra Metropolitan Survey: The 1988 Season. In *Vijayanagara: Progress of Research 1987–1988*. Edited by D.V. Devarajand C.S. Patil. Mysore: Directorate of Archaeology and Museums, 1991, 55–80.

Sircar, D.C. "Eduka." *Indian Historical Quarterly* 29 (1953): 302–303.

———. *Studies in the Religious Life of Ancient and Medieval India.* Delhi: Motilal Banarsidass, 1971. First published 1953.

Smith, Vincent. "Relics (Eastern)." *Encyclopedia of Religion and Ethics* 10 (1918): 658–662.

Snodgrass, Adrian. *The Symbolism of the Stupa*. Delhi: Motilal Banarasidass, 1992. Heidelberg, Germany: South Asia Institute, University of Heidelberg, 1982.

Somasundaram, Ollilingam, A.G. Tejus Murthy, and D. Vijaya Raghavan. "Jainism–Its Relevance to Psychiatric Practice; with Special Reference to the Practice of Sallekhana." *Indian Journal of Psychiatry* 58 (2016): 471–474.

Srinivasan, C.R. *Kanchipuram Through the Ages*. Delhi: Agam Kala Prakashan, 1979.

Srivastava, K.M. *Buddha's Relics Form Kapilavastu*. Delhi: Agam Kala Prakashan, 1986.

Stoker, Valerie. "Conceiving the Canon in Dvaita Vedanta: Madva's Doctrine of 'All Sacred Lore.'" *Numen* 51, (2004): 47–77.

———. *Polemics and Patronage in the City of Victory: Vyasatirtha, Hindu Sectarianism, and the Sixteenth-Century Vijayanagara Court.* Oakland, CA: University of California Press, 2016.

Strong, John S. *Relics of the Buddha.* Princeton, New Jersey: Princeton University Press, 2004. Delhi: Motilal Banarasidass, 2007.

———. *The Legend and Cult of Upagupta: Sanskrit Buddhism in North India and Southeast Asia.* Princeton, New Jersey: Princeton University Press, 1992.

Subrahmanyam, B. *Buddhist Relic Caskets in South India.* Delhi: Bharatiya Kala Prakashan, 1998.

Sundara, A. "New Light on Religious Trends in Anegondi Region during Vijayanagar Period." In *Early Vijayanagara.* Edited by G.S. Dikshit. Bangalore: B.M. S. Memorial Foundation, 1988, 101–112.

Swahananda, Swami. *Monasteries in South India.* Hollywood, CA: Vedanta Society of Southern California, 1989.

Talbot, Cynthia. "Golaki Matha Inscriptions form Andhra Pradesh: A Study of a Saiva Monastic Lineage" In *Vajapeya. Essays on Evolution of Indian Art and Culture – K.D. Bajpai Felicitation Volume*, Vol. 1. Edited by A.M. Shastri and R.K. Sharma, Agam Prasad. Delhi: Agam Kala Prakashan, 1987, 135–168.

Tapasyananda. *Bhakti Schools of Vedanta.* Madras (Chennai): Sri Ramakrishna Math, 1991.

———. *The Greatness of Sringeri.* Bombay: Tattvaloka Publications, 1991.

Thapar, Romila. *Early India: from the Origins to AD 1300.* Berkeley: University of California Press, 2004.

Tekumalla, Achyuta Rao. "Andhra Literature in the Vijayanagara Empire." *Journal of the Andhra Historical Research Society* 17 (1946): 45–64.

Tirumalai, R. "The Mathas in Pandyan Townships." In *Vajapeya. Essays on Evolution of Indain Art and Culture. K.D. Bajpai Felicitation Volume*, Vol. 1. Edited by. A.M. Shastir, R.K. Sharma, Delhi: Agam Prasad, 1987, 395–407.

Tobert, Natalie. *Anegondi: Architectural Ethnography of a Royal Village.* New Delhi: Manohar, American Institute of Indian Studies, 2000.

Torcinovich, Giovanni. "The Custodians of Truth." In *Guru: The Spiritual Master in Eastern and Western Traditions.* Edited by Rigopoulos, Antonio. Delhi: DKPW. 2007, 137–156.

Trainor, Kevin. *Relics, Ritual and Representation in Buddhism: Rematerializing the Sri Lankan Theravada Tradition*. Cambridge: Cambridge University Press, 1997.

Tripathi. *The Sadhus of India: A Sociological View*. Bombay: Popular Prakashan, 1978.

Turner, Victor. *The Ritual Process: Structure and Anti-Structure*. Chicago: Aldine, 1969.

Upadhye, Adinath Neminath. "Nisidhi- It's Meaning." In *Memorial Stones: A Study of their Origin, Significance, and Variety*. Edited by S.Settar and G.D. Songheimer. Dharwad: Institute of Indian Art History, 1982, 45–46.

Upasaka, C.S. "Cultural Significance of Udayana (Uddyana)." In *Vajpeya: Essays on the Evolution of Indian Art and Culture, K.D. Bajpai Felicitation Volume*, Vol. 1. Edited by A.M. Shastri and R.K. Sharma. Delhi: Agam Prasad, Agam Kala Prakashan, 1987, 93–95.

Uttangi, C.D. *Anubhava Mantapa: The Heart of Lingayat Religion* (Reprint 1982). Edited by S.R.Gunjal. Dharwar, India: Uttangi Centenary Commemoration Committee, 1955.

———. "Some Aspects of Lingayat Ideology and Monastic Organization." *Eastern Anthropologist* 33, no. 4 (1980).

Vaisali, B. Subrahmanyam. *Buddhist Relic Caskets in South India*. Delhi: Bharatiay Kala Prakashan, 1998.

Vidyabhusana Baladeva. *Prameya-Ratnavali*. Delhi: Ras Bihai Lal and Son, 2009.

Wagoner, B. Phillip. *Tidings of the King: A Trranslation and Ethnohistorical Analysis of the Rayavacakamu*. Hawaii: University of Hawaii Press, 1993.

Williams, Monier. *Sanskirt –English Dicionary*. New Delhi: Munshiram Manoharlal, 1899.

Van der Veer, Peter. "Taming the Ascetic Devotionalis in a Hindu Monastic Order." *Man* 22 (1987): 680–695.

Vaudeville, Charlotte. *Myths, Saints and Legends in Medieval India*. Delhi: Oxford University Press, 1999.

Vedavyasachary, H.K. *Jagadguru Sri Raghavendra Swamy*, 4th ed. Trans. G.B. Joshi. Nanjangud. Bangalore: Sri Parimal Research and Publishing House.

Venkata Subbiah, A. "A Twelfth Century University in Mysore." *The Quarterly Journal of the Mythic Society* 7, no. 3 (April 1917): 157–196.

Verghese, Anila. *Archaeology, Art and Religion: New Perspectives on Vijayanagara*. Oxford University Press, 2000.

———. *Hampi: Monumental Legacy*. Oxford University Press, 2002.

———. "Krsnadevaraya's Monument of Victory: The Krsna Temple at Vijayanagara." *Journal of the Asiatic Society of Bombay* 71 (1997): 197–207.

———. *Religious Traditions at Vijayanagara: As Revealed Through its Monuments*. New Delhi: Manohar Publications and the American Institute of Indian Studies, 1995.

Verghese, Anila and Dieter Eigner. "A Monastic Complex in Vithalpura, Hampi Vijayanagra. South Asian Studies." *Journal of the Society for South Asian Studies* (incorporating the Society for Afghan Studies) 14, no. 4 (1998): 127–140.

Wijayaratna, Môhan. *Buddhist Monastic Life: According to the Texts of the Theravāda Tradition*. Cambridge: Cambridge University Press, 1990.

Wilkins, William Joseph. *Hindu Mythology, Vedic and Purānic*. Calcutta; London, 1900.

Williams, Monier. *Brahmanism and Hinduism*. London: J. Murray, 1891.

White, David Gordon. *The Alchemical Body. Siddha Traditions in Medieval India*. Ed. T.W. Rhys Davids and J.E. Carpenter, 3 Vols. Chicago & London: University of Chicago Press, 1890–1911.

Williams, Sri Monier. *Buddhism, in its Connexion with Brahmanism and Hinduism and in its Contrast with Christianity*. London: John Murray, 1889.

———. *Sanskrit-English Dictionary*. New Delhi: Motilal Banarsidass, 1899, 2002.

Yazdani, Ghulam. *The Early History of the Deccan*. Parts 1–VI. London: Govt of Andhra Pradesh and Oxford University Press, 1960.

Yetss, Perceval. "Notes on the Disposal of Buddhist Dead in China." *Journal of the Royal Asiatic Society* (1911): 699–725.

Yocum, Glenn E. "A Non-Brahman Tamil Shaiva Mutt: A Field study of the Thiruvavduthurai Adheenam." In *Monastic Life in the Christian and Hindu traditions*. Edited by Austin Creel and Vasudha Narayanan Edwin Mellen, 1990, 250–265.

Yogananda, Paramahamsa. *Autobiography of a Yogi*. Los Angeles: Self-Realization Fellowship, 1956.

Yun Hua Jan. "Buddhist Self-Immolation in Medieval China." *History of Religions* 4, no. 2 (1965).

Index

Ablur inscriptions, 36
ācārya(s)/ *upādhyāya*, 1, 6, 22, 25, 27, 55, 68–69; *pīṭhas*, 28
acyutapreksha, 58
adheenam of a Saiva Siddhanta *maṭha*, 115
adhyāpaka, 22
Ādi Śankarācārya, 5, 11, 24, 53–56, 91, 137, 160
adrisya, 74
Advaita: *maṭha*(s), 5, 21, 30, 53, 56, 58, 66–67, 69, 73, 157; monasteries, 11; philosophy, 160; School of Saivism, 54
Advaita, Viśiṣṭādvaita and Dvaita *maṭhas*, 5, 54–55, 156
Advaita Vedānta, 158; *maṭhas*, 11
Āgamas, 29, 31, 35, 41, 71
Agamic theism, 31
agrahāra(s), 6, 25, 27–28, 30–31, 40
aham brahmāsmi, 55, 160
aiduka, 158; was basically a Saiva structure, 110
Ajanta, 76
alankāra, 102
Ālvārs, 57, 71; saints, 119; Tamil saints, 57
amsa of *jeeva*, 144
ānanda, 2, 13, 57; in Dualist philosophy, 143; of *jīva* is different from *ānanda* of *brahman*, 143
Ānanda Tīrtha, 58
Ananta, 135
ananta rūpa, 141
ancient Indian education system, 5
Aniruddha, 140, 142
anthakarana, 145
anushthana, 33
anvīkṣikī, 23
Aphsad inscription of Adityasena, 20
apparent parallels between Buddhist *stupa* and Hindu *vṛndāvanas*, 12
archaeological evidences, 133
architecture of Dvaita monastery, 74
ascent of Saivism, 41
ascetic: Guru, 19; nature of the Guru, 160; pontiff, 91
ascetics of the Śaiva Siddhānta *maṭhas*, 33
Ashta *maṭha*(s)/Ashta *mathas*, 60–63, 66, 74–75
āśrama, 6, 135; system, 156
āśramas, 23, 27, 32
Āśrama Upaniṣad, 21
asthi, 105; *samarpaṇa*, 105; *samcayana*, 105; *sancayana srāddha*, 106
Atharvaveda, 23, 55
atimārga, 31
Ātman, 54
ātmavidyā, 23
avadhūta, 22

avatāra, 13, 140; theory, 56
*avatāra*s of Viṣṇu, 60, 95
ayamātma brahma, 55

bābā, 22
Badrinath, 54
Bāla Śivayogi, 1
Basaveshwara, 38, 91
Bauddha, 37
Bauddha-*vihāra*, 38
Baudhayana Pitru Medha Sutra, 117
beginnings of Hindu monasteries, 20
Bhagavad Gīta/, 21, 23, 53–54, 56–57, 64, 74, 138
Bhāgavata, 59; cult with Kṛṣṇa Vāsudeava, 56
Bhāgavata/Bhāgavat Purāṇa, 9, 136, 139, 143; also connects Tulsi and Kṛṣṇa to Tulsi and Rādhā, 138
Bhagavata rūpa, 141
bhakti, 57, 162; cult, 57; movement, 9, 145–46
bhaktivāda, 57
bhasma, 105
Bhatta Bhaskara, 54
bhikku, 22
bhikkuni(s), 25
bhiksha matha santāna, 35
bhikṣu, 22
Bhimasena, 145
Bhramara Gīta, 143
Bilhana, 142
bliss, 143
boarding, 91
bodily: features of the Guru, 143; relics, 109
body and life of the Guru is eternal, 160
Brahma, 37, 64, 106
brahmacāri(n), 22–23, 27
brahman, 23, 54
brāhmaṇas, 36
brahmānubhava, 145
brahmapuris, 27, 29
Brahma Saṁhitā, 140
Brahma Sūtras, 53–54, 59
brahmavidvans, 33
brahmavidyā, 23
brāhmin and non-*brāhmin maṭhas*, 35
bronze icon of Lokeśvara, 113
Buddha, 3, 21, 24, 37, 39, 91, 105, 107–8; was the first refuge or jewel of Buddhism, 24
Buddhism, 1, 25, 30, 36, 105
Buddhist: Chinese evidences, 119; iconography, 39; inscriptions, 40; monasteries, 5, 40; philosophers, 54; and pre-Buddhist traditions, 3; relics, 6, 93; *saṅgha*(s), 19, 24–25; *stūpa*(s), ix, 108, 113, 158; vestiges, 41; *vihāra*(s), 37, 64
Buddhist, Jain and Hindu monasteries, 11
Bukka Raya, 70
burial feasts, 101

caitya (s), 111, 158; was a religious edifice, 109; and *stūpa* have conceptual and functional similarities, 109
cakra, 101, 103, 143
Candellas, 30
caryā, 31
Caturvarga Cintamani, 67
celibacy, 29
cetiyas/caityas, 107–8
Chalukyas, 26, 117
Chalukyas of: Badami, 27, 30; Kalyana, 27; of Kalyani, 31
chatri, 116
chaturanana paṇḍitas, 34
Chinese: Buddhists practice of self-immolation, 115; ruler Xian-Chun, 113
Christian monastery, 4
circumambulatory path, 74, 144
Cola(s), 10, 27, 31, 39; king, 111
community feeding, 91
comparison: of the architecture of a *maṭha* and a *vihāra*, 76; between Hindu and Buddhist monasteries, 4

concept of: *bhakti*, 56; four *Vyūha* forms of Viṣṇu, 142
conflicts between the temple and *maṭha*, 77
connection between Kṛṣṇa and Mathura, 140
constant dependence of the *jīva* on *brahman*, 143
cult of: Gurus, 146; Viṣṇu, Nārāyaṇa, and Kṛṣṇa-Vāsudeva, 56

dagoba, 110
dakṣiṇapathapati, 10
dāna, 28
dandanāyaka Rupabhattaya, 38
daṇḍanīti, 23
darśan of the icon of Kṛṣṇa, 103
Darukacārya at Ujjain, 28
*dasanāmi sanyāsin*s, 54
Dasa Prakarnas, 59
dāsyanāma, 71
death markers for ascetics of the Viraśaiva order, 110
decline of Buddhism, 7, 11, 20; and Jainism, 56
decline of Buddhist: monasticism, 39; *saṅgha*, 27
demands of mass religion, 162
Desastha *maṭha*s, 60–62, 66
a detailed survey of *maṭha*s, 155
Devaśarma, son of Bhāradvāja Muni, 135
dhamādhikari, 68
dharma, 24, 55, 67, 77, 157; relics, 105
dharmarāya, 70
Dharmaśāstra, 28
Dharmaśastras Nibandha, 67
Dharmasūtras, 21, 66
dhātu, 105; *caitya*, 109
dhātu garbha/dhātugarbha, 105, 110
difference between: Buddhist and Hindu education system, 25; *maṭha* and another educational institution, 29; temple and *maṭha* architecture, 76
Digambara tradition, 114
diksha guru, 33
disciple, 145
divine play of *prakata* and *aprakata*/ divine play of *prakaṭa* and *aprakaṭa*, 148, 160
division between Advaita and Dvaita philosophies, 59
doctrine of: *māyā*, 56; qualified monism or Viśiṣṭādvaita, 57; spiritual monism, 57; Vaiśeṣika philosophy, 31; Viśiṣṭādvaita and Dvaita, 57
Dualism, 59, 161
Dualist thought, 91
duṣṭa nigraha, 41
Dvaita, 59, 156; *ācāryas*, 146; Guru(s), 74, 120, 142, 160; *maṭha*(s), 3, 6, 11, 13, 21, 53, 59, 66, 68, 73, 91, 101, 103, 138, 148, 160; adhere to the philosophy of Madhvacarya, 63; of Madhvācārya, 11, 67, 102; philosophy, 145; pontiff, 141; *sanyāsins*, 115; system of philosophy, 58
dvāparayuga, 145
Dvaraka, 54
dynamic traditions of asceticism and bliss, 4

early: formal educational institutions, 6; history of Hindu monasteries, 20; monastic architecture of Śaiva monasteries, 6
Eastern Chalukyas, 10; of Kalyani, 39
educational philosophy, theory and classification, 23
efficacy of the *vṛndāvana*, 13, 161
*eiduka*s, 107
*ekadandin*s, 36
Ekoramaradhya at Himavatkedar, 28
embalmed body of the Guru, 12
epigraphical evidence of *liṅga*s, 110
erection of: *aidukas* as memorials, 110; a *vṛndāvana*, 110
esoteric Shingon school of Buddhism, 112

establishment of *maṭhas*, 54
eternal form, 141
ethical foundation, 157
evolution of Buddhism, 24
exchange of philosophic and religious traditions, 10

Fa Hsien, 26
favorite god, 95
female *yogis*, 135
five: deities of the *panchayana*, 66; *mudras*, 65; original *maṭhas*, 38; pontifical thrones, 28; *prāṇas*, 144
flexibility and assimilative character of Vaisnavism, 56
followers of Śaiva traditions, 66
formal: educational system, 30; traditional Vedic educational system, 27
formidable institutions, 157
four: classes of Śaivism, 34; *Vedas*, 28; Vyūha forms of Viṣṇu, 141
fourteen divisions of musical science, 28
function and concept of the *stūpa* and *caitya*, 109
"functioned as centers of ecclesiastical teaching," 91
functions of a *maṭha* during the Gupta and post-Gupta periods, 20
funerary practices for ascetics, 93
funerary relics, 105

gada/*gadā*, 103, 143
Ganapatideva, 33
Ganapati/Gaṇapati, 106, 134
Gangas, 10, 27, 40; of Talakad, 39
Gangu, Hasan, 70
gap between God and Guru, 133
garbhagriha, 74–76
garland of *navaratnas*, 102
Gaudapada, 54
Gautama, 36
ghaṭikā(s), 28, 31
ghaṭikāsthana, 28
God: of life-breath, 144; Narayana, 145
Goddess: Tara Bhagavati, 38; Vṛndā, 138
God's form, 141
Gokula Vṛndāvana *dham*, 161
gopicandana, 65
gopis/*gopīs*, 92, 95, 138, 143
gotra, 54
Govardhana, 54
gṛhastha, 22, 63–64
growth of: Hindu (and Jain and some Buddhist) monasteries, 9; *maṭha*(s), 10, 20; as a kingdom, 69; monasteries into full-fledged independent seminal institutions, 157; Saivite *maṭhas*, 41; Vedānta *maṭhas*, 41
gulf between followers of Buddhism and orthodox Hinduism, 56
Guptas, 26
Gupta-Vakataka kings, 30
Gurjara Pratiharas, 30
gurudakshina, 28
Guru-disciple lineage, 30
guru/Guru, 1, 2, 101, 156, 160, 162; and his status of a God, 159; lineage, 3; *stotras*, 147; who was an *avatāra* of God, 161
gurukulas, 22, 25, 27
guru paramparā, 2, 9, 32, 60
Guru-sanyāsis, 55
guru-śiṣya paramparā, 30
Guru śiṣya relationship, 147
gurus of: Desastha *maṭha*, 63; Dvaita order, 146
guru's vṛndāvana, 137; relate to Vṛndāvana, 133
Guru vṛndāvana(s), 116, 141

Hanuman, 145
haridāsa movement, 146
haridāsas, 9, 146
Harihara, 36
Harihara I, 70
Harihara and Bukka, 67

Harivaṃśa, 9, 56, 139–40, 161
Harsa, 40
Hastamalaka, 55
head of a *maṭha* represents the institution, 134
heavenly form, 141
heterodox traditions, 55
hetuvidyā, 26
Hieun Tsang, 26, 40
Hindu: burial practice for *sanyāsins* and yogis, 101; burials, 93; *devālayas*, 1; initiation of studentship, 25; law, 66; *maṭha*, 27; and the Buddhist *vihāra* exhibit similarities, 76; *maṭhas*, 37, 155–56; model of hermitages, 26; monasteries, 5–6; monasticism, 27, 91; Sanskritic culture, 30
Hindu, Buddhist, and Jain monastic systems, 156
Hindu/Buddhist and Jain traditions, 23
Hinduism, 1, 3
Hindu monastery, 25, 27; eludes definition, 4; was an institution of the Guru, 13; known as a *maṭha*, 1
Hindu monastic: architecture, 72; system, 24
hiranyagarbhadāna, 70
historical: influences of Buddhism, 93; interpretation of Kṛṣṇa's Vṛndāvana, 139
historicity of: Kṛṣṇa, 139; *Mahābhārata*, 139
history of: erection of memorials and relic worship, 107; Hindu monasteries, 19; Śri Vaiṣṇava *maṭhas*, 6; whole-body relics, 93
holy basil, 136
Hoysala, 36; kings, 41; Yadava princes, 57
Hoysalas, 10, 28, 31
Huineng, 111
human mummified icon, 108

I am *brahman*, 55
icon of the *guru*, 12
iconographical connotations of the *vṛndāvana*, 13
iconography of: *guru*, 3; *vṛndāvana*, 158
icons of Tara Bhagavati, 113
ideals of Śankara *pīṭha*, 56
idea of constant meditation, 146
ideology of: *dana*, 67; equality and social justice, 39
immolation through meditation, 112
importance of the *guru* within the institution of the *maṭha*, 13
individual soul, 59
Indus Valley site of Dholavira, 110
influence of: Buddhist order, 11; Chinese Buddhists in South India, 112
influences of the Buddhist *saṅgha* and the Jain *maṭha*, 30
inner instrument, 145
inscriptional evidence from the Cola and Pandyan domains, 20
inscription of Samudragupta, 20
installation of the whole-body relic, 115
institutionalization of: deceased Guru, 3, 162; Guru, 155; living Guru, 68
institutionalized the system of monasticism, 41
institution of: Buddha, 3; Buddhist *saṅgha*, 24; deceased Guru, 77; monastery, 10
integrated educational-philosophical system, 55
inter-action between *bhakti* and the Dvaita Guru, 147
interlink between kings, Gurus, and community, 71
interpretation and systematization of Vedic philosophy, 53
Islamic: armies, 40; community, 57
issues of iconic and "aniconic"/non-figural forms in Indian art, 13
iṣṭa devatā, 95

jagadguru, 2, 54–55
Jain, 65; *basadis*, 37; images, 147; *maṭha ācāryas*, 38; *maṭhas*,

5; monasteries, 19; practice of *sallekhana*, 112, 114; saint Bhadrabahu, 20; *saṅghas*, 27, 114; *stūpas*, 109
Jain and Buddhist: *maṭhas*, 38; mendicants, 36
Jainism, 1, 36, 41, 55, 109
Jalandhara, 135
jangamas, 67
japa, 146
jāti and *varna* status, 40
Jayanti Prabudha *vihāra*, 113
jeevan samādhi, 112, 115–16, 119, 148
jeevātma, 59
Jina, 37
Jivaka, 26
jñāna, 31, 146
Jyotir *maṭha*, 55

Kadambas, 27, 39
Kadgas, 40
kaivalya, 63
Kakati Prola II, 34
Kakatiya, 36; king Ganapati, 33; kings of Warangal, 33
Kakatiyas, 6, 31, 39
Kalachuri kings of Chedi, 33
Kalachuris, 30–31
Kālamukha, 31; Gurus, 34, 67; heads, 37; *maṭha*(s), 38
Kālamukhas, 34, 41
kaliyuga, 145
Kallesvara temple, 34
Kalyani inscription of, 1476, 113
kāma, 135
kamandalu, 103
Kanaka Dāsa, 146
kanakana kindi, 103
Kane, P.V., 117
Kanheri, 26, 76
Kapālika, 34; Saivism, 31
karmayoga, 58
Karnataka, 27
Karunika Siddhantins, 34
Kazuo, Kosugi, 112
Kedaresvara *maṭha*, 36
Keladi: Nayakas, 6, 10; Ramaraja Nayaka, 68
kingly and religious institutions, 67
kings of Malava, 33
King Viṭhala Deva (Bitti Deva), 57
kīrtana(s), 146
Kōbō Daishi, 112
Kodiya *maṭha*, 36
kriya, 31
Kṛṣṇa, 66, 73–75, 92, 95, 102, 138, 145, 159–61; was the main deity of Vaiṣṇavites, 142
Kṛṣṇa's *līla*, 143, 148
ksapanakas, 36
kulaguru and *rājaguru* of Harihara II, 67
Kulottunga II, 144
Kumara, S., 6
kumbhābhiṣekha, 102
Kundinapura, 26

Lakshmidhara, 67
Lakshmi/Lakṣmī, 4, 135–36; Hayagriva, 102
Lakulāgama, 34
Lakulas, 31
Lakula Siddhānta, 36
Lakulisa, 39; Siddhānta, 34
language of *dhamma*, 24
law of Dharmśastras, 66
leadership of the Guru in the *maṭha*, 41
life of the Guru was a biography of knowledge, renunciation, and miracles, 160
līlā is the divine play of Kṛṣṇa, 161
lineage of: Gurus, 6, 103, 156; Mattamayuras, 32
liṅga, 110, 115, 158; as a symbol of *chaitanya*, 38; tied around their neck, 65
liṅgas, 107, 110
Liṅgāyat, 156; Guru, 38
Lingāyats, 31, 38, 119
link between Tulsi and Kṛṣṇa, 138

Lokayata, 36
Lord Kṛṣṇa, 13
Lorenzen, David N., 37
loyalty to one's husband, 136

Madhura Vijaya, 70
Madhva: *maṭhas*, 59; Siddhanta, 65
Madhvācārya, 3–5, 53, 58, 60–61, 64–66, 73–74, 91, 100, 138, 145, 147; had eight disciples, 60; was said to be an *avatāra* of Hanuman and Bhima, 159
Madhvācārya's Dualist philosophy and religion, 142
Madhva Dvaita: Desastha order, 63; Vaiṣṇava sect, 118
Madhvavijaya, 147
Mahābhārata, 59, 114, 139
*mahācaitya*s, 109
mahāmangalārti, 102
mahamunigal, 33
Mahaparinibbana Sutta, 108
mahāpūruṣa, 22
mahārāja, 22
mahātantra, 31
mahavidyālaya, 29
Mahāviṣṇu, 135–36
mahotsava, 102
Maitrikas, 40
maṇḍapa, 101
Maṇḍūka Upaniṣad, 23
mantramārga, 31
mantropadesa, 71
Manu, 23
marked factor for the growth of *maṭha*s, 30
maṭha/matha/math, 2, 4, 8, 19, 20, 30, 39, 64–65, 68, 75–77, 98, 102, 156–57, 161–62; *ācāryas*, 33; architecture, 72, 76; as an ecclesiastical system, 13; has parallels with a Hindu temple, 73; was an institution of the Guru, 77; of Maninagabhattaraka of Ekambaka, 20; organizational structure, 30; provided an institutionalized base for asceticism and teaching, 156
*maṭha*s, 12, 29, 32, 37, 55, 71, 156
Mathura and is said to be the birthplace of Kṛṣṇa Vāsudeva, 140
Maurya, Chandragupta, 20
māya, 59
meaning of *vṛndāvana*, 145
medieval: archaeological remains, 116; Vaisnavite literature, 133
memorial/tomb called *vṛndāvana*, 5
message of Dvaita philosophy, 147
Mīmāṃsā, 28
miraculous properties of relics of Buddhist and Dvaita Gurus, 108
Mishra, Mandana, 54
mithyātva, 59
moksha, 2, 63–64, 146
monasteries, 25
Monism, 91
moola vṛndāvana, 75
mountain of meditation unto death, 114
mritige: *maṭha*(s), 102; *vṛndāvana*(s), 74, 104
mudradharane, 65
mūla maṭha, 102, 108
mūla vṛndāvana(s), 74, 97, 101, 104
multifaceted Vedānta *maṭha*s, 11
multiple functions of Vedānta *maṭha*s, 157
multiplication of *vṛndāvana*s, 107
mummification, 3; and veneration of "whole-body relics," 7
mummified body of: ascetic Guru, 158; Zhiyi, 111
mummy of Huineng Xu Hengbin, 111
Mundesvari inscription of Udayasena, 20
muni(s), 22, 32, 117
Munroe, Thomas, 147
mythical, 142
mythological tale of Vṛndā, 134

Nadia or Navadvipa, 26
Nagarjunakonda, 76

naiṣṭhika: *brahmacāri*, 29, 36; *tapomārga nirata*, 36
naiṣṭhika-sthānam, 29
naividya, 102
Nalanda, 26
nama, 143
namaskāra(s), 143
Nammalvars, 144
Nandadasa, 143
Nandikesvara was referred to as *mūla sthāna maṭha*, 37
Nandivarman, Malladeva, 40
Narahari Tirtha, 142
Narasimha, 138, 159
Narasimha Varman II, 112
Nath *yoga* tradition, 158
nijarūpa, 148
Nimbarka, 142
nirvāṇa, 108
nisiddhi(s), 109
nistrika/naiṣṭhik, 36
nityarūpa, 148, 160
non-Christian Asiatic usage, 105
nyāya, 26
Nyāya, 28
Nyayasudha/Nyaya Sudha, 61–62

Odantapuru Mahavihara, 26
Olivelle, Patrick, 5, 21
organization: and architecture of Udipi *maṭha*, 6; of ascetics, 54
origin: and meaning of the icon of the *guru*, x; of Vaisnavism and Vaiṣṇava *maṭhas*, 56
origin, form, and meaning of the *vṛndāvana*, 10
origins of: institutionalized renunciation, 19; *vṛndāvana*, 115, 133; whole-body relic cult, 12

pabbjja (*pravrajya*), 25
Paditharadhya at Śrisaila, 28
padma, 143
Padmanabhachar, C.M., 5
Padmapada, 54
Padma Purāṇa, 9, 56, 134, 136, 140–41
pagoda, 113
painting in the Virupaksha temple, ix
pallakki, 69
Pallavas, 10, 27, 39–40
Pancāmṛta, 143
pancāmṛta abhisekha, 102
pancāryās, 28
pancha maṭha, 37
Panchamaṭha Hiriuyamaṭha, 37
panchamaṭha mūla sthāna, 38
paṇḍita(s), 1, 22, 93, 161
Pandyan, 31
Pandyas, 10, 27
parabrahma, 66
parabrahman, 38
parama-hamsa, 22
Paramaras, 30
paribhogikā/pāribhogika, 105, 109
Parimala, 62
parinirvāṇa, 107
parivrajaka, 22
Pārvatī, 134, 136
paryaya swamy, 66
pāśa, 31
paśu, 31
Pāśupata, 31; beliefs, 34; and Kālamukha *maṭhas*, 11, 21, 34; *maṭhas*, 35; Śaivas, 33; *sanyāsis* and brāhmins, 39; teachers, 110
Pāśupata, Kapālika, Kālamukha monasteries, 11
Pāśupatadarśana, 34
Pāśupatas, 37, 41
pāthaśala, 73–74
path of four *āśramas*, 22
pativratā dharma, 136
patronage of monasteries, 6
pattada form, 65
Peshwa, Bajirao I, 116
Peshwa, Madhav Rao I, 62
phala mantrākshate, 102
philosophical studies, 91

philosophy of: Madhvācārya, 93; qualified: monism, 56; nondualism with *bhakti*, 58
pinda pradhāna, 106
pontiffs of the Dualist school, 134
post-Gupta period, 40, 140
post-Harappan period, 139
post-Śankarācārya period, 55
post-Vidyaranya period, 56
powerful symbols of asceticism, 21
power of *liṅga*/consciousness, 38
Prabandhas of the Ālvārs, 57
Prabha Bauddha Balara, 38
Prabhupāda, Swāmi, 1
practice of: entombment and construction of *vṛndāvana*, 116; initiation, 64
practice whole-body relic entombment of Dvaita ascetics, 119
pradakshiṇapatha, 74–75
Pradyumna, 140, 142
Prajavani, 102
prajñānam brahma, 54
prākāra, 144
prāṇa, 144–45; *pratishthāpana*, 144
Prāṇa Devaru, 144
prāṇapratiṣṭhā, 159
prana-sakti, 145
prapati mārga of *bhakti* by Rāmānujācārya, 57
prasāda, 143
pre-Buddhist: *caityas*, 137; and medieval Hindu burial, 12; traditions, 107
principle of: Pacaratra, 58; Vedism, 162
puja, 57
Purāṇas, 31, 36, 57, 59, 140
Purandara Dāsa, 70
Puranic and non-Puranic Saivism, 31
pure form, 141
Puri, 54
Pūrnaprajna, 58

Qualified Non-Dualism, 91
quasi monastic institutions, 20

Rādhā, 161
Rāghavendra/Rāghvendra Swāmi, 94, 102, 115, 147; *maṭha*, 100
rājadharma, 67, 70
Rajaditya, 111
rājaguru, 66; to Kṛṣṇadeva Raya, 68
rājagurus, 32, 41, 64; of Kataktya kings, 36
rājapurohita, 66
Rāmakṛṣṇa Paramahamsa, 1
Ramana Maharshi, 1
Rāmānujācārya, 4–5, 53, 56–57, 60, 65, 91, 119, 144–45
Rāma/Rama, 102, 138, 145, 159
Rāmāyaṇa, 118
Ramesvara *paṇḍita*, 34, 36
Ranganatha, 66
rāsalīla, 161; with Gopis, 138
Rashtrakuta king Krishna III, 34
Rashtrakutas, 10, 26–27, 31, 39–40, 117
realization of *brahman*, 64
redefined concept of Guru *bhakti*, 147
relation between Kṛṣṇa and Guru *vṛndāvana*, 138
relevance of *aidukas*, 110
relic: cult, 102; veneration, 105
relics, 12
relics of: Buddha, 4, 108; Guru, 107
religious: movement of *bhakti*, 145; symbolism, 13
renaissance of monasticism, 10
renaming of an *agrahāra* as a *maṭha*, 30
renewal of ancient Upanisadic tradition, 10
Renukacārya of Rambhapuri, 28
Rgveda, 23, 59
rich heritage of Hindu monasteries, 14
rise of: militant Śaiva kings, 11; Śaiva *maṭhas*, 41; Saivism, 31, 39
ritual of commencement of studies, 23
role and function of *maṭhas*, 156
root of *bhaktivāda*, 146
round sacred stones symbolizing Viṣṇu, 93
royal *paṇḍita*, 66

a royal umbrella, 116
ṛṣi, 1, 22
rudra bhūmis, 109–10
Rudra Śiva, 32
rules of: Buddhist monastic education system of initiation, 25; *Śilpaśāstras*, 76, 157

sacralizing ritual of *pratishthāpana*, 101
sacred leadership of the Guru, 156
Sadarśana, 36
sadguru, 22
sādhu, 1, 22
saguṇa brahman, 146
Sahaji, 117
Śaiva, Vaiṣṇava, Vedānta, and Liṅgāyat *maṭhas*, 3
Śaiva and: Vaiṣṇava religious movements, 65; Vedānta: ascetic philosophers, 10; *maṭha*, 66
Śaiva/*Śaiva*, 66, 134; *Āgamas*, 33; institutions, 40; Kapālikas, 41; monasteries, 20, 40; Nayanmars, 145; recitals, 33; religious movement, 30
Śaiva/Śaiva *maṭhas*, 31, 36, 39, 53, 55, 60, 71–72
Śaiva Siddhānta, 11, 32; *maṭhas*, 21, 31, 35; *sanyāsis*, 31
Saivism, 57
Saivite: *maṭhas*, 31, 34; and Vaisnavite monasteries, 156; vows of renunciation, 33
Śaivites, 65, 119
Śākta, 66
Śaktiśiva, 32
Śaktism, 41
sālagramas, 93, 101, 107, 160
Saluva: Narasimha, 67; and Tuluva periods, 67
samādhi, 115, 142; *mandir*, 109; *maraṇa*, 112, 114; sites, 120
samadhi-betta, 114
samādhis, 116
samartha, 23
samasrayana, 71
Sāmaveda, 23, 55
Sambhulinga temple, 34
sāmpradayas, 5, 63; of asceticism and education, 30
samsāra, 2
saṃsthāna, 56, 157
Sangama rulers, 119
saṅgha, 26; of *bhikkus*, 25; and *dharma* were the *triśaraṇa*, 24
saṅghas, 26
Śankara, 54, 137
Śankarācārya, 54, 56–57
Sankarṣṇa, 140, 142
śaṅkha, 101, 103, 143
sannyasa ashrama, 64
Sanskritic *Vedas*, 146
sant, 1, 22
sanyāsa, 22, 25, 61, 63–64; within the *āśrama* order, 63; *maraṇa*, 114; as a value, 63
sanyāsāśrama, 63
Sanyāsa Upaniṣad, 21
sanyāsi, 4, 21–22, 38, 58, 67, 77, 117
sanyāsi(s), 22, 25, 64
sanyāsin(s), 22, 39, 64, 93
sapinda śrāddha, 106
Sarada center, 55
Saradamba (Sarasvati), 66
Sarasvati, Chandrasekharānanda, 1
Sarasvati, Dayānanda, 1
śārira, 105
śāririka/śārīraka, 105, 109
sarovara, 74
Sasanka, 40
śāstras, 23, 28, 55
śāstrī, 22
śāstrikā brahmacārin, 36
sat, cit, ānanda, 57
Satapatha Brahmana, 103
Satavahanas, 26
sattras, 64
Satya Sai Bāba, 1
Satyasamhita, 64
sāvitrī rite, 21

Sawai, Yoshitsugu, 5
Scharfe, Hartmut, 5
Schopen, Gregory, 6
Sears, Tamara I., 6, 33
sect embodies three essential features, 35
self-immolation, 112
sepulchral and mortuary icon, 3
servants of God, 146
Settar, S., 93
Sewell, Robert, 69
sexual love, 135
shakha maṭha, 102
Shantakumari, Leela, 6
Sharma, B.N.K., 5, 93, 143
Shastry, A.K., 6
Shikarpur inscription of, 1065, 113
Siddhata theology, 33
Śilpaśāstras, 71
śiṣṭa parigraha, 41
śiṣya, 145
site of early monasteries, 10
Śiva, 33, 37, 65, 134–35, 148; *liṅga*, ix; *maṭha*, 37; represented a militant quality, 39
*śivacārya*s, 32
Śivaliṅgas, 111
six: *anugraha* forms of Śiva, 41; systems of philosophy, 36
sixteen modes of worship, 58
sixth Patriarch of Chan Buddhism, 111
Sixth Platform Sutra, 111
smarak, 109
*smarta*s, 65
Smith, Vincant, 105, 109
social organization of the monastery, 6
socioreligious: conflicts, 66; network system, 157; power, 162; *sāmpradayas* of *sanyāsa* and *ācārya*, 21
sokushinbutsu, 112
Somesvara *paṇḍita*, 36
spirit of Hindu teachings, 158
sport of Rādhā and Kṛṣṇa, 142
spread of *vṛndāvana*-related pilgrimage sites, 162
*śraddhā*s, 146
śrāddha/srāddha, 101, 106
sravana, 146
Srinath *muni*, 57
Sringeri, 6, 54–56
Śri Vaiṣṇava, 4; *maṭhas*, 116
Śrī Vaisnavites, 65
sthānādhipati, 76
*sthanādhipati*s, 34
Stoker, Valerie, 6, 68
story of: Kṛṣṇa, 138; *samudra manthana*, 134; Tulsi Vṛndāvana, 136; Vṛndā, 136; Vṛndā's *vana*, 136
Strong, John S., 6
stūpa, 158; relics, 109; of tooth relic, 107
stupa and *vṛndāvana*: follow a canon, 107; have parallels in the worship of the relics, 158
*stūpa*s, 107–10
stūpa/vṛndāvana, 76
Subrahmaṇya, 134
Subrahmanyam, B., 109
Sudha, 6
Sunas, 28
superficial, 12
supreme soul, 59
Suresvara, 55
svādhyāya, 33
śvetadvīpa, 140
sveta rūpa, 141
Swāmigal, Saddhananda, 115
Swamy, Sadu Siddaiah, 115
Swamy, Veerabramhendra, 115
Swamy, Yadati Govinda, 115
symbolic articulations on the *vṛndāvana* recounts those on the *stūpa*, 107
symbolism of the *vrndavana*, 160
symbol of philosophical quintessence of puremonism, 54
symbols of: Nārāyaṇa, 66; Viṣṇu, 160

Taittiriya Upanishad, 144
Takshasila, 26
Tamil Prabandhas, 146

Tantras, 41
tapodhana, 37
tarka, 58
tatācāryas, 67
tat tvam asi, 55, 61
tattvavāda, 59
Tatva Prakasika, 62
teaching traditions, 158
temple of: Kadambesvaradeva, 29; Mallikarjuna, 34; Śrī Nārāyaṇa, 20
ten: *avatāras* of Viṣṇu, 5; names of *sanyāsins*, 54; philosophical monographs, 59; principal Upaniṣads, 54, 59; *sannidhānams*, 111
Tengalai school, 58
Tengalai subtraditions, 146
thades, 116
theories of *bhakti*, 146
theory of: *avatāra*, 148, 160; Hindu aesthetics, 13; *līla* and *avatāra*, 139
Thiruvalluvar was a Jain saint, 115
threat of Islam, 10
three: *dharma* traditions of India, 1; major Vedānta monasteries, 156; superimposed *bhadrapīṭhas*, 110
tilakas, 65
Tirtha *prasāda*, 102
tirtha yātrā, 146
Tirumaladevaraya, 118
Tondaradippodi Ālvār, 70
Toṭakācārya, 55
traditional school system of *gurukula*, 24
tradition of: erection of memorials or *nisiddhis*, 114; Nath yogis, 119; philosophical speculation, 1; self-immolation, 111; worshipping memorials and relics in Hinduism, 158
traditions of asceticism and: education, 5; teaching, 24
traditions of *gṛhastha* and *sanyāsi*, 63
training future priests, 91
transformation of: relic into icon and portrait, 13; Vaisnavism, 57
tretayuga, 145
Tribhuvanamalladeva, 34
true knowledge, 145
tulāpurusadāna, 70
Tulsi, the goddess, 109, 136
Tulsi plant, 116, 136
Tulsi Vṛndāvana, 92, 136
twelve *saṃhāra* forms of Śiva, 41
twenty-eight Śaiva Agamas, 38
twenty-two votive *vṛndāvanas*, 75

uddeśik, 109
underwater excavations at Dvaraka, 139
universal soul, 59
upādhi, 59
upādhyāya, 22
upajjhaya, 25
upakurvāṇa, 29
Upanisadic: philosophy, 57; theistic philosophy, 11; thought, 59; tradition, 23
Upaniṣads, 2, 8, 22, 38, 53, 57, 59, 64, 77, 93, 156
upavāsa, 146
urdhvapundra, 65
usnisa, 39

Vadagalai, 146; denomination, 58
vadakirutthal, 115
Vadavati, 62
Vādirāja, 115; Tīrtha, 59
Vaidik *dharma*, 119
Vaikhānasāgama, 58
Vaikuṇṭha of Viṣṇu, 143
vaikuṇtha rūpa, 141
vairagya/vairāgya, 21, 63, 67, 77
Vaiṣṇava, 3, 66, 109; Ālvār, 145; asceticism, 56; *bhakti*, 145; images, 147; *maṭhas*, 60; monasteries, 71; philosophers, 146; sacred marks, 101; *tilaka*, 65
Vaiṣṇavas, 92
Vaisnavism, 56–57, 148
Vaisnavite: Dualist order, 106; *maṭhas*, 33; symbols, 143

Vakatakas, 26
Vali, 118
Vallabha or the Gauḍīya Gosvāmīs, 140
Vallabhi, 26
Vamasakti, 36
vānaprasthya, 22
varṇāśrama dharma, 55
Vāsudeva, 140, 142
Vāyu, 98, 144–45; is also a personification of *tattvajñāna*, 145
Vayyartha-Candrika, 62
Vedāṅgas, 22, 36
Vedānta, 3, 28, 55–56, 156; ascetic head, 67; Dvaita: *maṭhas*, 72; order, 12; *maṭha*, 77; monasteries, 11, 91, 106; *sāmrājya*, 61; Vaiṣṇava Dvaita (Madhva) *maṭhas*, 92; and Vīraśaiva *maṭhas*, 157
Vedānta and Liṅgāyat: *maṭhas*, 157; monasteries, 157
Vedānta *maṭha*s, 2, 5, 21, 53, 64–65, 68–69, 72–73, 145
Vedas, 2, 11, 20, 22–23, 26, 28, 36, 53, 59, 64, 77, 93, 156
Vedavyāsa, 145
Vedic: beliefs, 1; Brahmanism, 40; fire-worship, 56; God, 145; hymns, 69; *mantras*, 98; seers, 21; teaching, 40; tradition, 56
Vedic and: Epic periods, 22; Upanisadic: thoughts, 13, 162; tradition, 59
Veeraśaivism, 37
veneration of whole-body relic, 91; *yatis*, 133
Verghese, Anila, 6, 67
vertical line on the forehead, 143
vibhuti or *tripundra*, 65
vidya, 23
vidyālaya, 28
vidyāpīṭha(s), 28, 30
Vidyāranya, 56, 61, 67, 69, 72
vidyāsthāna had fourteen *gaṇa*s, 28
*vidyāsthāna*s, 28
vidyopadāna, 23
vihara/vihāra, 38, 113
Vijayanagara: dynasties, 10; kings, 36
Vijayīndra Tīrtha, 59
Vikramaditya VI, 34, 68
Vikramankadevacarita, 142
Vikramasila, 26
Vimalaśiva I, 32
Viraballala I/ViraBallala II, 37
Virahamanjari, 143
virakta method of succession, 65
Viraśaiva: disciples, 65; *maṭha*, 65
Viraśaiva/Lingāyat *matha*s, 91
Viraśaiva *maṭha*s, 21, 38, 67
Vīraśaivas, 158
Virasaivism, 38, 67
Virasaivism/Lingayatism is an offshoot of Saivism, 38
Vishnu, 37
Viśiṣṭādvaita: *maṭhas*, 11, 21, 67; of Rāmānujācārya, 11
Viśiṣṭādvaita *matha*/Viśiṣṭādvaita *maṭha*, 53, 91
Viśiṣṭādvaitavāda, 146
Viśiṣṭādvait/Viśiṣṭādvaita, 65, 156
Viṣṇu, 4, 13, 66, 92, 134–36, 142, 147–48; *bhakti* became a unifying force in society, 57; as *paramātma*, 59
Viṣṇudharmottara Purāṇa, 110
Visnukara *brahmacāri*, 37
Viṣṇu Purāṇa, 9, 56, 139–40
Viṣṇu's vehicle Garuḍa, 134
Viṣṇuvardhana, 57
visual culture, 10
Visvesvara Śiva, 33
Viswaradhya at Kasi, 28
Vivekānanda, Swāmi, 1
Vividhatīrthakalpa, 140, 142
votive memorials, 74
vrata, 146
Vṛndā Devi, 138
Vṛndā's act of self-immolation, 136
Vṛndāvana, 136, 139–40, 142; appears as a *mandala*, 141
vṛndāvana of: Dvaita pontiffs, 120; Guru is symbolic of divine *ānanda*

of the Guru, 148; a Madhva, 119; Raghavendra Swāmi, 102, 104; Raghuvarya Tīrtha, 95; Yogindra Tīrtha, 95
vṛndāvana(s), 3, 6–7, 9, 12–13, 73, 75, 91–94, 99, 100–103, 105, 108, 110, 112–13, 115–19, 133–34, 140, 143–44, 147, 158, 160–61; appears to be unmistakably Buddhist in character, 107; being the *nityarūpa*, 148; are considered extremely sacred, 8; of eleven Gurus, 68; reinvented the meaning of Guru *bhakti*, 147; relic, 108; as a symbol, 148; whole-body relic, 108
vṛndāvana was a: substantiation of *bhakti*, 147; symbolic appropriation, 108
Vṛnda/Vṛndā, 92, 135–36
vyākaraṇa dāna maṇḍapa, 28
*vyākhyānaśālā*s, 32
vyākhyānasimhāsana, 56
vyāna which is conveyed by *udāna* as *tejas*, 145
Vyasaraya/Vyāsarāya, 102, 146
Vyāsarāya Tīrtha, 59

Western Chalukyas, 10, 40; of Badami, 39
whole-body mummification, 105
whole-body relic, 3, 115; entombment, 111; of Rāmānujācārya, 116; in the *vṛndāvana*, 112; worship, 12
whole-body relics, 112, 158
wife of Viṣṇu, 92
Wodeyars, 10
worship of Śiva, 31; *stūpa*, 158; *vṛndāvanas*, 98, 103; whole-body relics in Hinduism, 158

Xu Yun, 111

Yādava Prakāśa, 57
Yadavas, 117
Yagnyavalkya, 64
yajnasthana, 109
Yajurveda, 23, 55
Yaska, 22
yati, 1, 22, 133; *sanyāsin*, 117
yativṛndā, 133
Yocum, Glen, 111
yoga, 31, 55
yogapīṭha, 141
yogaśāstra(s), 26, 36
yogi, 22
*yoginī*s, 135
Yuvarajadeva II, 39

About the Author

Nalini Rao is professor of world art at Soka University of America. She earned her PhD in Art History from the University of California at Los Angeles and a second PhD in Ancient History and Archaeology from the University of Mysore. Some of her publications are *Sindhu-Sarasvati Civlilization: New Perspectives* (2014), *Royal Imagery and Networks of Power at Vijayanagara: A Study of Kingship in South India* (2010), *Contours of Modernity: An Exhibition of Contemporary Indian Art* (2005), *Sangama: A Confluence of Art and Culture during the Vijayanagara Period* (2005), and *Boundaries and Transformations: Masterworks of Indian and South East Asian Sculptures from the collection of Dr. and Mrs. William Price* (1997). She is the Chair of Dr. S. R. Rao Memorial Foundation for Indian Archaeology, Art, and Culture.

About the Author

www.ingramcontent.com/pod-product-compliance
Lightning Source LLC
Chambersburg PA
CBHW050904300426
44111CB00010B/1372
* 9 7 8 1 7 9 3 6 2 2 3 9 6 *